A BENCHMARK SERIES BOOK

# The Beagle

## An Owner's Survival Guide

Diane Morgan

Published by Doral Publishing, Sun City, Arizona
Printed in the United States of America.

Interior Design by The Printed Page
Cover Design by 1106 Design

Library of Congress Card Number: 2002103418
ISBN: 0-944875-77-7

**Publisher's Cataloging-in-Publication**
*(Provided by Quality Books, Inc.)*

Morgan, Diane, 1947-
The beagle : an owner's survival guide / Diane Morgan -- 1st ed.
p. cm. -- (Benchmark series book)
Includes index.
LCCN 2002103418
ISBN 0-944875-77-7

1. Beagle (Dog breed). I. Title.

SF429.B3M67 2002 636.753'7
QBI02-200328

*For Paige Adams*

# Contents

# Introduction

I came to Beagles by way of the Cold War. A friend who worked in a "sensitive capacity" for the United States government was always galloping off to various parts of the free and not-so-free world. I was Bruce's Beagle sitter when he was gone. Liz wasn't much to look at, from an aesthetic viewpoint. She was a muddy tricolor, and her proportions were not all what they might have been. She had a strange, strangled, rasping bark, which made people look at her funny and ask me if she had laryngitis.

Bruce's overseas trips lasted anywhere from two weeks to several months. While he was busy doing whatever people in sensitive government positions do, I was falling in love with his little dog. Gradually I began thinking of her as "my" little dog. One day, my friend informed me that he had to make a trip to Jakarta and would be gone for several months. He wasn't; he was gone four years. During that time, Liz became my dog in fact as well as fancy.

Still, Liz never really got over Bruce. If I mentioned his name, she'd look up sharply at me. Sometimes she'd run to the window to watch for his car. Other times I would find her in the back yard, her sad, delicate nose thrust between pickets as she stared hard down the driveway, as if willing him to return. When Bruce was able to make his few visits, Liz was beside herself in ecstasy. When he left, she mourned with a low keening sound. I could never replace him in her book. But that was all right; in fact, I admired that quality in her.

When the end came at last, at age 17, she quietly went to her little dog bed, and unassumingly lay down to die. I held her in my arms while she breathed her last uncomplaining breath. But her last look was one of faint puzzlement. "Where's Bruce?" she seemed to say. "Where's my dad?"

I think it was this combination of adaptability and loyalty that sold me on this breed.

The great thing about Beagles is that they love you for yourself utterly, and not your possessions. They don't care if you've gotten a trifle slow or creaky. (Although they don't excuse slowness if it makes dinner five minutes late.) Or that you've gained a bit of weight recently. Dogs know what's real, and so do you. That's why you have a Beagle. Good decision. You have chosen to share your life with a sentient, intelligent, beautiful being who will love you without question.

Beagles take a lot of work and a lot of love, but they give more than they take: happy days, snuggly nights, and warm memories forever. You will never, ever be sorry you shared your life with this most engaging of dogs.

Welcome to the world of the beautiful and beguiling Beagle!

*Louie*

*photo courtesy of Wally Jarratt*

# Chapter 1

# Bravo for Beagles!

It took the great cartoonist Charles M. Schulz (1922-2000) and his immortal Snoopy to show the world what Beaglers knew all along—that here is no ordinary Bowser.

Snoopy is, of course, the greatest fictional Beagle in history. He debuted on October 4, 1950, a date that should be celebrated as World Beagle Day. The early Snoopy was a slimmer and more snipe-nosed creation than the later classic character, but he is still recognizably a Beagle, with Snoopy's inimitable joie de vivre. Early in the life of *Peanuts*, shortsighted editors tried to convince its creator to reduce the strip's focus on Snoopy, but Schulz knew that like all Beagles, Snoopy was far more than a dog. A sort of canine Walter Mitty, the silent Snoopy fantasizes that he is the great World War I Flying Ace ("Curse you, Red Baron!"). He fancies himself a writer of immortal prose ("It was a dark and stormy night"), as a vulture, and as Flashbeagle. (He also obsesses about the cat next door.) In many ways, the dreaming, visionary Snoopy is the most "human" of all Schulz's creations.

In selecting a Beagle for a hero, Schulz chose wisely. Some breeds may be bigger, or more elegant. Some might be easier to train, or more dependable off lead. Others may have breathtaking beauty. Still, no other dog presents such a unique combination of charm, agility, and sweetness—along with a handsome profile and cheerful disposition. It's no wonder that Beagles are currently the fifth most popular breed in the country. Over 52,000 of them were registered with the American Kennel Club in 2000. And that number doesn't include the large number of pets and hunting dogs who are unregistered, or listed with different registries. Where did all these Beagles come from?

## Beagle Beginnings

Although everyone agrees that all modern dogs ultimately trace back to the wolf, *Canis lupus,* the precise ancestor of the Beagle remains controversial. It may be that several subspecies of wolves contributed to the Beagle's eventual triumph.

### Merrie Proto-Beagles in Merrie Old England

The first dogs that we can reliably call "Beagles" came from England. The legendary King Arthur supposedly possessed a pack of white scenting hounds resembling Beagles, but since the very existence of Arthur is questionable, his hounds can be only a rumor. Still, it's a pleasant notion that today's Beagles are the descendants of those ancient and royal hounds.

We do know this. In 1066, that year of years, William the Conqueror brought two types of hounds to England, gazehounds who hunted by sight, and scent hounds who hunted by nose. Since all kinds of game flourished in medieval England, the early aristocracy depended upon a variety of breeds as hunting assistants.

Always looking for something different, fourteenth century hound breeders fooled around with the genetic pool considerably. One of their products was a sort of toy hound, standing only five to nine inches high. This little Glove, or Pocket Harrier, as it was known, could be tucked neatly into a saddlebag and then carried along on a hunt. This dog was particularly noted for his elegant voice, and hence given the name "singing beagle." It was popular to add a singing beagle to a pack, as even today Basset Hounds are sometimes placed in a Beagle pack to improve the "tone" of the pack. (They certainly add nothing to the hunting ability.) Although faddish with the sporting set for a while, breeders finally caught on to the fact that Pocket Harriers weren't such a great idea after all, and eventually the tiny breed was allowed to die out.

Beagles proper may have begun as foxhounds or harriers during the time of Henry VIII and his daughter Elizabeth I, when fox hunting became popular among the wealthy. Before that time, royalty were given to chasing deer around in the woods and the hound of choice was a great big creature called a "buckhound." Some historians think that buckhounds were crossed with small rabbit-hunting dogs to create foxhounds, and that Beagles were subsequently developed from that group.

Other authorities, however, deny that Beagles were "bred down" from foxhounds or buckhounds, and point out that "Beaglish" dogs could be found long before fox hunting became a royal pastime. They suggest that foxhounds may have been "bred up" from Beagles rather than the other way around. (Terriers and spaniels have been implicated in both the "bred up" and "bred down" theories.) The truth will probably never be known; certainly, the surviving paintings upon which most of the "evidence" is based have more charm than breed accuracy.

For a while, Beagles were actually in danger of becoming extinct, as fox hunting began to replace rabbit hunting among the sporting set. These folks preferred using true foxhounds and Beagles survived only because rabbit hunting was still important among small-time farmers in southern England and Wales. They hunted not so much for sport but to supplement their diet.

## The Breed in Transition

By the mid-1700s, two Beagle-type dogs were in existence: one was the so-called Southern Hound, a large, deep-voiced animal (possibly resembling today's Basset Hound, although only loosely related to him). This dog may have been descended from the white Talbot Hound, one of the hounds brought over with William the Conqueror.

The other Beagle-type dog was the quicker, hard-running North Country Beagle, whose voice had a higher-pitched, "yappier" tone. Some researchers claim that there was yet a third Beagle type, one even smaller than the North Country Beagle (and hence an economical hunting companion). Probably all three types contributed to the development of today's Beagle.

## The Gape-Throated Dog

The word Beagle itself may derive from the French word *begle,* which in turn comes from the medieval *begueule,* or *bagoule* meaning "gape-throated." This was a derogatory term stemming from a Latin root for "gullet." It probably referred to the loud voice of the Beagle, although a rival derivation suggests that the throat, and hence the appetite of the dog, was small. I don't know about this. For a small dog, Beagles can eat a lot. It would be fun to make a connection between the words "beagle" and "bugle," but there isn't any.

A completely different explanation of the name draws upon the ancient Gaelic tongue. In Irish, for instance, *beag* means "of little worth." The term may not mean that the dog itself was of little value, but rather that the game he pursued, rabbits and hares, was of less significance than deer, elk, or boar. At any rate, the Irish word for Beagle today is *gadhar,* which means a "crying or shouting" dog. The other Irish word for Beagle, *pocadan,* may be related to the Irish word *poca,* or pocket, possibly harking back to the old "Pocket Harrier." (Harriers are called Harriers because they chase hares.)

Charles Schulz once said that he decided Snoopy should be a Beagle because *beagle* was a funny word. This is true, although I'm not sure it's any funnier than Poodle, Wirehaired Pointing Griffon, or Italian Spinone. To each his own, I guess.

## The Modern Beagle

We can credit the creation of today's Beagle primarily to an Essex County clergyman who bore the delightful name of Parson Phillip Honeywood. Honeywood assembled the first pack of sporting Beagles in the mid-1800s. He got his Beagles by mixing up some of the original stock with Otterhounds and Bloodhounds. This sounds like a strange combination, but it worked. Honeywood and his cronies got together a little club of sorts called the Merry Beaglers of the Meadows, and began to amuse themselves by chasing rabbits all over the countryside. The story goes that the good parson's hounds, while clever hunters, were not all that much to look at. However, a fellow Englishman,

Thomas Johnson, remedied the situation by producing a pack of hounds that were as handsome as they were good hunters.

The appearance of these early Beagles is controversial. Some contend they were leggier and rangier than modern examples, while others claim just the opposite. Judging from the contemporary paintings, whose accuracy, as I pointed out earlier, may be suspect, both kinds of Beagles were present. It's safe to say that the "Beagle type" had not yet been fixed, and breeders consulted their own preferences to a larger degree than is true today, when quality Beagles must adhere to a breed standard.

## Beagles in America

In the United States, the early Beagle was a mostly white hound, bearing only a few dark or tan markings. According to the American Kennel Club's official history, the dog wasn't very attractive and several American breeders sought to improve the Beagle's appearance. One of these breeders was General Richard Rowett of Carlinsville, Illinois. During the 1870s, Rowett imported some English Beagles and from them developed a line known as the Kerry Beagles, noted for their handsomeness. In 1896, James Kernochan of Rhode Island imported some hunting Beagles from the famous Royal Rock Beagle Pack of England. These animals possessed the desirable head and neck qualities that were lacking in the American types. The third breeder, also from Rhode Island, was a man known to history only as Mr. Arnold of Providence. Mr. Arnold apparently had the grave misfortune of losing his first name somewhere, but luckily he managed to hang on to most of his Beagles. He and Kernochan were great fans of field trailing, and they organized the first such Beagle events in America.

Breeders near Philadelphia established the first American Beagle Specialty Club in 1884, the same year that the American Kennel Club was founded. (The first Beagle registered with the American Kennel Club, in 1885, was a dog curiously named Blunder.) The new club worked hard to develop a single standard for their breed. With care and attention, a stable American Beagle type emerged.

Our National Beagle Club, later called the National Beagle Club of America, was created in 1888, two years before a similar organization started in England. (An Association of Masters of

Harriers and Beagles had formed in the United Kingdom in 1873, but we don't need to count that if we don't want to.) In 1900 the Breed Standard was revised to emphasize the "running gear" of the Beagle, and a year later the first National Beagle Club Specialty show was held.

### Canine Sniffing Machines!

Beagles are not only cute and charming, they are smart and useful working dogs. One Beagle named Peaches earned her living by sniffing out termites for a firm in Scranton, Pennsylvania. Her fame spread far and wide until she was issued a challenge: Could Peaches out-sniff professional human pest inspectors with fancy termite detectors? Peaches was pitted against the competition at a church with known termite problems in State College, Pennsylvania. Everyone stood by nervously as Peaches was given her cue. "Termites!" Instantly Peaches went into "attack" mode, trembling all over. She immediately discovered every known termite infestation, plus twelve other sites unknown to the judges. As a bonus she found some colonies of carpenter ants. The human pest inspectors were still lugging their equipment around the building by the time Peaches had completed her assignment. Her reward? Three chili dogs at a local fast food place.

## The Beagle Breed Standard: "Big for their Inches"

All dog breeds recognized by the American Kennel Club must conform to a breed standard developed by the national club of that breed. This club keeps studbook for its breed. Each club works hard to make sure that its show dogs approach the written standard. The standard is there for comparison. Beagles should look like Beagles, and not like Dachshunds or Basset Hounds, which is what might happen if people were left to create their own individual standards.

The breed standard is a written picture of the ideal dog. Since it refers to an ideal dog, most pet Beagles don't meet every criterion perfectly. In fact, not even a Westminster Best of Breed Beagle is perfect. Still, it's always interesting to examine the standard to see how well our own dogs compare with the imaginary ideal.

# Big for Their Inches

*Louie*
*photo courtesy of Wally Jarratt*

*Clancy*
*photo courtesy of David & Joan Dwyer*

*Hypo*
*photo courtesy of Lea Ward*

*Bailey*
*photo courtesy of Madlyn Schneider*

## Beagles Come in Two Sizes!

For competition purposes, Beagles come in two varieties based on size. The smaller Beagle cannot exceed thirteen inches at the withers (top of the shoulder), while the larger cannot exceed fifteen inches at the withers. Two inches may not seem like much, but when you're a little dog, every inch counts. (The Beagle is the smallest of all hounds.)

No matter what size the Beagle, however, he should conform as closely as possible to the Beagle standard. To read the complete standard, consult the latest edition of *The Complete Dog Book,* the American Kennel Club's official publication containing the standards for all recognized breeds. Here I'll touch on the important points and discuss them. Italics represent an exact quotation from the Breed Standard, ordinary type my comments and explanation. The current breed standard for the Beagle was approved September 10, 1957.

## The Standard in Detail

### Head

*The skull should be fairly long, slightly domed at occiput, with cranium broad and full.* A Beagle needs a good nose, and a good nose needs a good head. A flat or very narrow skull is a defect. In general, the head should be the same length from the occiput to the stop as from the stop to the muzzle. The occupit is the "bump" toward the back of the skull. The stop is where the muzzle meets the cranium, between the eyes.

Although the American standard makes no specific mention of a difference between sexes, it is generally acknowledged that boy dogs should look like boys and girl dogs should look like girls.

*Ears—Ears set on moderately low, long, reaching when drawn out nearly, if not quite, to the end of the nose; fine in texture, fairly broad—with almost entire absence of erectile power—setting close to the head, with the forward edge slightly inturning of the cheek—rounded at tip.* This explains why, at a dog show, the handler or judge pulls the ears forward toward the dog's nose—he's measuring the ear length. Even though the standard calls for "almost entire absence of erectile power," in point of fact, the Beagle can raise his ears to some extent when interested.

*Eyes—Eyes large, set well apart—soft and houndlike—expression gentle and pleading; of a brown or hazel color.* Beagles can manage to look pleading even when you are not chomping down on a hamburger in front of them. They can also look very merry, a word that is in the British standard but not in ours. In any case, sharp "terrier-like" eyes or protruding eyes are a definite fault.

*Muzzle—Muzzle of medium length—straight and square-cut—the stop moderately defined.* A sharp, "snipey" muzzle is a defect. The muzzle is not supposed to be turned up.

*Jaws—Level. Lips free from flews; nostrils large and open.* This means that the jaws should meet without being undershot or overshot. And of course a hard-running hunting dog needs big nostrils. A dark nose is preferred, although the American standard makes no mention of nose color. Red and white Beagles may have lighter-colored noses.

The standard does not specifically mention "bite," or the way the upper and lower teeth meet; however, it's generally considered that the best bite is a "scissors" bite, where the upper teeth slightly overlap the lower ones. A level bite, where the upper and lower teeth meet evenly, is also acceptable, although I personally don't like to see a level bite—it causes undue wear on the teeth.

Flews are the pendulous flaps of skin you find at the corners of the mouths of Basset Hounds and Bloodhounds. They are a defect in Beagles.

**Body**

*Neck and Throat—Neck rising free and light from the shoulders strong in substance yet not loaded, of medium length. The throat clean and free from folds of skin; a slight wrinkle below the angle of the jaw, however, may be allowable.* The word "loaded" refers to a dog who is just too heavy in the shoulders or neck. Beagles should not have a thick, ugly neck or a throat with the folds of skin (dewlaps) characteristic of a Basset Hound. Dogs with heavy throats like this are called, logically enough, "throaty."

**Shoulders and Chest**

*Shoulders sloping—clean, muscular, not heavy or loaded—conveying the idea of freedom of action with activity and strength. Chest deep and broad, but not broad enough to interfere with the free play of the shoulders.* It's important that the shoulders not be straight, since this interferes with good movement. A too broad chest causes the same problem.

### Back, Loin, and Ribs

*Back short, muscular, and strong. Loin broad and slightly arched, and the ribs well sprung, giving abundance of lung room.* You don't want to see a Beagle with a sway back or one that is humped or "roached," as they say in dog-language. The side view should reveal a straight back or topline, with a slight arch over the loin. Flat ribs are a defect.

### Forelegs and Feet

*Forelegs—Straight, with plenty of bone in proportion to size of the hound. Pasterns short and straight.* The pastern is the area between the front carpus or "knee," (which is really a wrist) and the feet. The leg should be substantial, with plenty of bone. Beagles are not delicate Toy Poodles. The front legs should be strong in appearance and straight; they should be parallel with the hind legs.

*Feet—Close, round and firm. Pad full and hard.* The elbows should not be turned out. The standard says it is defect if the "knees" are knuckled forward, or bent backward. As I mentioned above, however, the carpus is not a knee but a wrist. Dogs have knees only on the back legs. Both the front and back legs and feet are referred to collectively as "running gear."

### Hips, Thighs, Hind Legs and Feet

*Hips and thighs strong and well muscled, giving abundance or propelling power. Stifles strong and well let down. Hocks firm, symmetrical and moderately bent. Feet close and firm.* Viewed from the back, the hocks shouldn't be turned into each other. That's a condition called "cowhocks." The feet should be tight and cat-like, not open or spreading.

### Tail

*Set moderately high; carried gaily, but not turned forward over the back; with slight curve; short as compared with size of the hound; with brush.* That brush is very important! Judges don't like to see a "rat tail" with no hair on it. It is assumed that brush on the tail helps protect it from injury, although I am not sure this is true. It can also get caught in stickers more easily.

Although the American standard doesn't actually say this, it's generally conceded that the tail should have a white tip on it. This supposedly makes it easier for hunters to find their dogs in the bush; the tail acts as flag or signal. The British standard makes it a requirement that the tail (or "stern" as they quaintly phrase it) must be tipped white. The tail should be strong and tapered, and should be carried up; a lowered, or even worse, a tucked-in tail indicates fear and misery.

**Coat**

*A close, hard, hound coat of medium length.* This coat should be dense and shiny, and not feel "soft" to the touch. The Beagle is a hunting dog whose coat should be able to repel stickers and water. The British standard specifically states that the coat should be waterproof.

**Color**

*Any true hound color.* Beagles come in an amazing variety of colors, and most are of two or three different colors. As the original standard, written in 1884, admitted with charming frankness: "This arrangement is of course arbitrary, the question being one governed entirely by fancy." Most beagles are what we call *tricolor.* Tricolor dogs have a black "saddle," with a white chest and underbelly. Tricolor dogs often have brown or tan faces. I should note that many future tricolor puppies are born black and white; the tan color appears later. Beagles who remain black and white are extremely rare. Show ring judges seem to have developed a taste for red and white Beagles recently, but the standard doesn't prefer one color above another. In Beagledom "red" can be anything from light tan to very dark brown. There is also a "lemon" color, a pale unearthly shade. Lemon puppies are born all white.

Most beagles have some white on them. An all-white beagle is extremely rare, although it is perfectly permissible. Being hounds, you'll find Beagles with freckling (officially called ticking), grizzling, and mottling. All are acceptable. Stripes and polka dots are another matter. In general, dark or tri-colored Beagles seem to have fewer skin problems than those of lighter colors.

**General Appearance**

*A miniature Foxhound, solid and big for his inches, with the wear-and-tear look of a hound that can last in the chase and follow his quarry to the death.* A very vivid, if somewhat alarming description. Following one's quarry to the death is all very well in its place, I suppose, although the idea makes me a bit squeamish. This language derives directly from the original 1884 standard. In this instance, I prefer the British Standard, which merely says, "A sturdy, compactly built hound, conveying the impression of quality without coarseness." Nothing about following one's quarry to the death. The British standard also describes the Beagle as "A merry hound whose essential function is to hunt, primarily hare, by following a scent. Bold, with great activity, stamina and determination. Alert, intelligent, and of even temperament."

In general, it is best that a Beagle is "well-balanced," meaning that his front and hind parts look as if they belong to the same dog. The reason is not simply a matter of aesthetics, but of practicality. An unbalanced dog is not the sure, tireless runner that a Beagle must be to be worthy of the name.

## Temperament

The American standard does not refer to temperament; however, the British standard asks for a dog who is "Amiable and alert, showing no aggression or timidity." It is important for Beagles to possess what we call a "pack mentality," since age-old Beagle tradition requires them to hunt in packs. And indeed, most Beagles are the most sociable creatures imaginable, both

### Him and Her

Lyndon Johnson's famous pair of presidential Beagles, Him and Her, did their bit for educating the public about humane treatment of animals. When Johnson was photographed picking them up by the ears to show them off to reporters, animal welfare advocates quickly pointed out to the president that this type of manhandling wasn't a jewel in the crown of the Great Society. Otherwise, Johnson coddled his dogs, allowing them to swim laps with him in the White House pool and feeding them candy-coated vitamins.

with humans and with other dogs. This is one of their greatest charms. As a matter of curiosity, I asked at my veterinary office how often they ran into Beagles with aggression problems. The answer: "Never."

## The Joys of Beagling

If you like dogs, you must like Beagles! Beagles are versatile dogs who can fit happily in most households. They are a convenient size, for one thing, neither so large they take up the entire couch, nor so small that they can hide underneath it. With a modicum of care, and a great deal of love, the Beagle takes his natural place as a very special member of the family.

Like most dogs with a hunting background, Beagles need plenty of vigorous exercise, but a secure backyard and a dedicated owner can easily provide a sufficient amount. These dogs love to be outdoors and off on exciting adventures with you, but they just as easily snuggle up in your lap and snooze away the long winter evenings by the fireside.

Beagles are superb watchdogs. Alert and observant, they will bark noisily at the first sign of a trespasser, yet their cheerful, amiable disposition makes them entirely safe as pets. Although most breeds of dogs can *learn* to be sociable around children, kids and

*Louie Loo Eye*
*photo courtesy of Wally Jarratt*

Beagles are a natural team. Since Beagles are pack-oriented, they are not "one-person" dogs. Beagles like everyone in the family (and company too!) You don't have to worry about a Beagle sulking or going off his feed if his favorite person can't be with him every moment of the week.

Beagles also socialize well with other pets. They like cats, other dogs (especially other Beagles) and sometimes even weird little pocket pets. If they have a fault in this area, it's that they might be just a little *too* interested in Hopalong, the pet rabbit. That, of course, is owing to their heritage, since Beagles were developed primarily as a hunting breed.

As a bonus, Beagles live a very long time, for dogs, with an average life span of fifteen years.

# Chapter 2

# In Search of Your Ideal Beagle

Beagles are easy to find. In fact, it seems that everywhere you look, Beagles are either "for sale" or "free to a good home." But be careful. Choosing a Beagle isn't like picking up a quart of milk at the food mart. A dog is not a disposable commodity. A dog is for keeps. Your Beagle will be your companion, snuggle bug, and best friend for many years to come. Choose wisely.

*Bailey, 4 months*

*photo courtesy of Madlyn Schneider*

## Before You Beagle!

Incredible as it may seem, not everyone should own a dog, let alone a super dog like a Beagle. Adding a Beagle to your family is like acquiring a new child. He is a friend who will be with you as long as he lives. If you bought this book before you acquired your Beagle, you've already done one thing right: you've prepared.

Before you take the plunge, take this test to see whether or not a Beagle is right for you and your family. The purpose of these questions is not to scare you, but to help you decide how well a dog would fit into your life right now.

- Can you afford a dog? Sorry to be blunt, but finances are something that you need to assess realistically. Dogs are not cheap. Whether you spend a thousand dollars on a top show prospect or get one free from your brother-in-law, canine costs add up fast, especially in the first year. In fact, the initial cost of the dog is the smallest expense. You'll need to buy dog supplies such as a crate, bed, leashes, and neckwear. High quality dog food isn't cheap, and neither are veterinary bills. Your dog will need immunizations and regular health care—and there's no guarantee that he won't ever get sick or have an accident. Because obedience training is so important for Beagles, you should sign up for a class. If you're a first time dog owner, you'll learn more than the dog will. These classes are a terrific investment, but they're not inexpensive ($75 to about $250 for a series). If you plan on taking a vacation, and can't take the Beagle, you'll have to consider boarding costs. All in all, your first year's Beagle expenses, including regular veterinary bills and high quality dog food, will run about $1800. This figure doesn't include extras such as boarding fees or fencing.

- How much time do you have—realistically—to spend caring for a dog? Your Beagle doesn't stand quietly in the corner when you don't need him. You're the center of his life, and he requires your loving, regular attention. Although dogs can sleep an amazing fourteen hours a day, that leaves ten hours when they're wide awake, waiting for something to happen and someone to play with them. Some people feel that just being home around the dog is enough, but dogs thrive on personalized attention. Human beings developed dogs to be companion animals, and companionship is what they need. Having two dogs helps a lot, but dogs really need human company.

- Good dog ownership means devoting a fair-sized chunk of your day to feeding, exercising, playing with, grooming, and picking up after the dog. And besides those "fun" things you'll need time to go to the vet, the pet supply store, the puppy sitter, and the dog trainer. One of the main reasons that modern dogs have acquired so many behavioral problems is that they simply don't get enough company. They aren't being bad—they are just lonely and bored.
- Although the children will promise to be responsible for the dog, they have a habit of getting tired of or forgetting their obligations from time to time. If this happens, the job falls to you. If you have to be at work away from home ten hours a day, re-think your plan to get a dog.
- What is your career outlook? Do you have a job that may require you to move? What are your plans for your dog in that case? Unless you are determined to keep a dog with you as a permanent part of your family no matter what, it's best not to get a dog at all.
- Does everyone in your family really want a dog? Make sure everyone in the family truly wants a dog, and that the dog is a Beagle. Many dogs end up in shelters or with a rescue organization because they were purchased over the objections of one family member, who then gets saddled with walking, feeding, and cleaning up after the unwanted pet. Resentments build, and the dog may suffer as a result. So before you actually go out and choose your Beagle, get everyone's whole-hearted approval.
- Are you allowed to have a dog? Be sure you verify (don't just assume) that your covenant or rental agreement allows dogs. Get permission in writing. Don't take a chance on the welfare of your Beagle by trying to sneak him in, hoping you won't get caught. Sooner or later he will be found out, and you'll be in the uncomfortable position of having to decide between your dog and your home.

- How much room do you have? Although Beagles are small dogs and can survive quite well in an apartment setting, they need lots of exercise. You may want to take up jogging to provide it.
- Are you willing to be responsible for your dog and his actions? As far as the law is concerned Beagles are chattel—pieces of property. If your dog nips a child's finger, digs up a neighbor's garden, or kills the class rabbit you are babysitting over the weekend—you have to pay. It's a responsibility you have to take very seriously. The Beagle won't.
- What about the neighbors? Beagles can be noisy dogs, and although a well-trained Beagle is a joy to be around, some people are never satisfied. Although I wouldn't deny myself the joys of Beagle ownership because of some persnickety neighbors, it's still a factor to take into consideration. If you aren't on good terms with your neighbors now, the situation won't improve if you get a dog.
- Is anyone in your family allergic to dogs? If so, what medical care do you plan for the allergy? What would you do if someone suddenly *develops* an allergy to dogs? Beagle hair is technically classed as medium-length, by the way, not short, and they do shed quite a lot.
- Are you prepared for a Beagle? If your only canine experience has been with a Golden Retriever, you may be in for a shock. Hounds are psychologically different from other types of dogs, including learning response, propensity to wander, and interest in housetraining. You must be prepared to meet them on their own terms (which often includes bribery).
- When will you be Beagle-ready? Timing your Beagle acquisition is important. For most people, adopting a dog during a holiday can be a bad idea. With so much going on, and so many visitors tramping in and out, a holiday can be a bewildering time for new dogs and new owners. It's usually best to get a new dog during a more tranquil time.

*Hypo*

*photo courtesy of Lea Ward*

Okay, okay. You pass! You'll change jobs, sell your stock, and remodel the house just to get that Beagle. You're even willing to housetrain one. You waited long enough. Let's start looking. But where?

## Beagle Resources

Getting your Beagle from a reputable source will help insure a lifetime of happy Beagling. You can maximize your chances of getting a healthy, wonderful pet by selecting a responsible breeder, or, if you are willing to help an unwanted dog find a permanent and loving home, by going through a reputable Beagle Rescue organization.

### Finding a Breeder

The easiest way to find a good breeder, if you don't have personal contacts, is to visit the American Kennel Club Website (www.akc.org). This site will provide you with the names and addresses of Beagle clubs near you. If you prefer phoning to the Internet, the AKC runs a hotline, (900) 407-PUPS, that will direct you to breeders in your area.

You can also just call a nearby Beagle Club and ask for a list of reputable breeders in your area. The club will be thrilled to comply with your request, because wise buyers benefit the breed as a whole. Breeders who belong to AKC-affiliated clubs care about Beagles. They are proud of their handsome, healthy, well-bred puppies. They have agreed to a code of ethics that guides their actions with regard to both their dogs and their customers. This doesn't mean that AKC-registered Beagles are the only ones worthy of your notice. Other organizations, particularly those devoted to hunting, also register dogs, and care deeply about the breed.

Curiously enough, the best choice of breeder is the so-called "hobby breeder." A hobby breeder is no rank amateur, but someone who breeds for the love of the breed, rather than for financial gain. She doesn't depend on selling Beagles for her living. She probably takes her dogs to shows because she is proud of them and of her role in producing them. She enjoys breeding a litter occasionally, and is interested in improving her line of Beagles. Selling to the highest bidder isn't on her to-do list. You won't see dozens and dozens of dogs locked up in a pen in her backyard. A good hobby breeder has made her dogs part of her own family, and her pups will easily become part of yours.

If practical, join a local Beagle club before you even get a Beagle. What better way to learn about the breed and meet fellow Beagle enthusiasts? (If you get chummy enough with one of them, she might go along to help you find the perfect puppy.) A local club will also help you refine your goals about what sort of dog meets your needs.

You may also want to attend a few dog shows or field trials, depending on whether you want a hunting/field or pet/show type of Beagle. Some Beagles appear in competitive field trials, where they display their rabbit-scenting abilities. Information on when and where field trials are held can be found on the American Kennel Club's Website. Of course, some Beagles are used day-to-day in the field for really hunting rabbits. Most Beagles, however, like my old Liz, spend their days just hanging out, watching television, and barking at the neighbors.

Show-quality dogs (conformation dogs) are the ones you'll see trotting around a show ring, as at the annual Westminster Dog Show. Dog shows are held throughout the year, and you can find one near you by checking the American Kennel Club's Website. The world of dog shows is pretty mysterious, but go anyway. It'll give you an idea of how a nice Beagle should look. This is especially important if you think you might like to show your dog some day. If you find a Beagle you think is particularly handsome, ask his handler or breeder if an upcoming litter is planned or if there are dogs from related lines available. (Don't do this right before a class, however, since people tend to be a little tense then. Approach your target after the classes have been judged. I always start with a compliment to the dog in question.) Most breeders are happy to talk with serious students of the breed.

Good breeders usually have a line of people waiting to buy puppies, so be prepared to wait. Spend the time reading up on Beagles (and about dogs in general), so you can become an armchair expert. The more informed you are, the better choices you will make, and the happier you will be with your dog.

When you make contact with a good breeder, make a list of questions, and be prepared to answer a few questions as well. Responsible breeders have high standards about where, and to whom, their puppies go. Don't be offended if the breeder asks you "nosy" questions about your house, yard, fencing, working hours, dog-owning expertise, and planned sleeping arrangements for the puppy. While the only question a pet store clerk will ask you is "Visa or MasterCard?", a good breeder wants the best for her dogs, and she wants to make sure you and the puppy will be a good match. It's a bad sign if the breeder seems more interested in your pocketbook than in the way you interact with her dogs. If a breeder doesn't have the type of puppy you are looking for, she should be able to direct you to someone else. Be wary of breeders who don't seem to know any other breeders.

Even if you don't know a lot about dogs or dog breeding, you should be able to spot a top-notch facility. A good breeder will have a clean, sheltered facility, preferably indoors. Note that Beagles raised outdoors may come from a line of hunting Beagles who may not easily adjust to a more sedentary or indoor life.

## Picking Your Puppy

When visiting the breeder to select your puppy, bring along the whole family. Everyone should have some input into choosing the family dog. As difficult as it may be (especially for children), do not make an immediate decision. Steel yourself; buy with your head as well as your heart. To prevent impulse buying, go see the puppies before they're old enough to leave the litter (eight weeks at the earliest). And regardless of when you go, don't bring your checkbook on the first visit. One look in those eyes and it's all over. Make yourself go home, re-think your decision, and if you're *sure,* then go back and bring home (or reserve) your puppy. Of course, if you've traveled five hundred miles to see a litter, you'll have a hard time continuing your search. Before you make any long-distance plans, ask for photos. Unless you're looking for a hard-to-find bloodline or are planning a coup at Westminster, however, you'll be able to find a very nice dog locally.

Pay close attention to the mother dog, especially her temperament. Temperament is largely inherited. If the mother is merry, outgoing, and amiable, it's likely the puppies will grow up to be the same way. Shyness is a problem in Beagles; be careful to avoid a bashful mother or puppy. The temperament of the stud dog is also important, although the dad may not be on hand for viewing. Many high quality dogs are bred from parents who happen not to live together. (Family values in Beagles aren't all that they might be.) Seeing a photo or videotape of the father may have to suffice. Simply having both parents on the premises, however, is no guarantee of quality.

### Is An Adult Dog the Right Choice for You?

Consider getting an older dog! You can avoid housetraining and chewing problems. And you won't have to wonder how he'll look when he's grown.

## The Characteristics of a Good Breeder

A good breeder will be honest about the shortcomings as well as the glories of Beagles. No breed is perfect in every way.

One shortcut I have used to sort out good breeders from bad ones is to ask the simple question, "What are the goals of your breeding program?" If the breeder stares at you blankly, you may want to reconsider buying a dog from her. A responsible breeder, however, once you broach this topic, will not stop talking about it. Ask the breeder how long she has been breeding dogs. Although every breeder has to begin at some point, inexperienced buyers are best matched with experienced breeders. Ask the breeder how often she breeds. Breeders with large numbers of litters over a short period are suspect.

Be suspicious of breeders who seem too anxious to sell their puppies, who assert that all their dogs are show quality, or who seem reluctant to provide verifiable health information.

Notice how the breeder interacts with her Beagles. They should seem happy, cheerful, and comfortable around her. If her dogs seem shy, frightened, or reluctant to come close, reconsider. Dogs who are not loved are probably not well-cared for. And although Beagles are remarkably resilient dogs, it's a lot easier on you to choose one who has had a good start in life.

### But He Has Papers!!

Just because a puppy has AKC papers does *not* mean he is a quality or even a healthy dog. The AKC is a registration agency. It does not guarantee the quality of dogs in its registry. Some of them, in fact, are real "dogs."

A good breeder can provide references from previous customers. It's a good idea to call these folks, and ask questions about the health and temperament of the Beagle they purchased. A breeder who's unwilling to supply references may have something to hide. A good breeder will also agree to take the dog back at any time if you can no longer keep it.

You should receive a signed, written contract; veterinary records; and a pedigree from the breeder. The AKC requires the following information on a signed AKC registration application (called a blue slip), signed bill of sale, or signed written statement:

- Breed, sex, and color of the dog
- Date of birth of the dog
- Registered names of the dog's parents
- Name of the breeder

Don't let the breeder tell you that she will send you the papers later. You are entitled to them immediately.

The breeder will probably give you a few days' supply of the food the puppy is accustomed to eating, and an old towel or some other "home-smelling" item to take to his new residence. This will comfort the puppy.

# Chapter 3

# Beagle Belongings

Your Beagle may have come naked into the world, but by the time he's spent a few days in your home, he should have the same accouterments as the other Beagles on the block. (This would not include a rhinestone collar. Beagles just aren't a rhinestone kind of dog.) Even though the idea of purchasing so much equipment for such a small dog seems daunting, remember that you need to buy many of these items only once.

## Collars and Leashes

You should buy an adjustable, correctly sized buckle or snap collar. Check it periodically. You should be able to insert four fingers between the neck and the collar. If you can't, it's too tight.

Nowadays, head halters are becoming popular. These humane devices guide your dog gently by the head and they are wonderful for inveterate pullers. Even a small child can safely handle a dog wearing a head halter, but because Beagles are sniffers, they enjoy walking along with their noses to the ground. Sometimes they just never get used to the head halter. Give your dog some time to get accustomed to his halter, and check it frequently to make sure it doesn't rub. If you find that a head halter makes your dog miserable, don't use it. Head halters can also be tough to put on, at least until you learn how. And in rare situations, a halter can come off if the dog paws at it.

*Bonkers*

*photo courtesy of Christine Gaites*

Some people prefer harnesses, especially for puppies. Harnesses are also good for dogs with spinal problems, or for sensitive dogs who don't like collars and head halters. They are very safe, but provide less control than other methods.

With a well-trained dog, a buckle collar, harness, or head halter will be all you'll ever need. Never use a choke chain or a prong collar on a young dog. (In fact, I wouldn't use one on any dog.) Choke chains are especially dangerous because they can injure the trachea, and even strangle a dog. Modern training methods rely on positive reinforcement, not punishment, and make these devices unnecessary. This is a good thing, since Beagles respond to kind, loving encouragement, and not to chains and prongs. One reason some people consider Beagles "untrainable" is that inappropriate methods were used to train them.

## Legal Beagles: The Dog Tag

Purchase a license for your Beagle. It isn't expensive, and it's the law. A license also serves as a minimum form of identification.

It's best to get several leashes. One should be a regular four- to six-foot leash made of leather, waxed cotton, or nylon. Chain leashes are noisy, heavy, and unnecessary. They give no warning when they are about to break, and they can develop sharp edges. Cotton and nylon leashes are lightweight, but can give you a rope burn if your Beagle is a puller. (Of course, a correctly trained Beagle will never pull!)

Good leather leashes are durable and comfortable. Note that leather leashes are attractive to dogs' taste buds, so you should never let your Beagle take the leash in his mouth. Once he gets a taste for it, you're doomed. (Some owners spray their leather leashes with Bitter Apple or a similar aversive product to discourage chewing.)

Some people like using a sixteen- to twenty-foot long line or retractable Flexi-Lead. Others are less enthusiastic, feeling that they encourage a dog to pull. Some dog owners don't like them because they are heavy and uncomfortable to handle. I like them for walking, but people can trip over the thin, hard-to-see line.

A new concept in leashes is the stretch leash. Some are completely elastic, while others use elastic inserts. These humane leashes discourage pulling without putting too much pressure on the neck. They come in various lengths and strengths.

Another kind of leash, the British slip leash, is a combined slip collar and leash. I use one frequently around the property—they are perfect for taking the dogs out to the fenced-in field where they are allowed to run free.

If you have multiple Beagles who walk well together, get a coupler or tripler! This allows you to attach two or more Beagles to a single leash.

## Beagle Bowls

Provide your dog with a sturdy, non-tip drinking bowl. Stainless steel bowls, which are inexpensive, good looking, and non-breakable, are the best. Plastic bowls can develop tiny crevices where harmful bacteria grow. The same is true to a lesser extent with ceramic bowls. Plastic bowls can also leech chemicals that may give an "off-taste" to the water.

### Food Bowl Phobia

Believe it or not, some dogs are actually afraid of food bowls that are too shiny. I had a Beagle like that once. If you own one of these dogs, use a dull-surfaced ceramic bowl rather one made of stainless steel. Some dogs may also prefer one style of dish to another.

## Beagle Toys

Even though you're his favorite playmate, the right toys can fill a puppy's spare time admirably. The right toys are safe, interesting, and washable.

### Top Toy Picks

Wonderful, safe toys include Kongs and Buster Cubes—bouncy, hard rubber toys that can be filled with kibble, cheese, or peanut butter. These are fun for home-alone Beagles, since food always engages their interest. (After you fill a Kong with cheese, you can even microwave it and serve your dog a warm gooey treat that he'll love.)

> **Toy Tip**
>
> Clean your dog's rubber and plastic toys once a week in hot soapy water, and throw soft toys in the washing machine. Dirty, slimy balls and Kongs are neither pleasant to behold nor healthy for your dog.

Although dogs are not colorblind, certain colors are easier for them to distinguish than others. The most vivid colors in dog vision are blue and yellow, so choose toys of these hues rather than red or green. Beagles also enjoy toys that burble, bleep, squeak, squawk, groan or babble. So do I.

*Bonkers* *photo courtesy of Christine Gaites*

*Bonkers*
*photo courtesy of Christine Gaites*

*Hypo*
*photo courtesy of Lea Ward*

## Toys to Avoid

Safe toys do not contain parts that can be swallowed, sharp protuberances, or batteries. *Never* buy a dog toy with a battery. Dogs can swallow them, and if they do, the chemicals inside can kill them. Even non-battery toys frequently have a rubber squeaker that dogs can swallow, so if your Beagle is in the habit of ripping and swallowing his toys, avoid those with squeakers. Similarly, small balls, like golf balls, can lodge in your Beagle's throat. Don't allow your Beagle to play with anything smaller than a tennis ball, and always supervise your dog's play.

Don't give your Beagle puppy anything that looks or smells like human clothes as a chew toy. Dogs can't distinguish your best silk blouse from your discards. Panty hose or nylons are extremely dangerous to leave around, as dogs can't resist them, and terrible things happen when they get twisted up in your Beagle's intestines.

### Beware!

Many dangerous swallowed items may not show up on an X-ray. Clothing, plastic toys, balls, and string often escape detection. In these cases, the only solution may be exploratory surgery.

## Canine Confinement

You'll need to restrict a puppy's access to certain parts of the house while he is being housetrained. And when he's grown, there may be a room or other area you want to keep off-limits. There are several effective and humane products that will help.

### Crates

Your Beagle's crate is his home, hiding place, traveling compartment, refuge, and housebreaking tool. Crates come in many varieties—heavy-duty wire, sturdy plastic, fiberglass, and even fold-up nylon kinds that are super for travel. Many dogs prefer the wire crates, which offer good visibility and top ventilation. Others seem to prefer plastic crates with their close, den-like atmosphere. All crates should be well ventilated and provided with comfortable, easy-to-clean bedding.

Whether or not your puppy should sleep in his crate is a matter of individual preference. Certainly your dog should learn to accept being crated; otherwise travel, surgical recovery and other eventualities may be unduly trying. Your puppy is safe in his crate (and so is your house), but there's nothing wrong with having your puppy sleep in a bed with a family member—if it's agreeable to the family member.

No puppy should be in a crate for longer than a few hours except at night. It's too confining for a lively young dog and will stunt his mental and physical growth. Dogs need stimulation.

### Baby Gates

Baby gates are essential for keeping the dog out of any room you don't want him in. They generally run about $25 each. If your puppy is a major chewer, though, don't get wooden ones.

### Exercise Pens

This portable puppy playpen is a compromise between the isolation of the crate and the free range of the kitchen or living room. During times when you want your puppy around you, but not out of sight, the so-called x-pen ("x" is for "exercise") is a tremendously useful way to oversee your puppy. While you are cooking dinner or cleaning the refrigerator, your puppy can watch you. Even more important, you can keep an eye on him.

### Dog Houses

Even if your Beagle sleeps indoors at night, which is what I recommend, an attractive doghouse will be a pleasant addition to your dog's backyard experience. It gives him his own safe and shady den, away from winter winds and summer sun. You needn't be concerned if the roof comes to a point—Snoopy is the only Beagle I've ever seen lie on top rather than inside.

## Doggie Doors

Although not feasible for every household, a doggie door opening into a fenced yard makes life easier for both you and your Beagle. It even acts as housetraining aid by letting your Beagle come and go as he likes. Most wood or composite doors can be installed in minutes. The easiest ones for dogs to use have just a clear, flexible plastic panel, but you can also purchase high-tech models that you can adjust mechanically, so that you can prevent the dog from going out or coming in. A pet door will cost from $35 to $100.

## Beagle Beds

Unless your dog will be using the sofa or his crate as his regular bed, you will want to purchase a special, comfortable dog bed for your Beagle. Many experts believe that it's important for a dog to have his own bed, designated for his use alone. Beds come

*"Tucker"*
*Wynborne's Tucker Box, NA, NAJ*

*photo courtesy of Nikki Berrong*

in an almost unlimited variety of styles, colors, and fabrics. Buy one that is as long as your dog is when he's stretched out. (If your dog is chewer, stay away from wicker.) There's even an allergen-resistant bed, made from "breathable" Cordura nylon, a washable fabric tougher than cotton or fleece that traps dust and other allergy causing particles.

If your Beagle likes to sleep curled up, a bed with raised sides might be just the ticket. Dogs who prefer to stretch out at night generally like a rectangular bed. Of course, dogs tend to sleep curled when they're cold, and stretched out when they're hot, and some people even provide winter and summer accommodations for their pets. In the summer, Beagles don't appreciate a deeply cushioned hot bed; they like something cooler, just as we do.

### Vehicle Barriers

If you'll be riding around much with your Beagle, consider getting any of the various brands of barriers available; these will keep your dog safely in his own section of the car and out of your lap. The price of these barriers varies widely, from about $50 to $150, depending on model and size.

## Clean Up

You will definitely want to be ready for the less pleasant aspect of dog ownership by having certain items in the home before your Beagle gets there.

### Pooper Scoopers

I use my hand inside a plastic bag, but some people prefer to save their backs and noses by using a pooper scooper. These come in many styles, so browse the pet supply stores and catalogs until you find one that strikes your fancy. The fancier models retail for about $15.

### Cleaning Supplies

Assume your puppy will make lots of mistakes, so be armed with state-of-the-art odor removers. Some, like the enzyme cleaner Nature's Miracle, are designed specifically to eliminate the smell of urine. A gallon of good pet stain cleaner costs about $20. It's very important that you get rid of all traces of the odor; otherwise, your dog will assume he's found the proper place to eliminate. (Never use an ammonia-based cleaner for pet stains. It smells too much like urine to a dog.) It's really a good idea if you can just remove all carpeting altogether. You can even go all out and put in nifty artificial wood floors. Or tile, as we did. It makes a world of difference.

## Grooming Equipment

Luckily, Beagles don't require much brushing—a simple hound mitt will do the trick. A hound mitt is a rubber glove with protuberances that slips easily over your hand. It's designed to stimulate the blood circulation, remove dead hair, and give a good finish to the coat. You might also add a soft bristle brush, rubber brushes, or a slicker brush. There is even an "ionic" brush (operated by battery) that claims to emit "cleansing ions." This item supposedly removes odors from the dog's fur and replaces baths. It doesn't. A shedding blade is good to remove dead hair during a serious shed.

You'll need nails clippers, so buy a pair appropriate to your Beagle's size. The Dremel grinding tool is another nail-trimming option. For ten years, we have used nothing but a Dremel grinder for shortening our dogs' nails. The Dremel comes in both plug-in and battery models. It works great, and it's easier to use safely than clippers, with which you can cut a nail's quick.

A good brand of fancy shampoo for dogs can be expensive; you can get by with cheap shampoo for humans for a lot less. Either is fine for your dog.

You'll also need to buy a dental kit for your Beagle. This means canine toothpaste and a small brush or "finger brush." You can buy different toothpaste flavors like chicken or beef. Or even mint or peanut butter. (You may like the mint—the dog prefers the meat-flavors.)

# Chapter 4
# The Backyard Beagle

Beagles enjoy human company, and like to sleep inside at night. Although Beagles are happiest when kept as house pets, many people also provide runs and outdoor kenneling for their dogs. And of course, people who keep a large number of hunting Beagles must perforce keep them outside. Imagine twenty Beagles in a house! (Sounds like heaven, doesn't it?) There's a world of difference between an outdoor working dog, by the way, and a lonely "pet" relegated to the backyard. Hunting dogs are not deprived of human companionship, and lead exciting lives doing what they love best. Sleeping in a kennel is not a hardship for them, for they get lots of company and attention all day long. Besides, they are *very* tired at night. But unless you are actively outside all day interacting with your dog, bring him in at night.

Evenings aside, Beagles like to be outdoors (a lot), and they need a good amount of exercise. This exercise should not include his running free on the freeway. It's your job to keep him contained in his safe, fenced, authorized area, so confine your Beagle! This isn't as easy as it sounds. Beagles can dig under fences, climb over gates, and weasel around you as you come home from work. Some say that they can become temporarily invisible.

Don't leave your Beagle unattended in the backyard in the hope that he will get enough exercise on his own. Unless you have a supply of rabbits for him to chase, he'll spend his lonely hours digging holes, barking at the neighbors, trying to escape, and standing pathetically at the door waiting to come in.

Leaving a dog unsupervised in your backyard may also be dangerous. It puts him at risk of thieves and annoying children. It's fine for your dog to be outside for an hour or two without being watched every second (unless he's a true escape artist). But unless you have an exceptional facility, and excellent neighbors who would come to the dog's aid if anything went wrong, it's usually not wise to leave your dog in the backyard when you go out.

If you have a gate that faces the road, and your Beagle is in the yard, put a padlock on the gate. I know this may seem like a waste of time, but I know of three separate incidents where passersby "liberated" dogs—and the dogs were struck by cars.

## Beagle Barriers

A fenced backyard is a necessity for a happy Beagle, but Beagle owners must make sure that the fence is secure. Beagles are good at digging under, pushing through, and climbing over obstacles. Even if you have a sedentary, unadventurous Beagle, a low or insecure fence is no match for a fierce neighboring dog. A standard wood and wire fence provides the best protection for your dog, but other options are available, depending on your financial situation, your aesthetic sense, your local covenants, and the escape artistry of your particular Beagle.

### Electronic Fences

The so-called invisible or electronic fence is trendy nowadays, but it has several serious drawbacks. In the first place, dogs need to be correctly trained to heed the fence. Often a professional from the company will come out to help you do so. Only you, however, are responsible for obeying the instructions. Reasons I'm not crazy about electronic fences include:

- Some dogs will brace themselves for a shock and run right through the thing.
- Clever dogs will also know that the power of the fence is connected to their collars, and once the collars are off, they can make a break for it.
- Electricity isn't always as reliable as it might be.

- The collars that go with invisible fencing rely on batteries. You need to check the batteries every few weeks.
- Electronic fences rely on pain for the accomplishment of their objective.
- Electronic fences don't keep other dogs or nasty kids out.
- Although the electronic shock collar may not keep your dog in the yard if there's a rabbit to chase on the other side of the street, it most certainly *will* keep him out after he has broken loose.

## Kennels and Runs

Preferable to a tether is a sturdy kennel and secure run large enough for a Beagle or two. The run should be at least fifteen feet long and ten feet wide, with a six-foot high fence. The safest runs have concrete poured in a thin strip at the inside base, which will prevent your Beagle from digging out. The run should be secure, with good drainage and plenty of shade. It's best if you can divide the pen into two or more areas. That way you can add another dog, move your Beagle in order to clean one section, and so on.

I like a plain earth floor for a run, because clean dirt gives your Beagle a comfortable natural footing, and allows him to indulge his natural habits of digging. Of course, if your dog is a very skilled digger, a dirt floor might just invite him to escape. Moreover, dirt floors provide an increased problem with pests

*Bonkers* *photo courtesy of Christine Gaites*

and parasites, but keeping your dog on heartworm pills and flea/ tick control can reduce or eliminate these concerns.

Many people like an easy-to-keep concrete floor. This flooring helps to keep toenails down to a reasonable length, but it's cold in the winter, hot in the summer, and hard on feet. Other choices include pea gravel and brick.

## Bad Backyard Practices

A chain is not a replacement for a fence. Dogs kept on a chain feel vulnerable and scared. They don't get exercise. Furthermore, they are prime picking for dognappers and abusive children. Dogs can tangle themselves in a chain and do themselves serious injury as well. A brief supervised period on a stake is acceptable, but your dog should not be left unattended. (As a matter of fact, the U.S. Department of Agriculture announced in 1997 that keeping dogs on a tether is a cruel practice.)

On the other hand, a few people still believe that because it's "natural" for dogs to run free, they should always be allowed to do so. Natural it may be, but legal and safe it is not. Dogs who are allowed to run free get lost, poisoned, hit by cars, shot by hunters, and attacked by bigger dogs. They also eat garbage, get into hornets' nests, roll in dead things and tree sap (often at the same time), pick up contagious diseases, and destroy your neighbor's garden. To keep your dog safe and your own life simple, keep your dog in a secure area.

## Fixing Up the Joint

Of course, you will provide clean fresh water for your Beagle at all times while he is outside. Several buckets are better than just one, and deeper buckets keep water cool longer. Many water dishes come in a "no-tip" variety. You can also buy "self-watering" buckets. Keep the water in a shady place, and check on it frequently.

Keep interesting, sturdy dog toys in the yard, like tennis balls, a Buster Cube or Kong toy filled with peanut butter.

Having said all this, I want to reiterate that the most luxurious backyard in the world, with all the accouterments, is no replacement for your care and company. A Beagle left alone day after day in a pen or yard is the saddest sight in the world. If you need to be

*Bonkers* *photo courtesy of Christine Gaites*

gone during the day, keeping your Beagle in a safe pen is certainly acceptable, but consider getting another Beagle to keep him company. And when you're home, it's time for walks, runs, games, and lots of attention from the one he loves most in the world: you. Always remember that though your Beagle may not be the center of your life—you are the center of his.

## Recovering a Lost Beagle

If your Beagle extricates himself from your yard, don't just wait for him to come home. Think about your dog's personality and start looking. If you have a shy Beagle, chances are he isn't roaming around the city park trying to make friends. Head for the backcountry, and check under bushes. On the other hand, if your pet is Miss Congeniality, she might hanging out at the schoolyard with the children. Ask yourself, "If I were Tippy, where would I go?" Follow your instinct. Try baiting the area with food, the most powerful Beagle motivator known. Use a strong scented, flavorful food like barbecue or liver to draw him back.

Notify all dog-related businesses—groomers, shelters, pet sitters, and the like, that your dog is lost. Check out the shelters yourself—don't be satisfied with a phone call. Some shelter personnel don't know a Beagle from a Basenji.

If you have lost your dog in a strange place, put down your shirt or jacket—something imbued with your scent to leave as an attractant. This is an old hunter's trick that works more often than you think. Your local humane society will probably lend or rent you a humane box trap. Although some dogs are clever enough to back out of the trap without releasing the spring, you still have a fair chance of catching him.

Get out recent color photographs of your Beagle and put up posters everywhere. Don't be stingy about offering a reward; it's a powerful motivator to children who are often the ones to find the dog. Include a written description—but leave out at least one critical piece of information. It's disgusting how many unsavory people will pretend to find the dog, in hopes of parting you with your reward money.

Don't give up hope. I have known of Beagles who were returned to their rightful owners after months on the lam.

## Dog Tags

Here's the deal. Keep a buckle collar and visible identification tags on your dog at all times. Forget any stories you may have heard about dogs getting strangled by their collars, or abducted by aliens who used the tags as a magnet to get the Beagle on to their space ship. The truth is that collars, like seatbelts, save lives. For every dog who may have an accident involving a collar (and the right collar will come off in most emergencies), dozens are lost or killed. Dogs without collars are hard to catch. And every minute your lost dog goes without being caught increases his chances of being hit by a car or getting into some terrible trouble. Identification tags are too cheap not to own them.

You can certainly add tattoos or micro chipping as an additional method of safeguarding your pet, but the simple truth is this: Most lost dogs who wear visible identification tags are returned to their owners. Most lost dogs without visible identification tags are not. I recommend, in addition to tags, that you use a laundry marker to clearly print your phone number on your dog's collar. Or you can order a personalized collar from many pet catalogs.

## Backyard Perils

Although your Beagle will enjoy time in the backyard—lying in the sun, playing with you—you must be vigilant about making the yard as safe as possible.

### Pests

Dogs are nosy creatures, and that gets them into trouble with spiders and snakes. Although you might not find the rotting woodpile behind the shed all that interesting, your Beagle probably does. Rotting woodpiles are home to black widow spiders, who are not averse to biting your Beagle right on the nose. Black widow bites are agonizing, and although your dog will probably recover, he will need veterinary care. Mice like woodpiles, too, and mice draw snakes. Snakes also bite investigatory Beagles right on the nose. Even non-venomous bites are filthy and lead to infection. Dogs are also at risk from attack by hornets, bees, and fire ants. (If your dog *is* stung by a bee, scrape out the stinger with a stiff piece of paper or credit card. Don't try to pull it out, since you may end up injecting more poison into the animal.)

### Gardening Dangers

The greatest backyard perils, however, may come from you. Lawn chemicals are dangerous, especially the kind that a professional lawn care company sprays around. These aerosols tend to hover low over the grass—exactly the height of your Beagle's nose. You must keep your dog inside, away from the lawn for a specified period after spraying is done. It's much better to avoid the situation altogether by using organic lawn care products.

### Natural Flea Management

To safely rid your yard of fleas, use nematodes. These are microscopic worms that devour flea larvae. They are safe for people, pets, and plants. After they kill all the available fleas, they die, so you may need to reinvest in nematodes once in a while. You can buy them at a garden supply center.

*"Louie in Leaves"* *photo courtesy of Wally Jarrett*

Even too much organic gardening could be a bad thing, if you're not careful. For example, your trusty compost heap harbors a whole passel of nasty organisms you don't want your Beagle to touch, including those responsible for Salmonella and botulism. Keep it securely contained, away from a prying dog.

### Swimming Pools

Dogs can swim and dogs can drown. If you enjoy having your Beagle racing around the rim of your pool barking like a maniac while you and the kids are taking an afternoon dip, that's fine. However, someone responsible must be appointed to watch Buster the dog, because sooner or later he'll fall in. So teach him how to find the stairs if he happens to end up in the pool. If he can't, he'll rip the vinyl lining of your pool to complete shreds while trying to get out. Then he'll drown.

## Climate Concerns

Just like people, dogs are subject to the effect of the seasons. Using your common sense will go far to keeping your Beagle comfortable and safe year 'round.

### Summerizing Your Beagle

Dogs suffer heatstroke easily. They can't sweat, except a little through their paw pads. Dogs cool themselves by panting, a rather inefficient temperature regulation system.

One way to help keep your Beagle cool is to provide him with a child's plastic wading pool. (Make sure it's constructed of heavy-duty material!) But if your Beagle is just a puppy, be sure you supervise him—a little dog can drown in a wading pool.

An adequate supply of cool water is also essential for your summertime Beagle. It is important for him to have plenty to drink, and some dogs are reluctant to drink a sufficient amount, especially if their water supply is warm or stale. They are then in danger of becoming dehydrated. To see if your dog is dehydrated: Gently pull the skin on the back of his neck. Then release. Healthy skin springs quickly back into place. If the skin stays loose, your dog may be dehydrated.

When out for a stroll on a fry-an-egg-on-the-sidewalk day, keep your Beagle on earth or grassy areas. If you'd be uncomfortable walking barefoot on hot pavement (or asphalt!) so would your dog. Early morning and evening strolls are more comfortable than noonday hikes.

## Winterizing Your Beagle

Pet Beagles should be inside dogs. An inside dog is one who sleeps inside at night, and is generally in the house except when exercising or playing. Beagles are small dogs, and they are not designed to handle the extremes of cold weather common in the so-called "temperate zones" of the United States. If your Beagle is outside in the winter, provide him with a plastic rather than metal

*Wynborne's Tucker Box, NA, NAJ* *photo courtesy of Nikki Berrong*

water bowl. His poor tongue could actually stick to the metal on a cold day and cause him no end of grief.

Be aware that products that melt ice can be dangerous to a dog. Most of them are poisonous and nearly all are bad for your dog's feet. Even if you don't use ice melts, or use a brand that is "pet friendly," your dog can still be exposed to the poisons other people leave around. Keep your dog's feet safe by applying Vaseline to his paw pads before you set out on a snowy walk through suburbia. On your return, bathe his paws with a damp cloth and monitor him for skin infection. If you suspect he may have eaten chemical ice melts, watch out for the common signs: vomiting, diarrhea, salivation, and depression. Some people even put booties on their dog for these winter walks! (If you think they're for sissies, check out those Iditarod dogs sometime. They all wear them.)

# Chapter 5

# Bringing Your Beagle Home

Beagles are cheerful, gregarious dogs who will bond with your entire family. That's why it's extra important that everyone in the home be prepared to receive an unlimited amount of wiggly Beagle love. Owning a Beagle is truly a family affair.

## Before Your Beagle Arrives

The old Boy Scout motto "Be prepared" was never so apropos as it is when talking about Beagle ownership. Or, as my old drill instructor used to say, "The more you sweat in peacetime, the less you'll bleed in war." The way to avoid disaster is to prepare for it. Puppy-proof your house!

### Puppy-Proofing the House

Like children, but worse, puppies are into everything: books, magazines, fireplaces, electrical wires, household plants, medications, remote controls, pillows, Oriental carpets, tonight's dinner, old photographs, knickknacks, trash cans, table legs, income tax refunds, and dissertations. (Yes, dogs do eat homework; they pee on it too.) Some of these items are expensive, some irreplaceable, some dangerous. Chomping on the household is normal behavior, of course; all young mammals are curious about their environment. Unfortunately some of their experiments are bad for the house and worse for the Beagle. A penny minted after 1983, for example, has enough zinc in it to poison your dog. So do metal Monopoly pieces. Aluminum foil can do serious damage to your Beagle's innards, and plastic food wrap (irresistible to Beagles) can block the intestines. This means keeping non-digestible items out of your dog's reach.

## Lock Your Cabinets

To prevent your dog from getting into cabinets that may first charm, then harm your new pet, buy childproof locks on your puppy-reachable cabinets.

Check your store of cleaning supplies. Most of the household chemicals we use are really unnecessary. Even carpet fresheners can be dangerous. Dogs enjoy rolling on carpets. Then they lick themselves, and swallow what they lick. If you must freshen your carpet, use a non-toxic, natural product like baking soda. Baking soda, along with vinegar, are dog-friendly products that do a super job of cleaning. New products (called green cleaners) are also excellent and smell a lot better than the harsh cleansers of the past.

Keep your dog out of the bathroom, or if you can't, at least keep the toilet lid down. Even if you keep it sparkling clean, the chemicals in the thing can kill your dog.

Put everything that is valuable or dangerous out of the puppy's reach. (Puppies can reach further than you expect. An agile Beagle can get on top of the kitchen table with ease.) Sharp and heavy objects can fall and strike your Beagle. Plastic bags can smother him. Toddlers can fall on him. Cover trash cans tightly and move them out of the dog's reach. (We keep ours behind the cellar door.)

If an item is not removable, make it as inconspicuous as possible. Attach electrical cords closely to the wall and barricade them behind furniture. Keep the remote on top of the TV. At least then you'll know where it is. Instead of letting the unpaid bills pile up on the coffee table, you'll be compelled to read, respond to, and file them as soon as possible. Otherwise the dog will eat them. Think of it this way. Having a dog makes you a better, more organized person.

I have found, for example, that keeping the mini-blinds rolled up prevents them from being bent out of recognition by an eager

Beagle. In her haste to view the passing street traffic, our Liz would leap on the sofa, and stick her pointed little nose through the slats. If that didn't give her enough breadth of vision, she would toss her head around until she had wangled a sufficient space. By then, of course, the blinds were history.

## Deadly Flora

Many household plants are deadly to dogs. While adult dogs often show no interest in them, puppies may. Common and hazardous plants include aloe, amaryllis, caladium, cyclamen, daffodil, dieffenbachia, geranium, mother-in-law's tongue, and philodendron. Remove these plants or keep them well out of the reach of the most agile puppy. For more information about household poisons, contact the National Animal Poison Control Center at (800) 548-2423.

## Prepare Your Dog's Personal Space

Make sure you have your Beagle's crate, his own private room, in view and open. Unless he has had a bad experience with a crate in the past, he'll soon find his way in there. And if you've made it soft and comfortable, and perhaps added a dog biscuit or two, he'll quickly feel right at home in it. Perhaps he'll even curl up and go to sleep.

*Wynborne's Tucker Box, NA, NAJ*

*photo courtesy of Nikki Berrong*

## Decisions, Decisions

You've puppy-proofed the house, bought the supplies, and made the first appointment with the vet. You're ready! Whoops, not quite. The one thing you may have forgotten is the Family Discussion about Cosmo. Every family has different Dog Rules. (Even though dogs sometimes end up making their own rules, you can at least give it the old college try and decide what the rules should be.) As a family, you all need to agree on the Dog Rules. If one member of the family thinks it's fine for Cosmo to be on the couch and another is always chasing him off, and putting him on the floor, it's no wonder that the dog gets confused. Here are some things you need to agree upon:

- Responsibilities: Who will feed the dog in the morning? In the evening? Who will walk the dog? Who will take him to the vet, and who will be responsible for paying his expenses? Who will be primarily responsible for training the dog? Who will pick up the Beagle poop in the backyard? (This is something you don't want to leave to chance.)
- Dog privileges: Will the dog be allowed to come into every room, sleep in a person's bed, snooze on the sofa? Or is the dog expected to sleep in his own crate or bed? If Brother Walter doesn't want Trey in his room, Brother Walter needs to be responsible for keeping his door shut. Beagles really love furniture, and some people provide their dog with his very own couch. Others just throw a dog bed on the floor. The same is true with lap sitting. It's tempting to have your baby puppy curl up on your lap, but if you allow this, get ready for a lifetime of it. Undoubtedly, your guests will also be subject to the same treatment. It's possible, although not easy, to teach your dog to come onto laps only when invited. If you decide to do this, make sure everyone in the family (including the dog) knows it's going to be by-invitation-only.

- Where will the Beagle eat, and more important, where will he be while you're eating? Will you allow the dog to hang around under the table, hoping for a piece of broccoli to fall to the floor? Of course, feeding your dog *from* the table is a pretty bad idea as a rule. Pretty soon, he'll be demanding to be fed. On the other hand, it's perfectly possible to train a dog to eat only when invited, using a command word such as "Treat!" Be forewarned, though. This is a lot of work. It is much easier to not feed the dog from the table.

The important thing to remember is that dogs need rules, and everyone, including the dog, needs to know what the rules are. Although some dogs are smart enough to figure out that Cathy won't allow him on the couch but Caroline will, this type of inconsistency is confusing to most dogs.

### Get it in Writing

Whatever your family decides upon as good rules for Rover, write them down and stick them on the refrigerator. This will help to resolve differences of opinion that occur later on.

## Baptizing your Beagle

What's in a name? Lots of things. Although dogs probably do not understand their names the same way people do, they do associate the sound of their names with themselves. That's why it's important never to use your dog's name when giving any negative command like "No." "Good boy, Charley!" or "Come on, Smudge!" are pleasant things, but—"Time for a bath, Buster," is not. The key is that you should always use your dog's name for something pleasant. Of course, you'll slip up on this once in a while—we all do. But it's nice to make an effort.

If you have adopted a dog who has been abused, you might want to change the dog's name—it probably has only bad associations for him. Because dogs think of their names as signals for getting their attention, changing his name is a good start for rehabilitating your dog.

To help your dog get accustomed to his name in a positive way that will help in obedience training later on, get him to associate his name with looking directly at you. Whistle or cluck at your dog, and when he looks, say his name in a happy tone, praise him, and throw him a treat or a toy. This way he'll not only learn his name and associate it with something good, he'll also look at you when you say it. And that becomes important later.

## The Ride Home

At last the day has arrived! Now the real fun and thrill of Beagle ownership begins. Believe me, your life will never be the same again. Nor would you want it to be. On the ride home from the kennel, hold your new puppy closely in your lap (you'll be sitting in the back seat with him, of course) while someone else drives. This is the oldest and best bonding device in the world. Speak sweetly to him, but don't be alarmed or react in any negative or over-solicitous way if he cries. Likewise, if you both should be unfortunate enough for him to throw up on you, remain nonchalant, and clean it up later. If you make any kind of commotion about it now, the whole incident will be imprinted on his little puppy brain; in fact, it might create a nervous habit.

## Day One at Your House

The first day in your home is a very momentous one for your Beagle. Take it slow, let him get acquainted with his environment, and try to make it as stress-free as possible.

### The First Walk

Before you even enter the house, take your new family member for a stroll around the grounds. Let the puppy take his time to sniff around and get his bearings. Talk gently to him, and when he finishes smelling everything (this may take a lot longer than you want), he'll be ready to pay attention and toddle along after you.

Praise him mightily with every step he takes in your direction. This is an important way to get him to bond to you. And when he pees or poops, as he most certainly will, praise him still more, as long as he's still outside! Give him a bit of biscuit. Beagles are not subtle when it comes to these matters.

## First Meals

Your breeder or rescue group should have given you a diet sheet and perhaps even a sample of what your puppy has been eating. Keep your new Beagle on this diet for at least a few days.

Changing diet and changing homes at the same time can put a puppy under physical and emotional stress that will make itself known by diarrhea and other unpleasant effects. If you want to put your dog on a different diet, you can do so gradually after a few days. Contrary to what many people think, so-called puppy food is not very different from "adult dog food." Puppies and adults require the same basic nutrients, but pound for pound, puppies need more calories. Don't supplement your puppy's diet with vitamins, calcium, or other minerals unless so advised by your veterinarian.

Locate your pup's eating place as far as possible from heavy foot traffic, but as close as possible to the door—if you can find such a combination. Near the door is important, since you'll want to make a quick transition to the outdoors as soon as possible after Sammy eats.

Your puppy will make many mistakes; we all do. He is bound to pee on the floor, chew up a book, or steal somebody's sandwich sooner or later. It's part of growing up. Never use any physical correction on a Beagle. Hitting, cuffing, screaming, or shaking result in a traumatized animal, not a loving, confident pet.

### Picking Up Puppy

Of course, it's fun to pick up and cuddle your new puppy. It's great news to learn that this natural action is also good for his training. Studies have shown that puppies who are picked up at least five times each day from the age of six weeks to at least fifteen weeks show much less aggression and are better bonded to people than dogs in control groups.

## The First Night

I hope your dog will be a real part of your family, and integrated into all facets of your life. I used to believe that puppies should sleep in their crates from the first night onward, otherwise they would be "spoiled." I've changed my mind. Your new little puppy needs love and comfort. He has just been torn from the only home he has ever known. His mother and littermates are gone forever. He has come into a new place among a bunch of strangers. Everything looks, sounds, and smells different. It's not surprising if your puppy is a bit scared. Letting him sleep with you won't ruin him, and it's very easy to transfer him to the crate after a few days. The strong bonding that will develop between you now will help in future training.

Like human beings, dogs dream. Please do not wake up your Beagle when he's dreaming, even if you think he's having a nightmare. He'll forget about it in the morning anyway, and it's best not to disturb his natural sleep cycle.

If your puppy must sleep in a crate, keep it right next to your bed. Don't banish your Beagle to a far distant room. Tire him out with fun and play just before bedtime. His closeness to you will allow you to comfort him, and assure him that everything is all right. Talk to him gently just as he is falling asleep.

During the night, your puppy *may* whine to signal that he has to go out, but I wouldn't count on it. If he does, get up and take him out to use the "bathroom." You'll probably have to get up again very early in the morning. Your puppy has a tiny bladder that doesn't hold very much. In addition, the sphincter muscles controlling eliminatory functions don't fully "get in gear" until he is about four months old. Don't expect a housetrained Beagle before then. (See Chapter 8: Housetraining for more details.)

## Veterinary Check

Make sure you have selected a good vet before you bring home your puppy, and take him there for a checkup as soon as possible. The best choice is a nearby animal clinic; location can be critical in an emergency. Your veterinarian should be willing to take the time to answer your questions. Your dog should like him too. The first vet visit can go far to establishing a lasting impression (good or bad) on your dog. Never use a vet who seems rushed or insensitive. If you don't have the feeling that he really likes your Beagle, go elsewhere. For guidance in choosing a veterinarian, see Chapter 15, Beagle Well Being.

### Bringing Home an Older Dog

Although puppies tend to bond naturally with their new owners, it may take a little longer when the new family member is an older dog. This is natural. If a dog has been abused by people, he may be terribly shy; in other cases, the dog has had only one beloved previous owner. Patience is the key. One method that works well to help your new Beagle bond to you is by hand-feeding him. For the first week or so, forget about food bowls. Use your hand to establish a strong bond. Every meal should come from a family member—especially those with whom he seems reserved. Beagles are so food oriented that this time-honored method of getting connected works even better with them than it does with other breeds. Granted, this takes a little longer than throwing the food in a bowl and walking off, but it really pays in the long run.

## Out and About with Your Young Beagle

Beagles are probably one of the most easily socialized of all breeds! It's in the genes; remember they were bred as hunting dogs. Still, genetics or not, all puppies need to be socialized. You'll want to take your Beagle out with you whenever possible. Most people and most other canines enjoy the company of a friendly dog, but always ask before you arrive at a friend's house with Binky in tow. Luckily, Beagles are so happy-go-lucky and gregarious that getting permission to bring them is usually no problem, as long as you have a well-behaved pet. (I'll focus on puppy socialization in this chapter. The following chapter will discuss managing dog-dog relations and keeping children and dogs happy in the same home.)

Until your veterinarian assures you that your Beagle puppy is fully immunized, however, limit his access to strange dogs. Several deadly diseases are lurking about that your dog can catch through contact with other dog's feces, urine, saliva, or nearby presence. Don't allow your puppy to sniff the feces of strange dogs. That's a good way for him to contract parvovirus and other diseases. And there's really no upside to it. At all.

It's not a bad idea to check the bottom of your own shoes after being away from home. You can bring home something very nasty to your puppy. Some people even keep a very shallow pan of bleach to step in on their arrival back home, since bleach kills the parvovirus, one of the worst. It's not a bad idea.

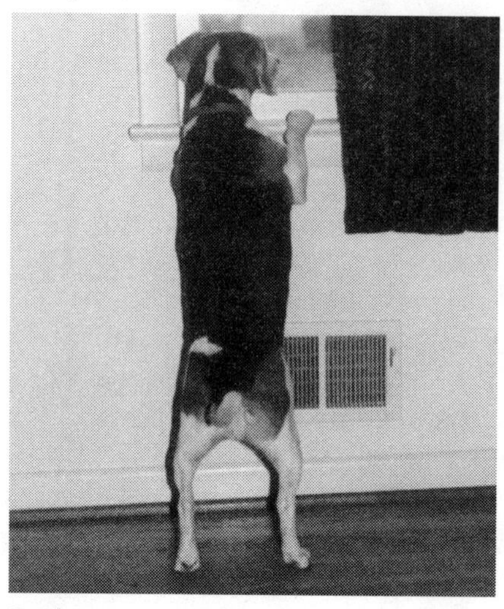

*Bonkers*
*photo courtesy of Christine Gaites*

Totally isolating your puppy until he's four to six months old, as a few people recommend, is not a good idea. Dogs are meant to be with other dogs, and hiding your Beagle away will hinder or destroy his normal socialization processes, bringing lots of trouble down the road. One solution is a well-regulated puppy kindergarten and play periods with dogs and owners you know well. Invite people and their vaccinated pets over frequently, and enjoy each other's company.

Your puppy should socialize with both vaccinated, friendly older dogs and healthy rambunctious puppies of his own age. Don't allow your puppy to associate with another one who looks sick. And keep your eye out for bullying dogs (including your own). Puppies bullied from a young age grow up to be timid adults. If you see bullying occur, separate the dogs briefly, and let them try again. Fight the urge to pick your puppy up and carry him away from a frightening situation. If you "rescue" your puppy, he'll learn that he's helpless. Try to get the other dog to move. For more specifics on Beagle socialization see Chapter 6: Socialization: Beagles, Kids, and More Beagles.

## Dog/Dog Socialization

If your puppy is less than nine or ten weeks old when he was separated from his litter, he may be insufficiently socialized with other dogs. The period between eight and twelve weeks is when puppies best learn how to manage with others in their group.

*Tuny*

*photo courtesy of Polly & Wilson Palacios*

Inadequately socialized puppies may not have learned responsible play behavior, and as a result may be "nippy" with their humans. These puppies simply never had a chance to learn how to play bite. Play biting is a normal puppy activity, but puppies can bite too hard. (Never encourage nipping. If your puppy does play bite, cry, "Ouch!" in a reproachful way. Refuse to play with your puppy for several minutes. Repeat until he learns not to bite. You can also roll some antiperspirant on the wrist or other vulnerable spots. Dogs hate the taste, and the experience should discourage nipping.)

## Human/Beagle Socialization

The very best age for puppies to develop socialization skills with humans is when they are six to eight weeks old. However, their socialization with other dogs develops best when they are between eight and ten weeks old. This creates something of a dilemma. Puppies who are not removed from the litter until they are older need to be handled and played with frequently by the breeder to insure that they develop human socialization skills. On the other hand, puppies leaving the litter earlier will need to keep up their interaction with other dogs.

Beagles like human beings just about as well as they like other dogs, so you have an easy job. Still, make sure you do that job by

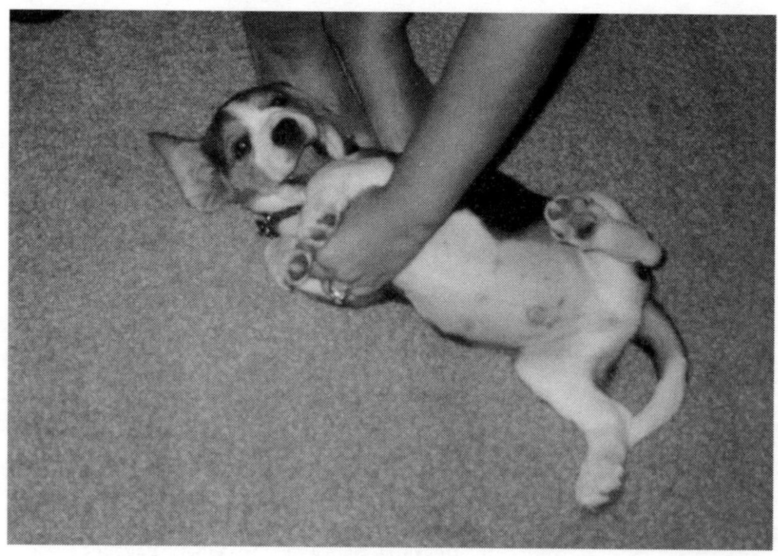

*Tuny*

*photo courtesy of Polly & Wilson Palacios*

having your Beagle puppy meet as many new people as possible. Don't isolate him in the backyard when company comes—allow him to greet the new arrivals in a warm (but not wild) way. Be sure to take your Beagle on frequent walks where he can meet lots of friendly folks. This is a critical stage in your dog's development. I'll talk about special techniques to help shy Beagles get over their timidity in the section on "Bashful Beagles" in Chapter 14—but for now make it your goal to have your Beagle meet a hundred new people in the next few months. Think of what it will do for your own social life!

## Puppy Kindergarten

Too many people wait until their puppies are several months old before they decide that yes, the pup could use some training. That's like waiting until a child is eight years old before you teach him to say "please" and "thank you." Get your Beagle pup registered in a good puppy kindergarten class as soon as they'll take him (which will be when he is fully immunized), and get started on the road to happy dog ownership. Good training is as much about training you as it is about training the dog.

# Chapter 6

# Socialization: Beagles, Kids, and More Beagles

Everyone wants a dog who is a pleasure to be with—a dog who is friendly toward other dogs and happy to be with people—old friends and strangers alike. By working with your Beagle to fine tune his social skills, you'll have a pet who is a joy both at home and in public.

## Beagles and Children, Children and Beagles

Children and Beagles are a natural match, and Beagles are one of the most highly recommended breeds for families with kids. Few dogs are so happy to be around children, or so trustworthy with them. This doesn't mean that Beagles (or any dog) should be left unsupervised with small children. Beagles have floppy ears and waggy tails, both irresistible to some kids. And Beagles, though small, are natural roughhousers; in their exuberance they can easily knock over a toddler. Beagle pups may consider children fellow puppies and will play with them as they did with their littermates, which includes playful nipping and chewing. Because of their hunting heritage, Beagles are "mouthy" dogs. This doesn't mean that they talk back; it means they investigate everything orally. Everything includes children's tiny hands.

Be aware that children can unwittingly hurt a dog, especially a small puppy. Dogs can get so excited playing with kids that they over-exert themselves, and puppies have actually been known to die in their efforts to "keep up." Kids can also pull ears and/or tails and make a dog shy or aggressive. When it comes to dogs, children need some socializing too. With good examples to follow and loving supervision, children with pets learn to develop their powers of empathy and sensitivity. In fact, having a dog helps kids become better adults.

### Cruel Kids

If you have ever observed your child being intentionally cruel to any animal, you should not have a pet. It is not normal for kids to be mean to animals, nor is it just a part of growing up.

Use playtime as an opportunity to work with your kids and your dog, teaching them to interact acceptably. Although Beagles are the most loving of dogs, don't allow your young child to hug your Beagle—or any other dog—until you're sure the dog doesn't mind. Not only do some kids hug too hard, but dogs and people don't interpret hugs the same way. To dogs, hugging may feel like a threat rather than affection. The same is true for kissing or even patting a dog on the top of the head. Teach your child to stroke (not pat) the dog gently on the back or chest instead. (Some dogs, however, interpret chest stroking as a sexual signal, and may initiate mounting behavior.) Scratching a dog lightly beneath the chin is also an acceptable and friendly gesture. Have your child stand tall and straight around all dogs, and have her speak and move slowly and in a reassuring manner.

Dogs often signal their dislike of something by walking away. Teach your child that this is the dog's way of saying he is tired of playing, and that he should be left alone. Never permit your child to chase or pull at your Beagle. Nothing good will come of it.

Likewise, dogs who mouth, guard, or try to mount children are showing dominance over them. Do not allow this behavior to continue. Don't allow the puppy to lick the baby. Licking easily progresses to chewing and mouthing, then to nipping. Playful puppy nipping can leave a scar or permanently frighten a small child. Sniffing only, please.

Every dog should have his own private place that is completely off-limits to the child. The rule should be, "When Buddy is in his bed, leave him alone." This is absolutely essential for good relations between child and Beagle. It's also best if the child and the dog have separate toys. A dog can easily lunge for "his" toy and unintentionally hurt a child. Children can become upset that a dog has "his" toy and may try to grab it from the dog. (It's a good idea if you can teach your child to keep his toys off the floor and out of Buddy's reach. Obviously you can't teach the Beagle.)

## Children and Beagle Training

The best way to make sure your child and the family Beagle will remain best friends is to integrate your children into your training plans for the dog. Children need to become dog trainers for a variety of reasons.

- It teaches them the basic principles of dog psychology. Children often think the family dog can understand fairly complex sentences, for instance, or they believe the dog "knows" it is wrong to chew clothes or fingers. Working with your child to train the dog gives you a chance to explain what dogs "know," what they do not know, and what they can learn.
- It makes you a better trainer and a better parent. There is nothing like teaching to learn something well yourself.
- It teaches the dog that children are not just playmates, but figures of authority who need to be obeyed. Just as children tend to think of dogs as small children, dogs tend to think of kids as large puppies. Until they learn better, they are apt to nip, jump on, or chew children, just as they would their own siblings.
- It teaches children how to correctly handle their pet.

Very young children, under eight or nine years of age, should not be allowed to "train" the dog themselves. Make the child your "helper" instead. It's also a good idea to enter your child and dog together in a positive-reinforcement obedience class. Both will benefit!

### Feeding the Dog

Children should learn how to feed the dog. Feeding the family Beagle gives the children an intimate connection with the pet, and until they actually participate in this task, children may not truly understand that a dog is a living being who needs nourishment.

You can also use the dinner hour to teach the child how to prepare the food (even if it's just opening a can or pouring out kibble) and how to serve it. Explain to the child what foods dogs require and the frequency and time of when you feed your dog. As the dog sees the child getting his dinner ready, it will strengthen the bond between them. He will begin to see the child as a source of food and hence authority, rather than as just another playmate. This concept is important for their future development.

### Other Tasks

Children can participate in dog ownership by picking up the yard. That way they learn the trials as well as the joys of dog ownership. They can help brush and bathe the dog. They can brush his teeth and help you clean ears and clip nails. They can shop with you for dog items. They can go along on routine trips to the veterinarian to learn about pet health. They can take photos of the dog and draw pictures of him for an album. They can write a story about the dog for fun or as a homework assignment. And of course they can walk the Beagle. All these activities help bond children and dogs.

### Dog Walking for Children

Although most adults can easily manage a Beagle, young children may have trouble controlling a dog on a walk. If your Beagle is a confirmed "puller," you can use a head halter such as the Halti-Collar or Gentle Leader. Head halters are both humane and effective and although Beagles usually object to them at first, they soon get used to the idea.

## Beagles and Babies

Everyone knows that older children should be prepared for the arrival of an infant into the household. Not so obvious, perhaps, is the fact that the family dog also needs to learn to accommodate himself to the new situation.

*Bailey (3 months) and a friend* *photo courtesy of Madlyn Schneider*

Beagles are extremely unlikely to be jealous of a new baby or aggressive toward one. Still, you can make the transition even easier with a little energy and forethought.

Practice your obedience routine with your Beagle. Make sure he knows how to sit, get down, and remain calm. If you have young children, have them practice commands with the dog too. They will probably find it boring, but then so are fractions.

As you bring in the baby supplies, let the dog sniff them. Some people even buy a life-sized doll and practice carrying it around. This not only gives the Beagle a hint about what "Life with Baby" will be like, but it gives you a chance to practice doing things one-handed!

Some people get a recording of a crying baby, and play it for the dog. This will accustom your dog to the noise, and if you jump up at the sound and rush to the nursery, the dog will get used to that routine also, and not think anything is especially wrong.

Take the opportunity to let your Beagle meet babies—with the parents' permission, of course. It's a curious thing, but your dog may not understand immediately that a baby is a small

## Adding a Dog to the Family

If you are planning to add a dog to a family with a baby or a young toddler, choose an older animal. Many people make the mistake of getting a puppy for their baby, hoping "they'll grow up together." But an older dog is almost always a better bet.

person. For one thing, babies apparently don't smell or sound anything like adults or children, and the first time your Beagle meets one, it's going to be a surprise. Keep your dog on a leash so you can grab him quickly if he does something odd like jump into the child's stroller or crib.

When the baby actually is due home from the hospital, get someone to take the dog for a walk, so that he is out of the house when the child arrives. Your Beagle will accept the baby even more readily if he senses that the child is part of the household rather than a visitor.

Make your Beagle feel that having a baby is a great thing. The best way to do this is to give him extra attention and treats when the baby is present. When you bring the child into the room where the dog is, hand out a treat and make a fuss over the dog. He'll soon associate the child's presence with good things, and bond quickly to the baby. Please don't change the dog's sleeping spot, or exile him to the backyard when your new child arrives. That would only stir up resentment, and produce an unpleasant result.

## Beagles and More Beagles

Beagles are by nature the friendliest of dogs. This is because Beagles were meant to live in packs. Even though your human family can replace the company of their fellow dogs to some degree, nearly all Beagles would like to have at least one canine companion, preferably another Beagle. Remember that two dogs will be more expensive and more time-consuming than one dog. But they will also be even more fun!

*Tuny* *photo courtesy of Polly & Wilson Palacios*

*Hypo and friend* *photo courtesy of Lea Ward*

Of course, you shouldn't get a second dog unless you are reasonably sure your present Beagle would welcome a companion. You can gauge his reaction easily enough by trips to the dog park or to Beagle gatherings, or by borrowing a friend's dog for a few days. Dogs who were correctly socialized with other dogs as puppies are much more likely to make new friends easily. Very dominant or very submissive dogs react less well to new dogs than dogs who are in the middle range of the scale.

When introducing a new Beagle to your old Beagle, or when introducing your new Beagle to an established pack—or even to a heterogeneous canine group at your local dog park, be on the lookout for telltale body language that signals acceptance or rejection. Contrary to what some people say, the best way to introduce strange dogs is *not* on a leash. Dogs on a leash feel constrained and defensive. Moreover, leashed dogs have no opportunity to flee, and they know it. Hence dogs on a leash are much more likely to lunge, posture, and even bite at a strange dog. It's all part of self-protection. Additionally, it's really easy to get yourself, your friend, and the two dogs all entangled in the leashes during opening maneuvers. Still, because of circumstance and leash laws, most dogs today meet on leashes. During introductions keep the leash as loose as possible.

Allow the dogs to meet on their own terms. This usually means the animals, after making a quick initial eye contact, will wander slowly toward each other, as if they are in no hurry. In

*Miss Pickles and Bonkers* *photo courtesy of Christine Gaites*

dog language, this means, "Hey, I'm not aggressive. I'm just wandering over that way anyhow." If they're not looking at each other, take it as a good sign.

When the meeting actually occurs, most dogs start sniffing at the mouth or ears, and then move toward the rear. All these body parts are packed with interesting orifices that contain vital information for dogs. I am not sure precisely what they learn from this, but it seems an important part of canine protocol. Most dogs don't seem to mind a bit. Observe the dogs carefully. Expect to see cheerful wagging tails. Tails held "half-mast" and stiff, however, signal that trouble may be brewing. So are "pinpointed" eye pupils on the part of the aggressor. If trouble starts brewing while the dogs are on leashes, each person should simply walk in opposite directions. Encounter over.

## Planning for Another Dog

So you've decided to take the plunge, and fulfill your Beagle's natural destiny by getting another dog! Give the new relationship time. It takes at least four weeks before the various dogs sort out their responsibilities and obligations in the pack order. You may see some squabbling before everyone understands who's who. On occasion, the new dog will "lie low" for a few weeks while checking out the competition. Then bingo! He begins to show dominance. This may come as a surprise to everyone, but it does happen.

It's often best if the second dog is a puppy. If he's not, try to get one who is the same size or smaller than the first. This will reinforce a natural dominance pattern. Dogs of opposite sexes usually get along better than those of the same sex, but then Beagles are so amiable it doesn't usually matter with them. Some people want to get a puppy to enliven an older dog's life, but a puppy might only confuse the older animal. A calm, middle-aged or senior dog is often a better companion.

*Louie and Buster playing around* *photo courtesy of Wally Jarrett*

## Pack Behavior

If a group of dogs is together for any length of time, a complicated hierarchy will develop. This is the ancestral pattern of wolves. A hierarchical structure decreases conflict, and low conflict is a very desirable arrangement for a pack. The Beagles will arrange this pecking order themselves, and there is nothing you can do about it. Don't try to interfere with the process so long as it remains non-violent. Don't try to equalize the dogs. Dogs are not democratic. They want a leader. If you don't accept the "alpha" dog as the leader, you'll create confusion among the pack. Gently reinforce the established order.

Interestingly enough, dog hierarchies are complex, not linear. A dog dominant in one context, such as eating, is not necessarily dominant in another, such as who gets the best bed. Males are apt to fight over territory, while females are more likely to quarrel about possessions. Dogs of both sexes will fight over food. Dominance squabbles between dogs who are close in rank can be dangerous. A fight may start because a younger, more agile dog is trying to taking over a dominant position from an older, slower animal.

Status in the pack is also fluid, depending who's feeling "bull-ish." Interesting things also happen when a previously dominant animal has died or left the residence: the rest of the pack find themselves at loose ends and scramble to re-create their pack. You may be surprised to see who emerges as the alpha dog!

In a group situation, most adolescent problems can be boiled down to the three major Beagle concerns: food, sex, and security. If your Beagles argue over food, feed each dog in a separate corner—facing away from each other. Don't throw treats around haphazardly; you'll incite a riot. Dogs also quarrel over favorite sleeping areas, and petting rights. Beagles are more likely to engage in this kind of bickering than in dominance fighting. It all has to do with security. By making sure each dog has his own bed, and by making sure each gets plenty of attention, you can reduce friction.

The most common and serious dog battles are between two dogs of the same sex. Many people think females give the most trouble in this regard, but I find that intact male dogs inflict the most severe injuries. The best way to solve this problem is to neuter your pets (male and female alike). However, if fighting has already become an established activity between rivals, neutering won't help much; behavior once driven by hormones has now become habit.

Once the hierarchy has developed, things are generally pretty stable unless you interfere. Your support will convince everyone that this is the way things should be. Pet and feed the "alpha" dog first. Allow him to go through doors before the other dogs. Don't scold him if he nips at subordinate dogs to keep them in line, unless you fear that some real damage is going to be done.

## Battling Beagles

Every once in a while, even the most peaceable Beagle may get into a brawl. Don't panic; let the dogs work things out for themselves. It may look awful, but there's not usually much damage done.

Strangely, most fights break out when the owner is there to observe. And most fights take place indoors in close quarters. Dogs left outside unattended rarely quarrel. So if a fight begins, immediately throw the disputants outdoors. This usually brings them to their senses. The banishment should be very temporary, however, only about two minutes. Any longer than that and the dogs will forget why they're out there.

If you have a continual problem with rivals, keep a spray bottle filled with water and a dash of lemon juice or vinegar to use on the fighting pair. A chair leg or broomstick inserted between serious fighters may be necessary, but never interpose any part of your body between two fighting dogs. You can also throw a coat or blanket over them. If you have to pull them apart, grab the tail or hind end of the aggressor. Beagles almost never do any serious harm to each other. Although blood may be drawn, it's usually flowing from a nip on the ear; ears bleed a lot.

If fighting occurs during times of high excitement, such as your arrival home from work, keep the homecoming low-key. When you arrive, *ignore* all dogs until they are calm.

Another good practice with fighters is to take them out long, calm walks. This enjoyable, distracting activity makes everyone, including you, more relaxed. If you are tense your tension transmits directly through the leash to the dog. If possible, get someone to help you walk the dogs. It's good for your dog to associate the fun of a walk with the company of his rival.

## Your Beagle and Other Pets

Beagles are generally good with other animal family members, as long as you take sensible precautions.

### Cats

Cats and dogs can be best friends, especially if dogs are socialized to cats early. I have had cats and dogs all my life, and no dog I have ever owned has had the slightest propensity to hurt one. Unless your dog is a determined cat hater, or plays too hard, your cat is generally safe around dogs. Cats have a habit of using their claws to let dogs know when they are playing too hard. Dogs respect that. Other reasonable precautions include:

- Give the cat a safe place to "lay up." Dogs can't climb very well, and cats can get through tiny places. So make sure your cat has his own safe sleeping haven where he can retreat when things get rough.
- Introduce the cat and dog slowly—with the Beagle on a leash. Let the dog know that your cat is part of your family by petting him, and speaking gently to him. Never chase your cat; the Beagle will certainly follow the lead.
- Secure the cat's bowls and litter box away from the dog. Somewhere high up is the best choice. (It helps if the dog is not allowed on furniture, but the cat is.) If that's not practical, try putting the bowls and box in the bathroom. Keep the bathroom door half-closed with a latch or short chain that allows the cat to sneak through, but not the Beagle.
- Socialize your dog to cats early. The younger the puppy is when he meets his first cat, the less chance there will be of any inappropriate behavior around them.
- Praise the cat and the dog whenever they are behaving well around each other. Cats are naturally suspicious and need lots of time to adjust. If you are lucky, however, you may actually see them sleeping together. When that happens, you'll know you're over the hump.
- Until you know that your cat and dog are friends, separate them when you're not home.
- Keep a squirt bottle handy in case of emergency. Aggressive behavior is the only time that I wholeheartedly recommend such negative reinforcement.

## Rabbits and Other Small Pets

Let's face it. Beagles were bred to find, and in some cases kill, rabbits. Never allow your pet bunny to be unsupervised with your Beagle, no matter how much your Beagle appears to like him. The same is true of any other small, scurrying creature you own as a pet.

# Chapter 7
# Nutrition: The Beagle Buffet

Taxonomically, dogs are classed as carnivores, or meat-eaters. This classification, however, is based more on tooth structure than on actual eating habits. Dogs can and do eat almost anything. This makes dogs, like human beings, omnivorous, rather than obligatory carnivores like cats. And they will eat a surprising variety of things, as you may have discovered for yourself if you ever played the old, "Let's see if Molly will eat this!" game.

## The Right Food for Your Beagle

A high-powered marathon runner and a diabetic great-grandmother in a nursing home need different quantities, content, and frequency of meals. Similarly, no two dogs have the same nutritional needs. Even two Beagles of the same size and age may need different types and amounts of food depending upon their activity, heredity, and stress levels, among other things.

The most important thing is to find a food that your dog enjoys and thrives on. Pay attention to indicators of nutrition like coat quality, energy levels, and bowel function. A dog with constipation, bad breath, diarrhea, gas, or vomiting may be eating the wrong food.

## Commercial Foods

Although most commercial foods provide adequate minimum nutrition for your dog, feeding him an optimal diet is more of a challenge. If you are absolutely dedicated to providing perfect nutrition for your dog, the only way to go is a home-prepared, well-researched diet. However, most of us can't reasonably make the effort this requires, and the option is a top quality commercial food.

Unfortunately, truly premium foods cannot be found on the aisles of grocery stores, or even in many pet supply stores. This is because most quality foods are produced by small companies that can't afford the large-scale advertising and fees it costs to get shelf space in a grocery store. Instead, they spend their money on developing and producing good foods. However, many of these companies can be found on the Internet, and most will deliver their product to your doorstep. California All-Natural, Canidae, Flint River Ranch, Innova, Wellness, and Wysong, are some of my own favorites. You might also check out the *Whole Dog Journal*, which frequently evaluates commercial foods and makes recommendations. Still, the best commercial dog food in the world doesn't match a homemade meal. If you don't believe me, offer any a Beagle a choice between Brand X and Mom's meatloaf.

Almost any kind of meat can end up in dog food. In many places, pet food manufacturers are free to use road kill, cows dead from disease, or any other source of protein that suits them. In fact, even highly reputable companies who use only human-grade meats in their dog food are not legally permitted to so state on their label. This regulation is obviously not designed to protect the consumer, but the farmer—who now has an outlet for his diseased and downed cattle.

However, you can avoid the worst food by sticking to some simple guidelines.

- Do not buy any dog food containing "by-products." Meat by-products are the part of the animal not deemed fit for human consumption, and while a few by-products are healthy and tasty to dogs, many more are not. Avoid them.
- Avoid food laden with grain or cereal by-products. These ingredients are the part of the plant left over after the

milling process; they are technically called "fragments," but appear in many guises on the label. The carbohydrates in food should be whole grains. Many dogs are allergic to soy; stay away from it.

- Good food should not contain sweeteners, artificial flavors, colors, or preservatives. The best dog foods are preserved naturally with vitamin E (tocopherols) or vitamin C (ascorbates or ascorbic acid).
- Ingredients are listed on the labels by their quantity, so select food with the specific name of a meat (beef, chicken, turkey) as the first ingredient. Foods that just say "meat" or "poultry" should be avoided. Unfortunately, just because a product has "beef" as the first ingredient doesn't mean that the product is mostly beef. Some companies engage in a practice known as "splitting." If they can possibly do so, they will divide the cereal products up into separate categories, like "rice" and then "brown rice." Added together, there may be more rice than beef. But because the companies are allowed to list them separately, beef is listed first.

Although the label declares the amount of protein in a food, it doesn't say where the protein comes from. Some kinds of protein are much more usable than others. Hair, for example, is just about all protein, but try living on a hair diet and see what happens to you. Plant proteins are much lower in quality than animal-derived protein, but reading the labels on pet products leaves you guessing as to the protein source. You need to check with the companies themselves.

## Storing Food

Food improperly stored can become loaded with molds and other deadly toxins. To reduce the chances of your dog becoming a victim, be sure to use the freshest foods available. If you use a commercial food, check the manufacturing date. Do not buy in bulk because smaller bags get used up more quickly and stay fresher long.

Store the food in a dry, cool place away from sunlight. It's best if you keep the food in the house or some other place with a stable temperature. Temperature fluctuations can produce moisture in the container that may lead to the development of mold or toxins. Most food should be kept in its original packaging, or in a special airtight container.

If the food smells bad, or if your dog suddenly refuses to eat it (while retaining his appetite), throw the stuff out, or take it back to the point of purchase for a refund.

## Supplements

If you are feeding your dog a balanced diet, he doesn't need any vitamin or mineral supplements, and some supplements can actually be harmful. The best vitamins come from the food your Beagle eats naturally, not in pills and capsules. Since many commercial processes destroy the natural vitamins and minerals that should be available to your pet, manufacturers have to add them back in.

Some common supplements include "super green foods" like alfalfa that aid digestion, omega 3 fatty acids (best gotten from marine fish), and "health-blend" formulas that provide enzymes, amino acids, fiber, "good" bacteria, phytochemicals, and vitamins.

A controversy rages over the function of vitamin C in the canine diet. Unlike human beings, dogs can manufacture vitamin C themselves, so conventional wisdom tells us that dogs don't need it added to their food. Some nutritionists claim it can actually be dangerous to the kidneys. Other experts, however, tout the value of vitamin C. They argue that although dogs can make their own vitamin C, they seem less efficient at doing so than all the other mammals who can make their own, and because vitamin C has antihistamine properties, some theorists believe it helps protect against certain canine allergies. Others think that along with vitamin E and the mineral selenium, it plays a role in fighting arthritis. Vitamin C may even fight cancer—both by preventing the occurrence of the disease and as a dietary supplement for cancer patients. However, dogs who receive large supplements of vitamin C may lose the ability to manufacture it for themselves.

### Clean, Fresh Water—All the Time

The benefits of drinking lots of water are too numerous to count, and they apply both to humans and to dogs. Make sure that your Beagle has lots of fresh water available at all times, whether he's inside or outside.

## Varying the Diet

Don't get trapped into feeding your dog only one food, even if it's a good one. Here's why:

- It's unnatural. Dogs are hunters and scavengers by nature and are designed to feed upon a wide variety of foodstuffs.
- It's boring. Dogs don't like the same food day in day out any more than we would.
- It may be unhealthy. Mix your dog's favorite food up with other high quality food to be sure your pet is getting all his required nutrients.
- It may cause allergies. Researchers believe that one of the best ways for your dog to avoid a food allergy is to consume a wide variety of foods from puppyhood on. A monotonous diet begs for a reaction.
- It may be impossible. What if your dog becomes allergic to something in the food, or the company goes out of business, or they change the formula, or you are vacationing in Upper Skoodookie where Fifi's Special Braised Cuts of Emu are not available?

### People Food

Considering what the commercial pet food market is like, it's all right to feed your dog most food that is healthy for human beings. The old business about "don't feed your dog table scraps" was a masterpiece of propaganda served up with relish by dog food manufacturers. Dogs thrive on fresh vegetables, chicken, beef, and fish. Many dogs also like fruit, including apple slices and melons, bananas, and berries. (I once had a dog who carefully picked blackberries from our bushes.) Low-fat yogurt and cottage cheese are also delightful treats. Avoid cramming your dog with junk food you shouldn't be eating yourself: cookies, potato chips, chocolate (which is toxic to dogs), hot dogs, and pickles.

## Homemade Diets

Nowadays, many people have opted to prepare their dog's diet at home. The advantages of a homemade diet are obvious: you can tailor the diet to your own dog's particular needs, and you'll be using quality ingredients that don't include artificial preservatives and by-products. Although it is often claimed that home-prepared diets are more expensive than commercial ones, you can largely offset this factor by including healthy leftovers from your own meals.

However, preparing a diet at home does require some training. The main dangers from such diets are a calcium/phosophorus imbalance, and inadequate levels of calcium, copper, iodine, and certain vitamins, especially fat-soluble and some B vitamins. On the other hand, many excellent books, such as Cheryl Gianfrancesco's *Doggie Desserts: Homemade Treats for Happy, Healthy Dogs* (Doral Publishing) contain recipes for healthy homemade diets that you can adopt for your own purposes.

## Bones

Dogs adore bones, but cooked bones are dangerous, since they can easily splinter, and can damage your dog's throat and digestive system. The sterilized bones you can buy in the store are very dangerous in this regard: they are unnaturally hard and can cause broken teeth.

Raw bones may carry bacterial dangers of their own, but I must confess to having fed fresh raw chicken bones (wings and necks) to my dogs for many years without incident. The nutritional advantages are without par. It is important that the bones be both fresh and meaty for your dog to benefit. Start your dog off gradually, and watch him carefully.

Bones are naturally balanced sources of calcium and phosphorous. People who decide to feed their dogs a diet of fresh meat and vegetables without the bone must artificially supplement the food with a calcium source such as bone meal. The exact amount is difficult to gauge; in addition, not all bone meal supplements are safe; some contain dangerously high levels of lead. It is better to use a commercially prepared food or to feed raw, meaty bones.

If you do decide to feed your dog bones, get the freshest ones available. Your best choices are chicken legs and wings; these bones have a perfect calcium/phosphorus ratio. Beef and even turkey bones may be too hard. Common bacterial components of raw meat include campylobacteria, E. coli, Listeria, and Salmonella. Trichinosis, tapeworm, and protozoal infections are also possible. Still, it's rare for a dog to contract these diseases. Their systems are equipped to handle them.

The most dangerous consequence of bone consumption is a perforated intestine, which allows toxins to escape into the dog's system. To eliminate this risk, grind the bones thoroughly in a food grinder or feed a commercially prepared raw diet. To learn more about a raw diet for your dog, read Ian Billinghurst's classic *Give Your Dog a Bone*.

## Treats

At first glance, treats seem to have no downside—people enjoy giving them, and dogs enjoy getting them. Still, not all treats are equal.

For example, cow hoofs are the number one cause of tooth breakage in dogs. Although wild dogs chew the hoofs of recent kills, fresh hoofs are much more pliable than the smoked variety commonly available in stores today.

Most dogs like rawhide, but they often chew it up like gum and then swallow it. The rawhide can stick in a dog's throat. Even if he gets it down, it's not doing the old digestive system any good. Moreover, some rawhide treats are basted with flavors that disagree with the canine digestive system, causing diarrhea. If you notice this, switch to plain rawhide treats, or omit them altogether.

Dogs also have strong opinions when it comes to the perfect flavor in treats, but despite the recent plethora or melon, vanilla, and peanut butter delights, most dogs like liver. There's no accounting for tastes.

The PetsMart Company has been marketing a product called "Shareables," dual-species treats designed for you and your dog.

These healthy snacks are just right for a joint backpacking trip. They include Peanut Butter Filled Pretzels, Crisp Rice Bars, and even Jerky Bites, a concoction of Salmon and Tuna jerky that I wouldn't eat on a bet but the dogs seem to appreciate them—as will your kitty cat. I have a feeling, though I can't prove it, that the treats are designed more for people than for dogs.

Still another commercial choice is Pet Botanics new product, Therasticks. These snacks come in a variety of formulas (Anti-Oxidant, Breath & Body, Anti-Anxiety, and Glucosamine Plus). They can be easily broken off to adjust to your dog's weight.

One interesting treat/toy combo is the Biscuit Ball, a "stuffable" toy. You can stuff the Biscuit Ball with biscuits, peanut butter, cheese, or any other favored treat. Dogs chew and chew the toy, which is especially desirable for Beagles suffering a touch of separation anxiety. The treats are available from Kong/Milkbone, Golden, Colorado (303-216-2626).

## Overfeeding

Sixty percent of all adult dogs in this country are overweight, a fact that affects their health, enjoyment of life, and ability to participate in normal dog activities. Beagles are particularly prone to obesity. No matter how much fun it is to feed your dog, and no matter how much he enjoys eating, remember: Obesity will shorten his life.

In dogs, obesity is defined as being 10 to 25 percent above the ideal weight. Look at your Beagle from above; he should resemble an hourglass. Too much bulge in the waist indicates that your dog needs to be put on a diet. If you place your thumbs along your dog's spine, you should be able feel each rib. If you must put pressure on the rib cage to feel the ribs, he's overweight. (If you can actually see your dog's ribs, he's too thin.) When viewed from the side, you should see a "tucked up" waist.

Although most cases of obesity are caused by the fatal combination of overfeeding and under-exercising, in a few instances, a medical condition like hypothyroidism, or insulin imbalance could be at fault. Don't put your dog on a weight loss program until you check with your veterinarian to make sure there is no underlying medical problem.

Once you find that your Beagle is in the clear, provide more brisk, aerobic exercise for him. A human-paced walk of a mile or two does almost nothing to burn calories for your dog. He needs to run, and if there is no fenced dog park or safe area near you, you'll have to help him out by active playing. Getting him an energetic doggy companion will help, also. Begin any exercise program gradually and use common sense.

Remember that all dog treats contain calories. If you use dog treats as a training aid, cut back on the amount of regular food you give your dog, and use treats that have some nutritional value. Try crispy carrots as treats, and add fresh vegetables, such as broccoli, to your dog's dinner. Just as with humans, the key is a low-fat, high fiber diet. Unless you're an expert on home-prepared foods, use a high quality weight loss commercial brand. The manufacturer has done the hard part by providing the correct amounts of vitamins and minerals. Change from one brand of food to another gradually over a period of a week or two, especially if your dog is a picky eater or has a sensitive stomach. For more information on dog nutrition, get a copy of my book *Feeding Your Dog for Life* (Doral Publishing, 2002).

## Gorging

Some dogs eat too fast for their own good. If this is the case with your Beagle, try feeding him in a separate, quiet place, away from stress and competition with other animals. You can also try spreading his food over a wider area (such as a flat tray) in order to coax him to eat more slowly. Some people report success by placing a tennis ball (or a rock) in the middle of his dinner and forcing him to eat around it. It may also help to feed several small meals rather than one large one a day.

## It Shouldn't Be on the Buffet

Being both scavengers and omnivores, dogs are frequently attracted to foods that are not in their own best interests.

- **Chocolate:** Chocolate can be deadly to our canine friends. Its active ingredient, theobromine, is the culprit. The amount of theobromine in chocolate varies: Baking chocolate is the most toxic, followed by semisweet, and then milk chocolate. Dogs don't seem to mind the bitter taste of baker's chocolate, and can eat a lot more of it than one would think. In some cases, one ounce of baker's chocolate can seriously poison a Beagle.
- **Corn cobs:** Some people think it's interesting to watch their dogs deal with corn cobs. Don't. Dogs are not horses, and the cobs can impact the intestines.
- **Onions:** A quarter cup of onions can induce hemolytic anemia, a severe, but usually temporary condition. Serious cases can even require a blood transfusion. Garlic has the same properties, but garlic in very small amounts probably does your dog some good. However, don't rely on garlic as a flea-fighter.

### Fecal Meals

The fancy term for eating feces is coprophagia. Unpleasant a habit as this may be, it's fairly common in dogs, especially puppies. Some experts estimate that about 10 percent of dogs develop this behavior pattern.

Eating feces can introduce some vicious internal parasites into your hapless Beagle's body. The danger is greatest if he eats the feces of other dogs, rather than his own. The waste of wildlife such as deer, and that of cats, is also quite dangerous.

Mother dogs routinely eat the feces of her young ones; this is an ancient device to keep the den clean and free of telltale odors. Puppies may be copying behavior they have noticed in their mothers, or, more likely, they are just going through an oral phase in which they eat anything that has an interesting smell or texture. Most dogs grow out of this habit, but a few do not. Some dogs even practice coprophagia to get attention from their owners. It works.

Some experts cite feces-eating as an example of allelomimetic behavior. "Allelomimetic" simply means to "copycat" (a poor word to describe canine behavior) another species' behavior and refers to the assumption that dogs watch their owners pick up feces and want to do likewise. I have always been suspicious of this line of reasoning. My dogs also watch me dust and vacuum and I don't see any of them volunteering to help with the housework. It's more likely that some dogs watch other dogs engage in this behavior and decide it looks like fun.

In a few cases, there's a medical excuse for coprophagia. Exocrine pancreatic insufficiency, pancreatitis, certain malabsorption syndromes, infections, and overfeeding a high-fat diet have all been blamed. Then again, dogs might just like the stuff.

Moreover, almost all Beagles (as well as most dogs in general) will eat cat poop if given the slightest chance. Apparently the stuff is irresistible to them, perhaps because of its high protein content. But cat feces carry *Toxoplasma gondii*, a nasty organism that causes nerve and muscle damage. The only solution is management; you cannot train a dog out of this disconcerting habit. See Chapter 6 for ways to prevent your dog from having access to the litter box.

Unfortunately, once dogs acquire this unsavory habit, it can be difficult to stop. You need to approach the problem systematically.

- First, keep the yard clean! This is not only for aesthetic reasons. Feces are attractive to a great variety of unsavory insects, many of which carry disease. Pick up the poop and dispose of it safely. Although some people recommend sprinkling hot pepper on feces to discourage your dog from eating them, it's really cleaner and easier just to remove the waste. And going around the block sprinkling hot pepper on strange dog poop is bound to earn you a few odd looks from the neighbors.

- If you simply can't pick up after your Beagle regularly, you can try products that discourage dogs from eating their own feces. Some, like *For-bid*, are designed to be sprinkled on your dog's food, apparently giving his feces an unpleasant odor—as if they don't smell bad enough already. *Deter* is a chewable pill that does the same thing. Of course, these products work only if the dog is prone to eating his own feces. You can also try adding meat tenderizer to the diet. The tenderizer supposedly breaks down the nutrients in the dog's system, and thus makes the feces less nutritious and therefore less appetizing to the dog. This is an "extra-label" use of the product, of course. You shouldn't expect the Adolf's people to brag about it on the bottle.

- Try feeding your dog more frequent (but smaller) meals so he won't feel so hungry, and ready to gobble anything. And feed your dog the very best food you can to make sure he's getting all the nutrients he needs.
- One thing that doesn't work is berating your Beagle for eating feces. It has no effect at all, except to hurt his feelings.

# Chapter 8
# Housetraining

One of the most challenging aspects of Beagle ownership is housetraining. Like all scent hounds, Beagles can be just plain hard to housetrain, and that's all there is to it. The bad news is that according to a study performed at the Animal Behavior Clinic, College of Veterinary Medicine at Cornell University, Beagles ranked as the Most Difficult dog to housetrain. (They were followed by their fellow scent hounds, the Bassets.)

Understand that your hard-to-housetrain Beagle is not being particularly stubborn, nor is he trying to get back at you for some imagined slight. He's not stupid either. He's just hard to housetrain. One possible explanation is that Beagles were historically kept outside in large kennel areas where housetraining is a pretty moot issue.

It's also possible that scent hounds, whose brains are organized so differently from our own, don't find the odor of urine and feces objectionable in the slightest. I think housetraining to some extent works against the basic hound nature. And since dogs are perennial wanderers, it's merely a way of marking your home as their own particular territory.

None of this means that you can't housetrain your Beagle, and many Beagle aficionados insist that their Beagles were a cinch to housetrain. But if your previous experience has been with sporting breeds, grit your teeth. You'll have to be savvy and patient. It's not unheard of for a Beagle to take one full year to become reliably housetrained, and a few can never be trusted at all. However, with the right techniques, your Beagle can be on his way to a better bladder and bowel!

## Paper Training?

Years ago, trainers would advocate "paper-training" a puppy, that is, teaching him to eliminate on newspapers before he makes the transition to outside. Most people no longer recommend this method. In the first place, it makes your job twice as hard—you'll have to train the dog twice. It's much simpler to train the puppy right from the beginning. Certainly, if you live on the tenth floor of an apartment building, or if you will be gone a very long time each day, you might want to consider paper training—on a permanent basis. Of course, there's no law that says you must actually use paper. Some people use a cat's litter box, which cuts down on the odor. There is even a doggie version of a cat litter box now on the market.

## The CRAPS System of Housetraining

Housetraining is not something to attempt in a haphazard way. The main reason people fail at housetraining is because they are not consistent. They try one thing one day, decide it doesn't work, and then try something else. This confuses Beagles. However, by developing a systematic approach, you can make this difficult job a lot easier. Hence, the CRAPS system of housetraining: Containment, Resolve, Attention, Praise, and Scheduling.

### Containment

A crate is a necessary tool when it comes to housetraining your Beagle. It is not some cruel torture device, but a portable home that helps your Beagle learn to confine his elimination activities to a suitable area—namely the outside world. The crate should be large enough for an adult Beagle to stand and turn around in. If you find yourself having problems with your puppy using a corner of a too-large crate as a bathroom, you can buy dividers that will discourage this behavior. Very few dogs can bear to soil their own bedding; to them it is an odiferous signal to the world that they are nearby, making them feel vulnerable. Dogs like to leave their mark on places they visit, but prefer to keep their sleeping places secret.

Some pet store puppies have been forced to use their crates as bathrooms. These dogs generally take longer to housetrain, and so need even more of your love and patience. At night, it's best to put the crate in your own room, near your bed, so you'll hear him if he begins to whine.

If your puppy uses his crate for a bathroom even though you give him plenty of outdoor opportunity and watch for every signal he gives, it's possible that the bedding is too absorbent and comfortable, in other words, too great a temptation. Try replacing, at least temporarily, that cushy bedding with something a bit more understated, and see if the problem improves.

## Resolve

Be patient. After all, how long did it take you to learn toilet training? Your dog will be at least twice as fast as you were, so keep thinking about yourself in diapers. Most dogs are not completely housetrained until they are three to four months old. Beagles often take longer. Their bladders are small and their sphincters are insufficiently developed before that time to "hold it."

When a dog makes a mistake in the house, he doesn't mean to annoy you or to create a mess. He does it either because he does not understand what you want, or because he can't control his behavior yet. At the age of eight or nine weeks, puppies need to use the facilities, so speak, up to ten times a day. The need decreases as they get older, although puppies who are six months old often need to go a half-dozen times a day.

## Attention

Pay close attention to your dog. Paying attention really means two things: observe and supervise. You need to do both well and consistently if you hope to housetrain your Beagle.

Your Beagle may be giving you subtle signs that he needs to eliminate. Watch your young puppy like a hawk so you don't miss them. Young puppies do not usually march to the door, whine or bark loudly, and then sit politely until you finish reading the comics. No. Your puppy may not make any noise at all. He may circle, look worried, stare at you, lick his lips or paws, or wander near the door. He may even simply yawn. You may not notice any of this. Then the Beagle pees or poops and bingo! You're upset.

It's up to you to learn to read your Beagle's signals. Once you understand them, you must respond immediately. Go out with your dog; don't just turn him out. Stay with him the entire time. Your presence is his reward. If you're out there with him, you can see what he does. If you just put him out and leave him there alone, he'll assume he is being punished. Taking your dog outside frequently is also beneficial to his health, because dogs who have to "hold it" for long periods are giving bacteria a chance to accumulate in the bladder.

## Doggy Doorbell

Lentek International, Inc. makes a very useful product called the Pet Chime Doorbell. It's portable and wireless, and shaped a like a giant paw pad mat. Place the mat by the door, and when your dog steps on it, a wall- or table-mounted chime will ring to alert you. The mat takes a nine-volt battery; the accompanying chimes require three AAA batteries.

If you can't be with your Beagle pretty much all day long while he is first learning housetraining skills, he is bound to make mistakes. And since it's counterproductive to correct a mistake after it's been made, you're pretty much stuck with the mess. And if you correct him only when you are home, he may get the idea that peeing and pooping is the wrong thing to do at all. Since he can't stop himself from doing either one, he develops the habit of peeing and pooping out of your sight. This is why it's imperative to work with your Beagle at home, even if you have to take time out from work, or hire someone to help you. The dog won't become housetrained by himself.

Some people have a lot of success tethering their dog to themselves while working on housetraining. To use this method, tie your dog loosely to you while going about your daily tasks. Here you accomplish a number of things:

- You are "containing" him
- You are bonding with him
- You are giving him exercise
- You are paying attention to him

Tethering can be combined with other methods of housetraining.

*Tuny* *photo courtesy of Polly and Wilson Palacios*

## Praise

Once your puppy does the right thing, praise him wildly. A mere pat on the head, and a subdued, "Good boy, Ralph," is not sufficient. Not for a Beagle. Beagles expect you to show true joy, even ecstasy, in their accomplishment. You must show this joy by delightedly jumping up and down, offering food treats, effusive gurgling praise, and other embarrassing behavior. It's worth it in the long run.

Wait until the puppy completes a peeing or pooping episode before you praise him, however. If you praise him too early, you'll interrupt his train of thought (so to speak), and he may not finish. Timing is everything in this business.

Punishment, on the other hand, never works at all. On the contrary, it does positive harm, and can contribute to aggression or shyness later on. Even a comparatively mild punishment, like shaking a finger in the dog's nose can facilitate a snapping response. Don't do it. Even if you catch your Beagle in the house right in the middle of The Act itself, don't punish the dog. Don't scream. Don't yell "No!" and don't rub his nose in it.

Not only will your dog fail to understand why you're rubbing his nose in excrement, he won't get the message that you are trying to send. It probably doesn't smell bad to your dog at all. Remember that dogs eat excrement on occasion, so he may think that this is what you want him to do.

If you catch your dog pooping or peeing inappropriately, say in an excited (not angry) voice, "Out! Out!" and then go outside with your dog. Carry him out the door if possible. Dogs are less apt to continue peeing while being carried (especially if you tuck the tail between his hind legs while you are doing so), so with any luck you can get him to finish his business outdoors, where you can praise him extravagantly for finishing. Only carry the dog, however, when it's an emergency to get him out. Otherwise, let him walk outside on his own, especially if you want him to use a particular spot in the yard. He'll find his way to it more easily if he walks along on a leash to get there.

Finishing the job may take fifteen or twenty minutes. Dogs often don't complete their toilet all at once. It's not unusual for a puppy to poop a little, forget what he's out there for, wander around, pee a little, then poop some more. Give it time. If, after fifteen minutes, he still doesn't go, bring him inside, and then, after about ten or fifteen seconds, take him back outside. He may have figured out during this time that he has to go after all. After he is done, and you have praised him to the skies, then take him for a longer walk as a reward. If you bring him in the instant he's done, he has every excuse for dawdling around, since he probably would rather be outside. Sometimes he may dawdle so long, you'll think he doesn't have to "go" and you'll bring him in. Guess what happens in the next minute and a half? Yep.

Once your pup gets the basic idea, you can teach him a cue phase, like "Hurry up" or some other verbal signal. Start by giving the signal when you can see he's about to begin. When he finishes, praise him. Eventually, he'll learn to associate "Hurry up" with his assigned mission, and eliminate pretty much on cue.

When you first start housetraining, you might want to leave a bit in the area where you want your Beagle to "go," to help clue him in. He'll soon understand where his "spot" is. Otherwise, keep the yard clean of dog poop.

To make sure he understands that his "spot" is not in the house, it's a bad idea to allow your dog to see you use the toilet. He may draw entirely the wrong conclusion.

## Scheduling

Keep your young Beagle on a strict schedule. Take him out within a few minutes after eating, and immediately after he wakes up or finishes playing. If you are gone all day, don't expect a puppy to "hold it." You probably can't do that yourself, and it's so unfair to expect it of a baby. Ideally, a young Beagle should be taken out on a lead every two hours for the first two or three weeks you have him. That is the only way you can prevent him from making a mistake. And don't withhold water while you are gone, either. If your Beagle is an inside dog and you are gone all day, you must do one of the following:

- Come home for lunch and a nice walk. This will give you both a break.
- Take your dog to work. You'd be amazed at how often you can get away with this, if you explain that your dog needs frequent medical attention. It's sort of true.
- Get a dog-sitter or a kind neighbor to come over during the day. You can water their plants in return.
- Take your dog to a doggy day care center. These facilities are springing up all over the country, and provide your dog companionship as well as potty breaks.
- Install a doggie door. Even a reluctant Beagle can learn to use one in a couple of hours, with gentle persuasion. (Don't shove the Beagle through the door; you'll only frighten him. Lure him with treats, and he'll soon get the hang of the thing.) Of course, doggie doors can only be used safely in connection with a secure backyard.

If any of this sounds too expensive or like too much work, remember that it's nothing compared to the time and expense of replacing your carpets every month.

If your previously housetrained dog suddenly begins soiling the house, something is very wrong. This new behavior might be caused by a stressful environmental change (all changes, even good ones, are stressful), or it might be caused by a physical problem.

Luckily, dogs are creatures of habit. They can be depended upon (sort of) to eliminate at the following times:

- When they wake up
- Before they go to bed
- After playing
- After riding in a car
- After meals
- Any other time they want to

**Regular Meals**

Scheduling applies not only to your dog's elimination schedule, but to his feeding schedule as well. Obviously, the two are related. Try to feed your dog at regular times, as often as his age requires. Young dogs should be fed three times a day; the number can be dropped to twice a day as the dog grows older.

Don't feed your dog right before you retire for the night. He'll just have to get up in the middle of the night to "go." And take him out the very last thing before you go to bed yourself.

"Free feeding" (leaving food out all day for your Beagle to snack on), is a bad idea all around. Not only is it completely unnatural—in the wild wolves need to dine the minute dinner is served or someone else will eat it—but it makes it impossible to decide when to take out the dog for his elimination walk. If your dog doesn't eat his dinner all at once, he is probably sick or doesn't like the stuff. It's a rare dog who will walk away from something really tasty like leftover meatloaf, for instance. (I am not suggesting your dog dine regularly on leftover meatloaf, although it's a lot better for him than some of the stuff you buy in the pet food aisle. Especially if you leave out the onions.)

**Regular Places**

Scheduling also refers to familiar places. Take your dog out to where you want him to "go" and have him use that spot, every time. This will discourage him from just pooping anywhere—something that will be easier on you as well.

## Quality Poop—and Quantity

You can learn a lot from looking at dog poop, unfortunately. Actually, the science of poop has an official name: scatology. Some people confuse the words "scatology" with "eschatology," the study of the end of things. There's an arguable connection.

In fact, get a group of devoted dog owners together for any length of time, and that subject will come up sooner or later. (This usually happens in a restaurant, for some reason. It's worth going just to watch the expression on the other diners' faces.)

The kind of poop your dog produces has an interesting—and somewhat controversial relationship to housetraining. Obviously, what comes out is largely dependent on what goes in. And the kind of food your dog eats is reflected in his stool. Here's the rule: the more "garbage" (non-digestible) elements in the food, the more is excreted from your dog. Good food produces smaller, darker feces; poor food produces larger, paler feces. High quality dog food produces fewer stools because it provides more real nutrition. Foods with a lot of fiber (often present in "weight-reduction" dog foods) also produce a lot of stool, as do foods with high fat content. Dogs need a fair amount of fat in their diet, however, so this is not necessarily a bad thing.

## Cleaning Up

Cleaning up is a very important aspect of housetraining. Your puppy is bound to make mistakes, and you need to destroy the evidence quickly—as much for your own sake as his. Obviously you should attack the mess as soon as possible. Some trainers, however, recommend cleaning up the mess away from the dog's view, under the theory that your "playing" with the mess gives tacit approval to the dog's creating it.

Use an enzyme-based product like Nature's Miracle that truly destroys the offending urine residue. A lingering odor will encourage your puppy to continue using that spot.

# Chapter 9
# The Beautiful Beagle

If you've ever owned a Poodle or an Afghan Hound, you may be tempted to say, "Thank heaven for Beagles." Beagles are truly low-maintenance dogs who can look their shining best with a minimum of fancy care. No dog, however, is completely free of grooming needs, and while good care may start with a thorough brushing, it certainly doesn't end there.

Good grooming benefits Beagle owners as much as it benefits Beagles, and for this reason: Beagles shed. Just because they have short hair doesn't mean that it doesn't fall out. It does, and it falls out all year long, although some seasons, especially spring, are worse than others. The fallen hair gets into everything in the house, weaving itself into upholstery, food, car seats, curtains, clothing, and computer innards. If you can't handle a fair amount of shedding, don't get a Beagle. They can't help it.

*Tuny*

*photo courtesy of Polly and Wilson Palacios*

*Wynborne's Tucker Box, NA, NAJ* *photo courtesy of Nikki Berrong*

## Good Grooming

Luckily, Beagles are very clean dogs, and do a lot of self-grooming. Still, a little human help will bring out the beautiful best in your Beagle's gleaming coat. And the younger your puppy is when you start grooming, the better behaved he will be during the process. Most grooming problems occur simply because the dog isn't accustomed to it.

I think it's helpful to follow a specific routine, and do your grooming tasks in the same order each time. Dogs are creatures of habit, taking comfort from knowing what's next, and this generally makes them easier to groom. Set aside some time each day, even if it's only a minute, so that your Beagle comes to expect grooming as a normal procedure like eating breakfast, only perhaps not quite as much fun.

Good grooming is important for several reasons.

- It helps control shedding.
- It's healthy for your dog's coat. By distributing the natural oils all along the hair shaft, you're adding an additional layer of beauty and protection.
- It helps his skin. Dead hair accumulates on the skin, and reduces oil gland efficiency. Unbrushed dogs have a tendency to develop skin problems like "hot spots."

- A good grooming gives you a chance to observe bumps, nicks, ticks, bruises, and the like.
- Brushing helps improve circulation.
- Grooming feels good to him, like a massage.
- It gives you an opportunity to bond with your dog.

A beautiful coat starts from the inside: good genetics and good nutrition. All the fancy shampoos in the world can't make up for lack of these. And although you can't do anything to change your Beagle's inheritance, you can provide the quality nutrition he needs to help his coat. (It's estimated that about 20 percent of the nutrients a dog consumes go to hair and coat maintenance.) Foods that contain omega-3 fatty acids (such as cold-water fish and flaxseed oil) are especially helpful, as are supplements like Mrs. Allen's Shed-Stop.

## Brushing Your Beagle

The best time to brush your Beagle is when he's tired. Serendipitously, that's usually the time he needs it most, too. Of course, you may feel less anxious to brush your dog after a whole day of romping through the meadows, but that's just too bad. The Beagle comes first.

Use a rubber hound mitt or medium length bristle brush and groom your Beagle thoroughly at least once a week. If your dog gets a lot of outdoor activity, and is exposed to environmental hazards such as ticks and thorns, you'll need to groom him more often.

Brush briskly, but be careful not to scrape the skin, which is sensitive. Be especially gentle around the tummy and inside the legs. Start brushing at the head and work backward. Use firm, short strokes, and be sure to brush all the way down to the skin. If your Beagle is shedding, or you want to do an especially thorough job, brush vigorously against the direction of the hair growth.

For a shedding Beagle, your best friend will be your shedding blade. Use it often. Lots of hair will come out like magic! Rubber curry combs and hound gloves will also remove dead hair. Once the hair is loosened, use a bristle brush to finish the job. Bathing also helps to get rid of extra hair. If you can get your Beagle to put up it, try vacuuming him. It takes a little time and patience, but it really helps.

## The Hair of the Dog

It seems against common sense, but shorthaired breeds like Beagles shed much more than longhaired breeds. The reason is that short hair has a shorter "life span" than long hair—and when it "dies," it falls out. The actual amount your individual Beagle sheds depends upon innumerable variables, including the dog's natural shedding cycle—the time it takes for each hair to grow, mature, and drop off. In dogs, it's about 130 days, although each type of hair has its own cycle. Other hair-shedding factors include stress, hormone levels, diet, lighting, and disease. Although dogs in the wild shed their hair seasonally, the artificial light of modern dwellings has "confused" the hair shedding cycle. That's one reason why Beagles shed all year round.

Actually, Beagle hair is technically classified as "medium" length rather than short. Compare your dog's coat to that of a Doberman or Weimaraner and you'll see how short "short hair" really is.

Dogs have three different kinds of hairs: guard hairs (longer and coarser), undercoat (soft, and thick), and medium hairs. Different breeds have different concentrations of each kind, but each individual hair follicle produces all three kinds of hair, usually one guard hair and several finer hairs. Although the hair follicles are living cells, hair itself is dead, no matter what they try to tell you in shampoo ads.

# Bathing Your Beagle

Dogs benefit from baths the same way people do. Don't pay any attention to old wives' tales about how baths remove essential oils, destroy the pH balance of dogs' skin, or any other silly charges. They used to say the same thing about people, after all.

Beagles are hounds, and hounds, if not bathed regularly, smell. Some people don't mind a hound smell, and perhaps you are one of these. I don't care for it myself. My dogs each get a bath at least once a week, and more often if they find something hideous to roll in. Which is often.

Have all your supplies ready at hand before you start bathing the dog. Nothing is worse than having a wet dog in the tub and realizing your left the shampoo in the cabinet. While you get it,

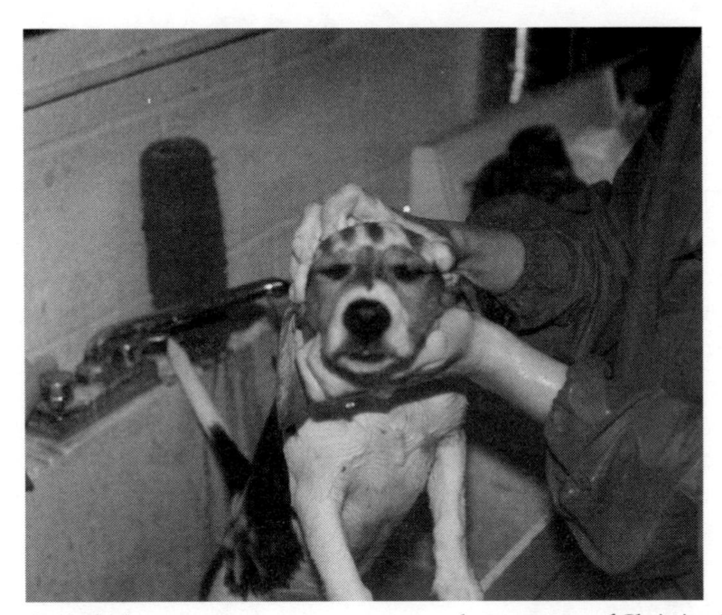

*Bonkers in the bath* *photo courtesy of Christine Gaites*

the Beagle will have leapt out of the tub and begun playing chase in the bathroom.

Use a gentle shampoo—either for humans or dogs. Some people go wild when I tell them this, and assure me that dogs must be shampooed with a canine-only brand. It is true that a dog's skin is more alkaline than ours, but no one has shown that using a special dog shampoo gets better results than using one made for people.

Put a rubber bathmat down in the tub to keep your Beagle from slipping, and pop a cotton ball in each ear to keep the soap and water out. Use a drop of baby oil in each eye in case wayward suds invade the delicate membrane. Use lukewarm water; you don't want to freeze or scald your Beagle.

Start with a ring of shampoo around the neck to prevent any fleas from trying to escape to your dog's head. (You don't need to use flea shampoo; any regular shampoo will kill the suckers.) Then scrub away, working the shampoo right down to the skin. (A hand-held shower attachment makes this job a heck of a lot easier.)

Work your way down his body—but don't forget to wash between the pads of the toes! If your Beagle is pretty dirty, then shampoo him again. Don't scrub your Beagle's face with shampoo. You can wash it gently with plain, warm water.

Afterward, rinse, rinse, rinse. Rinse again. It normally takes twice as long to rinse a dog as it does to soap him up.

Then towel dry vigorously. A regular terry-cloth towel is fine for this purpose, but you can also buy super-absorbent towels designed for dogs. These really work. If it's cold out, or you need to get your Beagle dry fast, put him in a crate and turn a blow dryer on him. Just make sure that it isn't too hot.

If you don't have time for a full-fledged bath, you can clean up your Beagle the fast and easy way, using a commercial "dry shampoo" or a homemade mixture of cornstarch and baby powder. Massage the stuff into the dog's fur, where it will absorb oils and odors. Then just brush it out.

## Beagle Boots

It is much easier and less painful to keep your Beagle's feet in good shape than to fix problems later. So give your dog's nails and paws a little regular attention.

### Nice Nails

Most dogs today don't get sufficient exercise to keep their nails short. If you can hear Bob's nails clicking on the floor as he walks, his nails are too long. You can run him on the pavement for twenty miles a day, or you can pick up his feet and trim them. Long nails can cause a dog's toes to splay and weaken his feet, and very long nails can even become ingrown. They can also catch easily in carpeting or fabric.

Most dogs dislike having their paws handled. It's important to get them used to this critical procedure from the time they are ten-week-old puppies. A few dogs remain so recalcitrant in this regard that you need to put soft muzzles on them or even tranquilize them, but eventually most dogs will learn to accept nail trimming.

Get your veterinarian or his technician to show you how to do it correctly so you won't cut the quick, or living part of the nail. The secret is regularity. Puppies should get their nails trimmed once a week while adult dogs should have it done every two weeks or so, depending upon the hardness of the nails and the amount of exercise the dog gets.

Get out your clippers, styptic powder, and a file for finishing. Use good quality nail clippers designed for dogs, not for humans. Clippers for human toenails aren't strong or sharp enough for canine nails. Most groomers consider the guillotine-type the best and easiest to operate; however, if your Beagle tends to have cracked nails, a guillotine-type clipper can crush them. Scissors-type clippers tend to be stronger and sharper.

If the nails are very hard, soak them in warm water for fifteen minutes before you start. Some Beagles aren't thrilled with this idea, either. Of course you could give your Beagle a warm bath first, having him stand his feet in the water. But then, you'd be trying to clip the nails of a damp Beagle.

If necessary, enlist a confederate to help you hold the dog. (If you live in the north, anyone will do.) Speak in a calm, gentle tone. If your Beagle's nails are very long, it may take several sessions to get them sufficiently short. Do just little bit at a time. The quick is the part of the nail that contains the nerves and blood vessels, so you need to be careful not to cut it. Unfortunately, the quick grows out with the nail, so the longer the nail, the more quick is visible. The quick will gradually retreat as you shorten the nail.

White toenails are the easiest to clip because the pink quick is usually visible. If the nails are black, you'll just have to clip right below the area that begins to curve. But clip quickly. Timid people usually clip too slowly, which may split the nail lengthwise. If you clip too closely, use a cotton ball or styptic powder to stanch the bleeding. To help keep the dog calm and comfortable during the clipping, give him something deliciously chewy to chomp on while you work. In cases of real fear, you are safer putting a soft muzzle on the dog. There's no point in getting bitten.

It also helps to place the Beagle high on a small table. If it's cold and slippery, like at your vet's, so much the better. If there's one thing dogs hate more than nail clipping, it's falling. A small, cold, slippery table keeps their attention where you want it—away from you. If you don't happen to have a vet's table, use the washer or dryer.

I don't clip my own dogs' nails at all any more: I grind them, using a Dremel Grinder. It's easy, quick, painless, and once the dog gets used to the vibrating sound, rather fun. One of my dogs actually goes to sleep during the grinding sessions. The Dremel comes in plug-in and battery-operated models. I prefer the plug-in variety, which, although louder and not so handy, seems to do a better job. But I have friends who have great luck with the Dremel 750 MiniMite Cordless Tool, using the 407 Drum Sander bit. For a smooth finish to the nails, whether you grind or clip, use an emery board.

*Tuny waits for a pedicure* *photo courtesy of Polly and Wilson Palacios*

## Perfect Paws

As tough as paw pads look, they can be torn, caked with tar, or embedded with thorns. Check the hair between the pads, also, and trim it out. Long hair can become matted with gunk and form an impenetrable mass that is painful to your dog. In serious cases, a foot infection could develop.

Tar can be removed from paw pads by applying Vaseline or mineral oil to the affected area. Follow with warm water and a mild soap. Never use turpentine or paint thinner to remove tar.

## Say Cheese!

Because Beagles are particularly prone to cardiac valvular problems, good dental care is critical. I mean it! The bacteria that accumulate in infected gums can go directly to the heart. Keep those gums clean. (A raw carrot every few days is great for scraping dog teeth; it also provides vitamins in a wholesome and inexpensive way.)

Brush Bowser's teeth with a canine toothpaste. Toothpastes designed for humans taste bad to dogs and are not meant to be swallowed. The only other item you really need is a baby or canine toothbrush. For extra protection get a canine-formula mouthwash. These mouthwashes contain stabilized chlorine dioxide, which breaks down the sulfur by-products produced by bacteria in the mouth.

If you prefer, you can use a "finger brush" that fits over your digit. Some people like using the corner of a washcloth. Rub gently, and don't forget to go all the way to the back teeth. Most plaque collects on the outside of the teeth, luckily, since that's all you can generally reach. As your dog ages, you'll need to schedule regular dental appointments for him with your veterinarian. Under a light anesthesia, your vet will clean and scale your dog's teeth right up under the gum line. You can find special instruction for dental care of senior dogs in Chapter 19.

It's really best to brush your dog's teeth twice every day, but even once a week will make a noticeable difference. Obviously, the ideal time to start brushing your dog's teeth is when he's a puppy, but even older dogs can learn to put up with a daily brushing, if you take it slow. You may have to start off by just using your finger.

### Easy on the Eyes

Gently clean away any gunk that has accumulated in the corner of the eyes with a soft bit of cloth. Don't use cotton balls, because the fibers can get into the eye and irritate it. Just use plain warm water for this task; nothing else should be needed.

## Keeping Ears Clean

Like many lop-eared dogs, Beagles are prone to ear infections. The inside of the ears are dark and humid—a perfect bacteria-growing medium. Individual dogs who happen to have hair growing in their ear canals are in particular danger, since the hair traps wax and moisture. Be on the lookout for signs of trouble, like scratching and head shaking.

Using a good alcohol-free commercial product, clean your dog's ears often. Follow the directions on the label. Never cram a Q-Tip down your dog's ears; gently swab with cotton balls or cotton wipes. Clean the outside of the ears clean with baby wipes.

Be aware that if your Beagles gets continual ear infections, he should be taken for a veterinary exam. He may have an allergy or a diet problem.

# Chapter 10

# On the Go with Your Beagle

If you are going on a trip, don't be Beagle-less. Take your best friend and most faithful pal with you. It's easier than you think, and more fun than you've ever dreamed.

## Backseat Beagle

Like people, dogs need to be restrained while riding. No one would think nowadays of putting a child in a car without a seatbelt. Dogs require the same consideration—not only for their sake, but for yours. Do you want your Beagle plunging into your lap at a critical turn in the road? Do you want your Beagle rocketing through your windshield? These are not pleasant thoughts, but they serve as a reminder that your Beagle is a precious being who needs your protection.

Your Beagle is safest in the backseat or cargo area of your vehicle. In cases of severe motion sickness, some dogs do better in the front seat, but unless you really have no other choice, keep your Beagle in the back—secured in a crate or seat belt. A deployed airbag can seriously injure your dog, even if he's in a carrier.

If your dog is claustrophobic, you might simply place a barrier between the back (or cargo area) and front of the car. You can mail- or web-order barriers, or even buy them at your local pet supply store. Many varieties are available, and some manufacturers, including Saab, Volvo, and Mercedes-Benz, make barriers specifically for their cars. (Most Beagle owners don't also own a Mercedes, but that's another story.)

**Beaglers Beware!** Standard car seat belts aren't designed for canine anatomy and can be dangerous. Purchase a pet seat belt or harness. You can find travel harnesses in any pet catalog or pet supply store. Some better known ones include: C.A.R.E. (Canine Auto Restraint Equipment); Easy Rider; Kwik Klip Care Safety Harness; The Roadie Ruff Rider; and Saab Auto Gear. Safety restraints also come in a multitude of sizes; measure your Beagle carefully according to manufacturer instructions, or bring him with you to the store to try it on. All are safe and comfortable for your dog, allowing him to both lie down and sit up. Most can be attached to the front or rear seats, and can fit any vehicle.

Even safely secured dogs should never ride in the back of a pickup truck. They are exposed not only to heat and cold and wind but also to flying debris that is extremely dangerous. If your Beagle absolutely must be transported in this way, he should be safely confined in a properly attached traveling crate.

It's also a bad idea to allow your dog to hang his head out the window. Dogs enjoy this mindless activity, mostly because it allows them to catch passing scents. Still, it's dangerous. Something awful can get blown in your dog's eye and besides, open windows are an invitation for your dog to leap out and disappear permanently. You can buy something called a window vent guard that can be installed or removed in seconds. It allows the dog to catch the scent without endangering his head or eyes. The guards are small enough to fold up and stick in your glove compartment.

If you're planning a long trip, here are the essentials:

- Dog food, especially if you use a "designer brand" not available everywhere.
- Water. Puppies in particular are less apt to develop diarrhea on a trip if they drink the same water they are used to.
- Paper towels. For everything.
- Veterinary first aid kit. Learn how to use it.
- Any medication your Beagle takes. A copy of your Beagle's medical records, including his rabies tag and vaccination record.

- Dog toys and treats. Familiar objects will make him more comfortable.
- Dog bed or blanket. Another reminder of home.
- A recent color photo of your dog—in case the worst happens. A picture of a lost dog is worth a thousand words. Saying, "I lost my tricolor Beagle" isn't enough.
- A flashlight.

## Carsickness: Avoiding Those Travel-Time Blues

Gas in the tank. Bags in the trunk. Rex belted safely in the rear seat. Key in the ignition. Ready to go. Then: B-A-O-F-R-G-H. That sound. That sight. That—that smell. Yes, Rex has just deposited his entire breakfast all over the backseat. And you're not even out the driveway. Sound familiar?

Carsickness is one of the most common (and aggravating) ailments of the modern dog. However, with the right techniques, you can prevent it. First, however, you need to understand the cause. It's possible that the first bout of carsickness was caused by strictly physical matters; however, that sickness triggered anxiety which triggered more sickness at even the thought of getting in the car. Dogs suffering from psychologically motivated carsickness become tense at the very sight of a car, and may throw up the minute they get in. They may betray their anxiety by salivating, trembling, and pacing before they are even asked to ride.

Dogs who suffer motion anxiety need retraining, and sometimes medication. Perhaps your dog associates riding in the car with something unpleasant, like a trip to the vet. To countercondition him, take him for short joy rides—perhaps to a neighboring park or play area. Get him to associate the car with something pleasant. Gradually lengthen the driving periods, or try feeding him in or near the car.

This is a problem that won't be cured overnight. Although some kinds of medication can help, they do have side effects. Tranquilizers can have an adverse effect on blood pressure, and antihistamines, although pretty safe, don't always have the desired effect of making the dog sleepy. In a few cases, dogs treated with antihistamines become hyperactive.

Dogs who suffer from simple motion sickness, on the other hand, have no such symptoms. They just barf when they start feeling nauseated. The physical cause of carsickness is a stimulation of the vestibular apparatus of the inner ear. The fluid-filled semi-circular canals are connected by nerve impulses to the brain and affect the sense of equilibrium. Some dogs (and some people, like me) are particularly sensitive to the sudden stops, starts, and swaying of cars.

With dogs who suffer simple motion sickness, there is a lot you can do.

- Travel light. Most dogs ride better on an empty stomach. Even if it doesn't stop the vomiting, at least you'll have less of it to clean up. Don't feed your dog six to eight hours before a journey—or, if he really has a fit—feed him very lightly. (A few dogs actually ride better on a full stomach than on an empty one. If your dog throws up a lot of bile instead of food, he's probably one of these.)
- Most dogs prefer riding in the front seat, and although I don't otherwise recommend it, it seems to help. Your Beagle gets a good view of the horizon from up front and it's usually less bumpy up there. Just attach his seat belt to the front and put the kids in the back where they belong anyway.
- Go slow and go easy on those turns. Pretending the family car is a ride at the amusement park is not calculated to relieve either your dog's travel sickness or his nervousness.
- Take a break every few hours to give your dog a breather and a walk, allowing your pet you relieve himself. Give him plenty of opportunity to do this.
- If your dog must remain briefly in the car, turn off the motor, unless you have to run the air conditioner. Gas fumes make pets sick.
- Keep the car ventilated with fresh cool air. Crack the windows. Dogs like it colder than we do. Crank up the air conditioning and put on a sweater.
- Crate your dog. It won't help with the carsickness, but it will localize the vomit and make cleanup easier.

- Herbalize. Many people use holistic remedies for carsickness. Chief among these is ginger, which can be bought in extracts at a health food store. (Extracts are better than capsules for dogs.) Give a Beagle one quarter to one half the amount recommended for a person. Alternatively, give your dog a ginger snap cookie. Peppermint also works well for this purpose.
- Medicate. Dramamine (Dimenhydrinate) is a commonly used over-the-counter antihistamine that can reduce or halt canine carsickness. The usual dosage is between twenty-five to fifty milligrams three times a day, or one or two milligrams for every pound of body weight. Give the medicine about an hour before traveling. Most dogs tolerate this drug best if you give a little food with it. Dramamine won't help if your dog is already sick, however. Do not give Dramamine if your dog has bladder problems, hyperthyroidism, seizure disorders, or glaucoma.

## Air Travel

Over half a million dogs and cats fly every year in our country. To maximize your pet's health and safety for the trip, do the following:

- If your Beagle is not used to being crated, be sure you practice with him before you go. No need to multiply traumas.
- Get your Beagle examined by a veterinarian within ten days of the flight, and ask him to issue you a health certificate. This is a requirement of most airlines and state health officials. Remember that some trips outside the continental United States will require you to quarantine your Beagle upon arrival. Know before you go.
- Be sure your Beagle is at least eight weeks old and weaned before the flight.
- Avoid giving your dog sedatives before the flight. They interfere with his heat-regulatory system.
- Identify your pet. He should have a collar and tags bearing your name, phone number, and where you can be reached.

- Your Beagle must be secured in an enclosed kennel that meets minimum standards for strength, size, and ventilation. The kennel must be large enough for the dog to stand, sit, turn around, and lie down. It must have a solid, leak-proof floor covered with a bedding material. The carrier must have grips or handles for the convenience and safety of cargo handlers.
- The kennel should bear a sign saying *"live animal"* and *"this side up"* in one-inch letters.
- Attach feeding and watering instructions to the kennel. Your Beagle should have been fed and watered within four hours of transport. Adult dogs must be given water every twelve hours (at minimum) and fed once every twenty-four hours. Food and water must be supplied to puppies (under sixteen weeks) every twelve hours.
- Try to book a direct flight for your dog (this reduces stress and the risk of "misplacement." If possible, don't plan to arrive on the weekend—if something goes wrong, there's never anybody around who can take charge. In summer, try to get an early morning or evening flight. It will be more comfortable for your pet.
- Put a familiar toy or an article with your scent in the kennel to keep your dog relaxed. I recommend some used underwear. The cargo handlers will get a good laugh, anyway.
- Your dog will be checked as excess baggage, an apt term if I ever heard one. Make sure your dog does not get checked as "freight"! He may end up in a different plane.

Although most pets fly incident-free, there are plenty of things to worry about on a plane ride. One well-known airline misplaced a friend's disabled dog, Lucy, for thirty-six hours. She was en route to Detroit, but was inexplicably left in Kansas City. Most animals travel in un-air-conditioned cargo holds, but if you are very lucky, your Beagle may be able to travel with you in the passenger compartment. Some airlines provide this on a first-come, first served basis. The upper limit for a carrier is usually nineteen inches.

Since the terror attacks of September 11, 2001, the rules of air travel are in flux. Please check first with the airline before sending your Beagle aloft.

## At the Destination

One of the reasons that dogs cause trouble when traveling is that their much-beloved routine has been shattered. Your Beagle is in a new place, with strange people all around. He may get unsettled, nervous, or downright scared. If you have to leave him alone for any length of time, he might also get bored. Any of these events can mean trouble.

Rules vary from place to place, but basic etiquette does not. Do not attempt to sneak your dog in to your hotel. Of course you will always clean up after your dog, in the room or out, and will respect all rules regarding animals. (Cleaning up after your Beagle involves both ends. Drool needs to be attended to, also.)

If you have to walk your male dog through the lobby, go quickly. Do not stop and allow him to sniff anything. The next step after sniffing something is peeing on it. It's best if you can go directly from your car to the room.

### Making Hotel Reservations

When making your room reservations, get confirmation in writing that having a dog in the room is allowable. You don't want to show up and be told that there must be some mistake and dogs aren't permitted. Your confirmation is your security.

Most motels will not allow you to bathe your pet in their bathtub. They also require your dog to be crated when you are gone. There's a good reason for this. I left my sweet wonderful dog uncrated in a motel room and he destroyed it. I was only gone five minutes, but that was enough for the dog to tear apart three pillows and chew a hole through the quilt.

Keep your dog clean and well brushed. The more you brush him outside, the less he'll shed inside, which is nice for the cleaning staff. Remember, you don't want dogs to get removed from the guest list. Make his stay hassle-free for everyone. And leave a nice tip for the chambermaids. Leave them with a positive feeling.

## Boarding Your Beagle

We can't always take our dogs with us. Boarding kennels are a fact of life for most owners. And since there are about 6500 of them across America—you should be able to find a good one near you.

Get a recommendation from friends or your veterinarian before deciding on a kennel. If you decide to try out an unfamiliar kennel, ask the management to give you references. Before you board your dog, however, be sure you check the place out personally. When you return from your trip, you certainly want your Beagle healthy and happy.

### Cleanliness and Comfort

The importance of a clean kennel can hardly be overstated. No one should board at places where the floor is littered with dog poop. Use your nose as well as your eyes to assess cleanliness!

Check out the water available to the dogs. It should be fresh and clean. The pails should sparkle. Dirty buckets half-filled with drooly water are a bad sign. Good kennels also provide plenty of clean, healthy toys for their boarders.

Kennels should be warm in winter, cool in summer, and free from drafts and flies at all seasons. Most top boarding kennels today are heated and air-conditioned. Expect no less. Some kennels go even further, and provide your pet with a truly homelike environment, complete with couches and rugs. Even so, bring along your dog's own bed.

Good kennels are also relatively quiet. While all dogs are expected to make some noise, the best kennels cut down on the racket by limiting the number of dogs in each building. On the other hand, dogs require socialization, and playtime with other dogs should be provided.

## Space

Kennels should provide runs that are worthy of the name "run." Your Beagle should have plenty of room to exercise. The best kennels are equipped with connected indoor and outdoor runs. The surface of the run should provide good traction. All exercise areas should have shade and shelter from the wind.

Each run should be separate from the next. This will prevent males from urinating on neighboring dogs, and help prevent the transmission of disease.

## Security

All fencing should be strong and in excellent repair. Beagles are escape artists, and the last thing you want is to have your dog run away in unfamiliar territory. The best kennel facilities have fences around the entire perimeter—not just the kennel runs. If your Beagle makes a break for it when the door opens, it's important to have another line of safety—just in case. Be sure to inform the kennel management if your dog is a runner. They will want to take extra precautions.

### Personal Attention

Good kennels have staff available to walk and play with your dog. Some come with extras like massage! Be sure to ask about the services offered when you choose a facility.

For more information, read the American Boarding Kennel's pamphlet: "How to Select a Boarding Kennel." It can be ordered from ABKA at 4575 Galley Road, Suite 400A, Colorado Springs, CO 80915. Or you can telephone (719) 591-1113, fax (719) 597-0006 or email: info@abka.com. Their website www.abka.com, provides a list of member kennels, sorted by city and state, along with tips and other information.

# Chapter 11

# The Brainy Beagle: Non-Violent Teaching

Most dog books refer to schooling a dog as "training," but I prefer the word "teaching." Training is a mechanical procedure that can produce the desired result; teaching is an interactive process that develops loving bonds between humans and their dogs. Training is concerned almost entirely with getting the dog to perform (or not perform) a specific action. Teaching lays the groundwork for desirable behavior in general. Teaching a dog not only helps him learn the desired behavior, it also sets up the conditions for him to want to learn more of it. Although I'll use the words "training" and "teaching" here pretty much interchangeably, think of the "training" process as a teaching one.

Teaching ourselves is really what teaching Daisy is all about. The first lesson we need to teach ourselves is that of patience. Dogs learn by repetition, and do not learn when they are yelled at. If you become impatient and unhappy, the only message your dog is getting is that you are impatient and unhappy. He won't know why. But he'll probably conclude that danger is near (possibly to himself) and he'll get stressed too. In a worst-case scenario, he'll decide you are angry with him, and get scared. Your dog should never, ever, ever be afraid of you. A stressful environment is not conducive to learning—or teaching.

To create the right environment, use a dog-centered philosophy. In the old days, most trainers relied on force, punishment, and negative conditioning. The order of the day included "swinging" dogs, using "alpha rolls," and whacking them with leashes. This doesn't work well for most pets, and it works not at all on Beagles. Not if you want a happy, joyful, loving, and fearless pet.

Nearly all behavior that we humans call "good" has to be learned. Dogs can manage "bad" behavior pretty much on their own. That's because "bad" behavior is natural behavior. "Good" behavior is taught behavior. It's that simple.

A well-behaved dog is one who has been provided with plenty of loving direction, and a sensible structure to his life. Teaching has another benefit—it establishes you, the human being, as the "teacher," and the Beagle as the "student." This is the relationship you want to create and to reinforce.

Since Beagles are fun-loving dogs, it makes sense that good Beagle teaching should rely on a Beagle's sense of play. Unhappily, a lot of dog teaching advice is written for Labrador Retrievers, Border Collies, and other workaholic breeds. What works for them won't necessarily work for Beagles. Beagles are dogs who are particularly interested in their physical environment; they are much more closely attuned to the smells and sounds of the woods than they are to you. This is part of their hunting heritage: They were bred to be independent searchers after game. To make your Beagle pays more attention to you than he does to anything else is a challenge. You have to provide a reason for him to listen. For Beagles, that reason usually involves food, although some respond well to praise, petting, or play. You have to know your own dog to decide what his strongest motivating factor might be.

You will also need to decide what you want your dog to learn. For each teaching session, write down a goal—what you want your dog to learn during that period. You might also want to create a Wish List that includes your highest hopes for teaching. You can use this list either as a personal reminder or something to give to a professional trainer.

## Finding a Teacher-Trainer

Although this chapter will help you learn some of the basics of obedience teaching, the very best thing that you can do is enroll in an obedience class. Not only will you yourself learn how to heel, fetch, and do figure eights, but you can pass along these same skills to your dog. It's fun. As a matter of fact, it should come as no surprise to know that Beagles already know how to do everything we want to teach them, unless you want to teach your dog to walk a tightrope or ride a bicycle. Beagles already know how to sit, lie down, get off the couch, and walk. They can stop. They can come. The trick is getting them to do these things when you want them to. Even though you can teach most behaviors yourself, it never hurts to enroll in a professional dog-training course.

When considering a training course, make sure you choose the right instructor. Not everyone understands the unique Beagle mentality, and some teachers have the erroneous idea that Beagles are difficult (or impossible) to train. This is because many of them do work primarily with Labradors and Golden Retrievers, dogs who, unlike Beagles, stand around waiting to be told what to do. Don't be afraid to ask questions before you begin the training course. Some questions you may want to ask include:

- What is the instructor's formal education or experience? The best trainers don't necessarily need a degree in applied animal behavior, but it doesn't hurt to have one either.
- What is the instructor's method of teaching? Does she rely on choke chains, force, or negative reinforcement? Or does she advocate kind, positive training with lots of rewards? (This latter type is the only one for a Beagle!)
- To what professional organizations does the trainer belong? One of my favorites is the Association of Pet Dog Trainers, an organization that advocates and specializes in non-violent, positive methods.
- Does she provide structured "homework"? Give out written handouts and summaries? Is she available for consultation?

Be sure you know what you want your dog to get out of class. Most Beagles are not great candidates for an obedience title. It's more reasonable to choose a class that emphasizes basic skills in a fun atmosphere. If your Beagle turns out to be that rare obedience natural, you can move up to a different class.

## Teaching Fundamentals

Whether you go to class or teach the dog yourself, there are some basic principles you must use to succeed.

### Never Punish Your Dog

Beagles are sensitive and do not respond to harsh treatment. Punishment of any kind makes them shy, nervous, and traumatized. It doesn't even work. Take the extra time to use positive teaching techniques—food and praise rather than leash jerking and punishment, and you'll go far in getting your Beagle trained.

#### Striking is Out

Never, ever strike your dog. Violence only begets violence. Not only is it counter-productive, but it teaches him to resent and fear your hand. Cooperation, not challenge, is the key to a happy relationship.

## Family Teaching

Everyone in the family should participate in teaching your Beagle. It's a group effort. One person should be the "training leader." She's the one who will make decisions about what commands are used, and, after consultation with the rest of the family, decide what should be taught (and how). Once the decisions are made, it's up to everyone to help out.

When only one person teaches a dog, the dog learns to listen to one person only, an extremely bad idea. In fact, I have a suspicion that many of the "one-man" breeds are encouraged to be that way by training as much as by nature. Many of these dogs are used for police and protection work. But most family dogs don't need or benefit from "one-man" teaching. Dogs taught by a whole family become family dogs. And Beagles are the ultimate family dog.

## Praise and Rewards

Praise is important for Beagles. Use it lavishly and immediately after the dog has performed the desired action. But few will do obedience work solely for praise. It's boring. You need to find out what your Beagle loves above all else. If it's a ball or a squeaker toy, use that. If it's food, use food.

For treats to be most effective, the dog should be just a little hungry. If he's too hungry, he won't be able to concentrate on the task. If he's not hungry (rare in a Beagle) he might not be sufficiently motivated to work. Besides, all the blood will be working to digest his food rather than feeding his brain. So a good time to practice teaching is before meals—but not right before. Because dogs are creatures of habit, try to do the training every day at the same time. Dogs work better when they know what to expect.

For treats, my favorite choice is bits of American cheese. Dog biscuits are not enticing enough to get Beagles to pay real attention, and liver bits are just *too* exciting. Cheese is a happy medium. Use tiny bits of food as treats—not huge chunks that are fattening or treats that have to be chewed.

Until good behavior is well established, reward your dog every time he succeeds in following instructions. Switch around rewards, sometimes using food, at other times toys or games. And always praise and stroke your dog for a job well done. For Beagles, praise means Exuberant Praise! A calm pat on the head and a quiet, "Good dog," is not enough to impress most Beagles.

As time goes by, you don't have to reward the dog for every single good behavior. As a matter of fact, research shows that random rewards are *more* effective than consistent praise, once the dog understands what he is supposed to accomplish. If praise is given randomly, it becomes more important to the dog, and thus is a more effective teaching tool. In addition, limit the frequency of the rewards if you have a pushy, always-needs-attention Beagle. Otherwise he will truly never leave you alone. Save rewards and rich praise for his accomplishing really difficult tasks like not barking, and being polite around company.

*Tuny sitting pretty*

*photo courtesy of Polly and Wilson Palacios*

*Bailey surrounded by pals* *photo courtesy of Madlyn Schneider*

*Louie sings for his supper*

*photo courtesy of Wally Jarrett*

## Brief, Calm Sessions are Best

Young Beagles learn best when coached in several brief sessions per day. Ten minutes per session, three or four times a day is a good schedule. (Older dogs can concentrate for longer periods.) Frequency helps them retain what you teach, and brevity keeps their attention focused. It is an interesting fact that while a Beagle can concentrate on finding a rabbit track hour after hour, even ten minutes of "heel" strains their brains.

Pick a quiet time when you are relaxed and stress free. Anger and frustration can be passed along all too easily to your pet.

## The Right Place

Many experts think the best place to train your dog is in the kitchen. Most dogs have very positive feelings about kitchens, and positive feelings help reduce stress. However, if your dog has very positive feelings about the kitchen, maybe you should select a more neutral spot. Start indoors in a familiar place. The living room or rec room may be good spots because they are generally large and familiar. Only when your Beagle becomes "perfect" inside should you take him outside. The yard has too many distractions. There's no way a dog treat can compete with the scent of a rabbit or the sight of a squirrel.

## Getting Your Beagle to Focus

The first thing your dog has to learn is to pay attention. If he doesn't pay attention, you can't teach him anything. And you can't get him to pay attention by counting on your beauty or winning personality. Beagles want food. While food isn't a guarantee your Beagle will pay attention to you, it's the best weapon you've got. Use a small tasty morsel to reward your Beagle for looking at you and paying attention to you.

While "obedience" breeds like German Shepherds and Poodles seem naturally to pay attention to their owners—Beagles are a different matter. Their scenting heritage bids them to keep their noses to the ground, not on your face. Beagles are extremely "distractible" from our point of view, but of course, to them we are the distraction! Holding small bits of food near your face and praise as reward, encourage your dog to look at you by saying, "focus."

### Expanding the Practice Field

Once your dog focuses well at home, take him to new places to practice. A dog who obeys in only one setting is not an obedient dog. Invariably, it's when something novel is occurring that our dogs most need to listen and so it's important to get your dog accustomed to novelty. Practice in different places and under different conditions.

In all teaching—take your time. Trying to pressure or coerce your dog into good behavior costs more time than it saves. It takes most Beagles as long to learn some "simple" tricks (like sitting quietly when something thrilling is happening) as it takes most humans to learn to solve a quadratic equation.

## The Balky Beagle

Beagles are stubborn dogs. There is no way around it, and it's pointless to whitewash the fact. Stubbornness, in fact, is a desirable characteristic in a scent hound, where it is called perseverance. Early breeders bred their dogs specifically to know their own minds, have confidence in their abilities, and go forth, with the human hunter trailing meekly behind. This is in direct contrast to retrievers and pointing dogs who are bred and taught to work in concert with human partners during the hunt.

*Louie still singing…*

*photo courtesy of Wally Jarrett*

The American Kennel Club Regulations for Small Pack Option field trials describes the Beagle in this way: "*The Beagle is a trailing hound whose purpose is to find game, to pursue in an energetic and decisive manner, and to show a determination to account for it.*" Further, it says "*the Beagle must be endowed with a keen nose, a sound body, and an intelligent mind, and must have an intense enthusiasm for hunting.*" Even if your Beagle never goes anywhere near a rabbit, he still possesses the innate, instinctive character to hunt them. Furthermore, he uses these traits all the time. You must take into account these qualities of energy, intelligence, enthusiasm, and determination when you begin teaching your Beagle.

Unfortunately for some pet owners, the celebrated stubbornness of the Beagle comes as a grim surprise during housetraining and obedience work. In fact, some so-called experts rate Beagles as low in intelligence simply because they seem less interested in heeling, fetching, and lying down on command than, say, Poodles. Since heeling, fetching, and lying down on command are of little use to rabbit hunters, however, this should not be such an amazing turn of events. Take a Beagle and a Poodle out on a rabbit hunt together one day and see which one finds the rabbit first.

## Beagles on the Job

The United States Department of Agriculture uses its famous Beagle Brigade at international airports to sniff out meats, fruit, and vegetables transported illegally into this country. By the way, the USDA uses food rewards for training Beagles. The dogs learn that if they find food, they get food. A similar program is in place in New Zealand, where the agriculture detection program does its own breeding. Even so, only one in twelve Beagles are good enough to make the cut. The dogs are tested for twenty-nine different characteristics, both physical and mental. The ones who pass the tests undergo a rigorous training program that costs the New Zealand government about $15,000 per dog. The dogs usually work until they are six or seven, at which time they go home to live with their handlers or are adopted by one of the many employees who have fallen in love with them and have applied to adopt. The top dog in the New Zealand program is Benny, who made 3,500 finds in just two years.

Beagles are also clever at "problem-solving," which paradoxically can cause difficulties for the trainer. One of the problems a Beagle wants most to solve is how to end the training session so you and he can go outside and do something really fun, something that involves a lot of running and barking, and not much heeling and sitting.

## The Three Field Commands

There are three critical commands for your dog to know. "Sit" isn't one of them. While owners like to teach their dogs to sit, "Sit" isn't going to save your dog's life. The three "field commands," originally designed to help control free-ranging dogs, just might. In the beginning, never give a command you can't enforce, and give only one command at a time.

### "Come!"

"Come on, boy, come on! Come on!" Whoops—there he goes—in the opposite direction. So much, it seems, for beckoning your Beagle. Teaching your Beagle to come when called is probably the most difficult and important command of all. Very early in your relationship with your pet, you are bound to notice that while Beagles excel in running fast, they seem to prefer running fast in any direction they choose, which may or may not include running fast toward you. And so, although I am going to tell you how to teach your Beagle to come on command, the chances are still pretty good that he won't do it reliably. By "reliably," I mean every single time no matter what the distraction. Beagles are genetically programmed to follow their noses.

To encourage your Beagle to come to you, you must make yourself the most inviting object in the area. Ideally you should start when your Beagle is young and most dependent. With luck, you can ingrain "coming on command (or request)" as a pleasant habit.

To teach your dog to come, attach a lead to your dog and choose a room that is small enough not to tempt him to run off. Kneel so you are close to his level and extend your hand. You might also open your arms in an inviting, sweeping gesture. Do not lean toward the dog, but lean away from him. Put your body at an angle to his, since to a dog, this is a more inviting stance.

## Hounds Will Wander Off

This very evening I was speaking with a man who lost his beloved Beagle of ten years, when he allowed him off-lead in a natural preserve. The Beagle found something to trail, and disappeared. He never came back. The suffering that results from having your Beagle lost or killed because you mistakenly believed he would stay close to you is not worth it.

Unless you are in a secure, fenced area, keep your Beagle on a leash. It's true that hunters must let their hounds off lead into order for them to do their jobs. On the other hand, hunting dogs are *always* getting away from their owners, and lots of them end up in shelters or the Humane Society until their chagrined masters can pick them up. Beaglers are always trading theories about how to lure their runaway Beagles back home.

Call him gently, and offer a treat. Chances are he'll toddle over. Praise him with every step. If he doesn't come, softly draw the lead toward you, still encouraging him. Don't tug or yank. The purpose of the leash is to help him focus. The ideal situation is that your Beagle never realizes it's even thinkable to go in a different direction than the one you're calling him to. When he responds by taking some steps in the right direction praise him. When he reaches you, give him a treat.

Practice three or four repetitions several times a day. When he gets really good at this, (at least two weeks of perfect behavior), experiment off lead in a secure area. Don't practice (yet) in times of high excitement or lots of distractions. He won't be able to concentrate, and that will guarantee a failure. It's all a matter of simple psychology. You need to be more interesting to your dog than anything else.

Dogs are extremely good at reading body language, so make sure that your posture, your tone of voice, and your commands are all saying the same thing. If you angrily call your dog to "Come!" while standing in a stiff, off-putting posture with your arms folded, your dog is reading the message behind the words. You're mad. Rover should stay away. Likewise, be careful about calling your dog to come to you for unpleasant procedures. What sensible creature would come to his owner to be punished, pilled, or given a bath?

Never chase your dog, not even in play. You can't catch him, and it only encourages him to run faster. Encourage *him* to chase *you*. This reinforces his "following" gene. In a larger area, begin by keeping your dog on a leash. You don't want to give him the opportunity to go in the opposite direction. The leash is not for pulling or yanking. It's a gentle restraint that keeps his attention glued to you.

When you first start teaching the "Come!" command off lead, move quickly in another direction (not toward him). Chances are he'll follow. Not only can dogs see a moving target quite clearly, but the allure of the chase burns in his blood when he sees you. Finally, don't overuse the "come" command. Especially at first, reserve it for very rare and excellent treats. If you overuse the command, your Beagle will get bored with it. Then he'll ignore it.

## "Whoa!"

This emergency field command is a life safer. Its purpose is to get your dog to stop immediately. It's most useful when your Beagle has escaped from the house and is headed directly into the street. Calling "Come" might tell your Beagle that you want him home, but he's apt to make a large circle while doing so—right into the traffic. "Whoa!" tells him to stop at once. When he "Whoas" you can walk over to him and snap on the leash.

To begin teaching, you need a plain collar (not a choke chain) a leash, and a Flexi-lead.

Start with the regular leash. While he is standing still, say "Whoa!" Then praise or treat him, but keep him standing. After a short period of praise, say, "Release!" and play (but don't run) with him. Then try again. Soon he should associate "Whoa!" with standing still, and receiving a treat. As time goes on, use the Flexi-Lead instead of the regular leash. This allows you more distance, but also control. If he doesn't respond to "Whoa!" stop him with the lead. When he stops, praise and treat him, or play with him some more. It's very important that his reward is not a run. You want to connect the whole procedure of "stopping and staying" with praise and food. When he "Whoas" reliably on lead, you can try him off-lead. Use your backyard or some other boring, fenced area for starters.

If you have done a good thorough job with "Whoa!" you just might save your Beagle's life. You can never absolutely count on a dog's obeying your commands, however, so even with an apparently completely obedient Beagle, it's not wise to allow him off lead in the hopes that "Whoa!" will automatically keep him out of the street.

### "Leave it!"

Dogs are forever getting into garbage, poison, and the like, not to mention your own dinner. Start teaching him by waiting until he is chewing on an object that he really doesn't care *that* much about. (It should also be one that's not important to you, either, of course.) As he's chewing, go up to your dog, and say, "Leave it!" Offer him a treat in exchange. Practice several times a day, and always offer the dog a treat that he likes (like bacon) better than whatever he is chewing. You want to reinforce that he'll be richly rewarded, not given a mere sop like a dog biscuit.

In real life, you would be most likely to use this command when the dog has gotten into something truly heady like a chicken carcass, so your established reward needs to be very powerful. Of course, you probably won't have any bacon actually on hand when the chicken carcass event occurs, but it's okay to cheat that one time and just reward him with a biscuit. Afterward, practice the "Leave it!" command several more times with your accustomed treat and plenty of praise.

## Pleasant Pup Commands

The following commands are helpful for general obedience and are useful around the house. They are essential for the civilized dog.

### Off!

It's a funny thing about Beagles. They tend always to be on what you want them off. The answer is not necessarily disallowing the privilege of furniture, but teaching your dog a positive rather than a negative command. Say "Off!" in a cheerful voice. Of course, if you never want him on that piece of furniture, you can use your dark, growly voice, but if you just want him to move temporarily, the "Off" command works very well. "Off" also works when you want your Beagle to get out of the car. In fact, your dog should only leave the car when you command him to.

## Wait

This calming command is useful when you have company. The dog doesn't have to sit, which can be very trying when friends have arrived, but merely to stand quietly and wait to be petted. It's also useful for keeping your dog from charging for the door while you are headed to open it—either to let someone in or to go out yourself. To teach the "Wait" command, begin by attaching a short leash to your Beagle. This will serve to give you a little control.

Touch your Beagle quietly on the rump and say "Wait" when a visitor arrives. Use the leash to restrain him if you have to, and reward him for quietly waiting to be petted.

## Sit

"Sit" is an easy command to teach, but it is often used inappropriately—usually when the owner really wants to dog to stay still, get out of the way, or not make a nuisance of himself. The catchall "Sit, boy" is supposed to magically cure all the bad habits your dog has gotten himself into. It doesn't of course, and it's much better to work on actually curing your dog's bad habits (like jumping up) than to tell him to sit every time he does them. Think of it this way. Most of the time, when you ask your dog to sit, you really would be happy if he just stood there quietly. If that's what you want, that's what you must teach him. "Sit" is a useful command, of course. I ask my dogs to sit before I give them a treat, because it's easier for me to find their little mouths that way. It's useful as a prelude to nail clipping. And it's a simple trick for children to practice with the family dog. But it's no substitute for good all-around behavior.

The easiest way to teach "Sit" is to say "Sit" is a cheerful voice while holding a treat over the dog's head, then gently start curving the treat backward. Most dogs will sit naturally. Praise him and give him the treat. In the few cases where this doesn't work you may press gently down on the Beagle's backside, saying "Sit." Do not *force* him—encourage him. Nothing about the

*Louie Loo Eye* *photo courtesy of Wally Jarrett*

training should be uncomfortable. Praise him softly, and while he is still sitting, give him a treat. If he gets up too quickly, refrain from treating him. He needs to learn that the treat comes only when he is actually sitting. Otherwise, you'll turn him into a jack-in-the-box. Never ask your dog to sit for more than a few seconds when you are starting out. You want to make success easy for him.

## Stay?

Some people teach "Stay" as a separate command. I don't. I prefer to use "Sit," which in our household vocabulary means "stay there in that place until I say "release!" Teaching "Stay" as a separate command is confusing to dogs, since you're not asking them to do anything new—you're just asking them to keep doing what you have already asked them to do.

## Lie down!

"Lie down!" is the next logical command after "Sit." At that point, you have half the body down, at least. The hard part is to come. Most dogs dislike being asked to lie down, although they are happy enough to do it on their own. This is because "down" puts them in a physically and psychologically vulnerable position.

Use the treat method again. While the dog is sitting, lower the treat slowly and move it toward the floor. Most dogs will lie down naturally. If yours doesn't after a few tries, you can gently extend his front legs and praise him as you ease him to the floor.

Don't push down on your Beagle's shoulders to force him down; you can actually dislocate his shoulder in trying to coerce a stubborn dog. Besides, you already know you're stronger than he is. You want him to perform joyfully, not out of fear or pain.

As your Beagle becomes expert at following commands while you are standing by, gradually increase the distance between yourself and the dog. Try adding one step further away each day.

## Walking on a Lead

Your leash is your dog's best friend. Don't think of the leash as a restraining device; think of it as a way to stay close to your dog. With only a little encouragement, your Beagle will look forward happily to the sight of the leash being taken off its hook: it means *walk-time!*

Since Beagles are rather small dogs, you'd think it would be a cinch to teach them to walk calmly on a lead. And it's really not very hard, although you'd never know it by the alarmingly large number of Beagle owners you see permanently entangled by their leashes, while their Beagles dart merrily all around them.

Beagles like to go first. Remember that they are bred to be leaders on a hunt. To some extent you are working against Beagle nature when you are asking him to follow you. You must replace his natural hunting instinct with an equally natural instinct of "follow the leader." When he becomes convinced that you are the leader, and that you know where the "pack" is supposed to go, he'll be more anxious to follow. Unless he scents a rabbit, and you don't.

So walk fast, at least at first. That keeps his attention directed straight ahead, where you want it while training. Begin your work with your Beagle when he is on a lead, not free. He should be responding to the "Come" command before you start teaching him to heel, (which means to walk nicely on a lead at your heel.) Enforce your command if necessary by kneeling and using a treat to lure him. Don't pull on the leash. Only use it to keep him from going in the other direction.

It is customary to have the dog walk on your left side. It doesn't really matter, but if you plan to engage in formal obedience training, you might as well start getting into correct practice right away. Start by keeping a little treat in your left hand. The point is to get the Beagle to believe that staying close to that appendage is likely to yield its rewards. Since a Beagle is pretty low to the ground, however, bend down when you feed him. You don't want to get him in the habit of jumping up for the treat.

Treat your dog frequently as you walk along, but only when he's in the correct "heel" position. To help position your dog, hold the leash behind your thigh. Start walking in a counterclockwise circle. Since your dog will be on the inside, you'll find it easier to guide him as you move along. Say, "Trooper, Heel!" in a bright voice and start walking. Don't scold him if he goes in the wrong direction—just don't respond to it. Stay still or move in a different way. Soon he'll realize that all the rewards come from staying near you.

## Mix it Up

Don't make every walk a lesson. Allow your Beagle plenty of time to snoop around and check things out, especially when you begin your walk. It may be exasperating to you, but Beagles really enjoy this part of the adventure. You can signal to your Beagle that a certain part of the walk is his turn to lead, but using some special command, (whatever you like) and loosening up on the lead. I say, "You lead!" and start following the dog. This is also very important if you plan to do tracking with your Beagle.

After your Beagle becomes accustomed to walking on the leash, and you don't have to give him a treat every two seconds for walking politely, ask him to "Sit" when you stop. Reward him when he does. Soon your Beagle will sit calmly by your side whenever you stop to chat with friends. If you do not want your Beagle to sit automatically at every stop, make sure you say "Sit" before you give him a treat.

For inveterate pullers, or if you have untrustworthy small children, you can always buy a no-pull harness. Several varieties are available, including the 4 Paws Anti-Pull Harness, and K-9

Pull Control. You might also want to try the Halti Headcollar or Gentle Leader. However, once you start using an anti-pull harness, you must keep using it. Otherwise, your dog will revert to his previous behavior. These devices are really problem-managers, not training aids.

## "No!"

Most people apply this useful command too often. Never use "No!" unless your Beagle knows very well that he is disobeying. Don't use it when you're trying to teach him a new behavior. Only when he is consciously disobeying a command is it acceptable to say "No!" or pull his collar to get him to change his behavior. And even then, the tug should not be painful, only firm. Never use negative reinforcement to train a dog except in the very rare circumstances where the dog is displaying hostile or truly dangerous behavior.

The bottom line is that Beagles can be trained. And so can their owners. It just takes time and love.

# Chapter 12

# Bonding with Your Beagle: Fun Things to Do

Beagles are happiest when participating in thrilling outdoor activities with their families, and you may be surprised to discover all the exciting things you can do together. You may never have to leave Clover alone again!

Just like human athletes, performance dogs need a training program. If possible, get a mentor for your activity, and have her help you design a reasonable schedule. Trying to achieve too much too quickly may not only ruin your dog's attitude, but also seriously damage his health.

Preparation is everything. Although you should teach your dog basic manners right from puppyhood, serious training should be delayed until your Beagle is a bit older. A dog is not mature until he is one year old. Before embarking on any athletic program, have your Beagle's health examined by a veterinarian. He needs to be in peak condition for hard training. Fat Beagles, and Beagles with heart or joint problems, are not suited to hard work or play.

And keep an eye on the weather, especially in the summertime. Dogs don't take heat well, as a rule. They need frequent access to fresh water to keep their heat regulatory system in good order.

Keep it fun. Almost nobody makes a living doing dog agility. Professional rabbit hunters are few and far between. There aren't many professional dog show handlers, either. For most people, dog activities should be a healthy hobby.

## Dog Shows

For dog people, the words "dog show" means "conformation show." Although showing dogs may seem like an occupation for the elite, this isn't really true. Every year, the American Kennel Club alone hosts 15,000 competitive events of all kinds. Many of these are officially called "dog shows," like the one the Westminster Kennel Club holds each February in Madison Square Garden. Some dog shows are formal competitions for titles (the AKC offers about 40 different titles—something for everyone); others, often called "matches," are informal events. A dog show is really a giant elimination contest, and while there can be only one Best in Show, there are lots and lots of ribbons to go around. I should reiterate, however, that you can't hope to do well at a dog show unless you own a show quality Beagle. You won't get one from the pet store.

The best way to learn about the sport of dog showing is to join your local Beagle or all-breed kennel club. You should get plenty of advice, and probably some helpful mentoring. Many clubs sponsors workshops, classes, and seminars on the fine art of dog handling.

## Obedience Competitions

In addition to classical obedience, there's a new sport on the horizon: Rally Style Obedience, called Rally-O by its promoters. In some ways the Rally is similar to traditional obedience. Participating dogs are expected to heel at different paces, make turns, do recalls, and jump. (Two levels are currently available. Level One is an entry level course that is performed on lead, and Level Two calls for more advanced exercises off-lead. Unlike traditional obedience trials, the Obedience Rally is a fast-moving event wherein the dog and the owner follow a predetermined course—not waiting for a judge to give commands.

*Hypo*
*photo courtesy of Lea Ward*

There are about forty-five different "exercises," and each specific course uses about twenty-six of them. Dogs can earn two hundred points for a perfect score, with point penalties assessed for errors. Unlike regular obedience competitions, the Rally allows the owner to repeat commands and to praise his pet for succeeding. This is *not allowed* in regular obedience classes. Verbal assurances are also permitted. This is great news for Beagle owners!

Rally-O is lot of fun for both owners and dogs, and even spectators, who find it an enjoyable change of pace. The Obedience Rally will be featured at AKC non-regular classes, and may soon become a "regular event."

## Canine Good Citizens

Dogs not ready for full-scale obedience can still take (and pass!) the Canine Good Citizen test offered by the American Kennel Club. To pass, a dog must successfully complete the following ten exercises:

- Accepting a friendly stranger
- Sitting politely for petting
- Appearance and grooming
- Walking on a loose leash
- Walking through a crowd
- Sit, Down, and Stay on command
- Coming when called
- Reacting appropriately to another dog
- Reacting appropriately to distractions
- Supervised separation

Canine Good Citizenship tests are conducted from time to time by many local kennel clubs. Contact the one nearest you for more information. There is no age limit for dogs taking the test, and dogs do not have to have AKC papers (or even be purebred) to pass. All dogs should have the necessary immunizations, however. For a copy of the Canine Good Citizens pamphlet, contact the AKC at (919) 233-9767 and ask for it.

## Tracking

Officially, tracking is part of obedience, but it's really its own separate world. Tracking offers all the thrill of the chase to people who aren't interested in actually catching anything.

In tracking, a dog follows a human scent left on an article, usually a leather glove or something similar. The dog, wearing a special tracking harness, then proceeds to follow the track of the article through a specified area. Dogs passing the test are awarded the title TD (Tracking Dog) after their names. Mastery of a more advanced test over more difficult terrain entitles the dog's owner to use the letters TDX (Tracking Dog Excellent). Another test is the Variable Surface Tracking Test, which is often given in an urban setting. (Large open fields available for tracking events are getting scarce, too.) Dogs who have attained all three of these titles are permitted to carry CT (Champion Tracker) after their names.

*Louie in flight!* *photo courtesy of Wally Jarrett*

The greatest tracking challenge for a Beagle is that he is expected to follow a human's, rather than a rabbit's, scent. And of course, it's not unusual, since the event is held outdoors, to have the track "crossed" by rabbit trails from time to time. Most self-respecting Beagles are tempted to abandon looking for the glove and start hunting rabbits the way they're supposed to. Only a good deal of training will overcome their inherited passion, but that makes it even more fun. A tracking event is not competitive, since everyone present can pass the test, but dogs who do the best are noted, as in an obedience trial.

## Field Trials: Beagles in the Brush

The wild woods and open meadows are a Beagle's natural environment, and if you can provide this kind of vigorous exercise for your dog, you and he are lucky indeed. However, before you undertake any new activity with your dog, both of you will need to prepare. (For every mile you walk, he'll probably run five.)

These competitive events are basically of two types: Brace and Small Pack Option (S.P.O.). In a brace trial, Beagles are placed in pairs for a contest to see which finds and tracks the rabbit best. I am happy to report to squeamish people (like me) that the rabbits are not killed in field trials. Many Beagle Clubs have frequent field trials, which you are welcome to attend as a spectator. Bring tick repellant with you. Unlike field trials for pointing breeds, you will not need to rent a horse to keep up with the dogs. The "gallery" as it is called, follows behind the dogs on foot.

It may seem that field work is very much the same as hunting (which I'll discuss in more detail later in this chapter), and it's true that dogs who excel in both have some qualities in common. However, in field trials the judges are looking from dogs who scent track more carefully and slowly than real-life hunters want. Take a look at the American Kennel Club's Regulations for Small Pack Options and check on the desirable characteristics for hunting and field trial hounds. Measure your own Beagle honestly against the criteria to see how suited he might be for field trial work or rabbit hunting.

*Bonkers* *photo courtesy of Christine Gaites*

## Searching Ability

This is the ability to recognize promising cover and eagerness to explore it, regardless of hazards or discomfort. Beagles who are afraid of rain, thickets, thorns, mud, and snow are too timid to excel in the field. Hounds should search independently of each other, in an industrious manner, with sufficient range. This means that your Beagle should not trail aimlessly after the other Beagles. He should be constantly searching, and not be afraid to go as far afield as necessary to find the game. In field trials where he is to be officially judged, he needs to stay within control distance of the handler, and should be obedient to his commands.

## Pursuing Ability

Here the hound must follow the trail closely. Game should be pursued rather than merely followed, and actions should indicate a determined effort to make forward progress in the surest, most sensible manner by adjusting speed to conditions and circumstances. Actions should be positive and controlled. Impetuous, heedless running around is not acceptable. Progress should be proclaimed by tonguing. Silent stalking of the prey is useless, since the Beagle's role is to draw the hunter and other hounds to the quarry. A Beagle can be hard to see in the bush, but his clear melodious voice should carry far.

### Accuracy in Trailing

Here the hound must follow the trail as cleanly and closely as possible. There should be a minimum of weaving on and off. He should take turns without problems. Some dogs are guilty of "ghost trailing," in which they give every evidence of having found a trail where none exists. This is very exasperating. Following the trail in the wrong direction is called "backtracking." Dogs who backtrack persistently in field trials are eliminated from the competition.

### Proper Use of Voice

Beagles let their fellow hunter know where the game is by "giving tongue" when he is in close contact with the scent. He is silent when he has lost it. This critical ability keeps everybody on track. Dogs who give voice unnecessarily are said to "babble." Dogs who don't give voice at all are said to "run mute." Insufficient voice is also known as "tightness of mouth."

### Endurance

Hounds are expected to be able to work all day. If your couch potato poops out after a stroll around the block, it's time to get him into a strenuous training program!

### Adaptability

Beagles should be able to *adjust quickly to changes in scenting conditions and be able to work harmoniously with a variety of running mates.* Beagles that quarrel with other dogs, or who need to work with one particular partner are not adaptable.

### Patience

Beagles don't give up. They don't run off the minute the track seems cold. They search diligently through bushes until they find it again. They don't "gamble" and they don't guess. They search until they find it or are called off by the master or another dog. When a dog fails to stay close to the lost scent and heads off in a new direction, it is called "leaving checks." It is a serious fault.

## Determination

Determination is desire in its most intense form. Determined dogs are not put off by distractions or discomfort. They are single minded and relentless. Dogs who are "quitters" show a lack of determination. Dogs who hesitate or dawdle are said to "potter," which may indicate lack of determination.

## Independence

Beagles need to be self-reliant and to refrain from becoming upset or influenced by the actions of faulty hounds. The proper degree of independence is displayed by the hound that concentrates on running its game with no undue concern for its running mates. A good hunter, of course, doesn't completely ignore his fellows, but will hark to them when they proclaim a find or indicate progress by tonguing.

## Cooperation

Good hounds work together. They "honor" each other and show no jealousy. They do not disrupt the progress of one another. Purposely leaving the trail to cut ahead of other dogs is called "skirting" and is an indication of lack of cooperation. Racing ahead of the other hounds persistently without noticing the true trail is "racing." This is a fault.

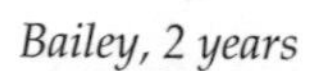

*Bailey, 2 years* *photo courtesy of Madlyn Schneider*

*Sage shows a competitive side* *photo courtesy of Blaire Healy*

### Competitive Spirit

Cooperative, yes, but every worthwhile Beagle desires to find the quarry first. This quality should never be at the expense of the others, however, and field courtesy is something that is actually judged. Dogs who plow into others in the quest to find the rabbit first are penalized.

### Intelligence

This is the master attribute that allows the Beagle to use all his abilities wisely. Stupid dogs are useless in the field.

## Hunting

I'm not a hunter myself, but if you enjoy this sport, you certainly can't go wrong with a Beagle as your hunting pal. Most authorities recommend that you start training your Beagle to hunt when he's a puppy. That way you won't have to train your adult dog out of the many bad habits he has probably acquired over the years.

Remember that you will have to train your hunting dog into getting used to gunfire. Dogs don't naturally take to loud noises, so this is something you'll have to work at. You can begin by

*Hypo* *photo courtesy of Lea Ward*

introducing loud sounds while he is eating. Eating is so important to most Beagles that it makes up for almost anything.

Of course, anyone who plans on hunting with his Beagle needs to learn the rules, obtain the proper licenses, and learn gun safety. I strongly urge beginning hunters to get a mentor, as this is really the only correct way to learn to hunt safely. For more information on training your Beagle to hunt with you, get copies of *How to Help Gun Dogs Train Themselves—Taking Advantage of Early Conditioned Learning,* by Joan Bailey and *Beagle Basics* by Bill Bennett, both published by Doral Publishing.

## Agility Trials

Agility has taken the dog world by storm! Here the handler runs the dog through and over a variety of obstacles including jumps, chutes, tunnels, weave poles, ramps, and seesaws. Many kennel clubs offer classes in agility, and if you are handy, you can even make your own agility equipment from PVC pipes, plywood, and children's tunnels. Beagles are smart and agile animals who do well in the game.

## AKC Agility Competitions

The AKC has its own agility competitions, limited to dogs with pedigrees, but other organizations offer contests to any and all breeds. Dogs must be one year old to compete. Because the jumps are adjusted according to the height of the dog, being small is not a disadvantage in this sport. The American Kennel Club offers bunches of Agility Titles for your dog to earn: Novice Agility (NA); Open Agility (OA); Agility Excellent (AX); Master Agility Excellent (MX). Other titles include Jumpers with Weaves Novice (NAJ), Open (OAJ) and Excellent (MXJ). The supreme title in agility is Master Agility Champion (MACH). For this title the dog needs to earn 750 points (based on the speed of sound—get it?) while double qualifying in each run through a course that requires both speed and accuracy. See AKC.org for more information.

*Wynborne's Tucker Box, NA, NAJ* *photo courtesy of Nikki Berrong*

*Bailey relaxes in the sand* *photo courtesy of Madlyn Schneider*

## Hiking and Camping

Hiking and camping are enjoyable family sports that require no special training classes, or even an admission charge. However, remember to keep your Beagle on a leash at all times. Most public land areas require it, and a loose is Beagle is a lost Beagle. You want to spend the day hiking companionably together—you do not want to spend it thrashing around in the brush screaming uselessly after your dog.

If you're hiking on a regular hiking trail, clean up after your dog. Don't forget those baggies. If you did forget them, use a stick or leaves and remove the offending residue well away from the trail. Unless dog owners keep trails clean, they will be banned from using them.

Use an insect repellent (either a natural spray or one with pyrethrins). Flea spray will work fine, but I wouldn't use a spray for humans that contains DEET. Although not shown to be dangerous, dogs do lick their fur, and ingesting DEET just can't be a good idea.

In very rough areas, you might want to consider booties for your dog, as they'll do wonders in saving your dog's feet. Take your time teaching your dog to wear them, though, and expect a little reluctance at first.

On any hiking trip with your Beagle, bring along plenty of water, and if possible, discourage him from drinking from streams and rivers—you never know what's in them. In hot

*Louie* *photo courtesy of Wally Jarrett*

weather, try to restrict the exercise to morning and evening hours, when it's likely to be cooler. If you're planning a vigorous workout, begin slowly; take at least ten minutes to "warm up." Watch your dog carefully for signs of overexertion. Beagles are anxious to go the limit, and they are very stoical about pain. If you sense your dog is tiring or has sustained an injury, take time out or quit. Dogs have actually been known to die in the attempt to keep up with their owners.

## Buoyant Beagles?

While most hounds will happily wade into water after game or even for the heck of it, they don't like swimming as such. Nor is it reasonable to expect them to dive into the water after sticks. They are not retrievers after all, and have entirely too much sense to go mindlessly in the water after something that's not even edible. One can hardly blame them.

If your Beagle is one of the few who enjoys water sports—or if you live near a lake or river, observe the basic safety rules. Keep a watch for swift currents, and never leave your Beagle unattended near water, including swimming pools and ornamental garden ponds. Although the kids may plead that they want to swim with Corky, it's dangerous to allow children to play in the water with dogs. Kids can unwittingly overwhelm a small dog with splashing, and dogs can do serious damage to close-swimming kids with their sharp nails.

## Therapy Dogs

Dogs are natural born healers of both the body and the spirit. By now, most people are familiar with the practice of owners and their pets making regular visits to hospitals, children's homes, psychiatric institutions, assisted-care facilities, and even prisons! All persons, no matter what their age, health, or status in society may benefit from having close contact with animals. In fact there's even a name for this activity—Animal Assisted Therapy (AAT).

Therapy dogs lower blood pressure, reduce stress, slow rapid heartbeats, and make people happy. Happiness is indeed a warm puppy, even if the "puppy" is fourteen years old. Beagles make no moral judgments about people and even those folks traditionally looked down upon by society (prison inmates, the mentally ill or disabled) have a chance to see their self-worth confirmed in the eyes of a trusting dog. In fact, workers in mental health facilities often report that a patient who has not spoken a word for years will suddenly begin speaking and interacting with a dog. It's a first step, but a giant one. Dogs have helped developmentally disabled children, and even helped stroke patients regain their speech.

Beagles are great for therapy work. For one thing, their small size makes them non-threatening, even to the smallest child or frailest older person. They can also be easily picked up and carried to a bedside or out the way of busy hospital traffic. Although German Shepherds and Rottweilers make excellent therapy dogs, many people have entirely negative associations with them. The cheerful Beagle, on the other hand, evokes a positive response from nearly everyone.

To participate in Animal Assisted Therapy (AAT), it's best to have your pet certified, either by the facility you'll be volunteering in or by a national pet therapy organization or its affiliate. In some cases, you'll just be making the rounds, visiting, and talking with residents (many of whom have literally no one else to talk to). In other cases your pet will be part of a specific treatment plan, with clear goals set forth on each visit.

Certification programs vary, but many require that your dog complete a full obedience course, a health screen, and be of a certain age (usually one year). Of course, a good therapy dog will be bathed and groomed (especially his nails), and be free of fleas.

You certainly wouldn't want your Beagle causing a flea infestation at the local hospital! As far as personality goes—two qualities are of the essence: friendliness and obedience. A dog who is just one or the other is not suitable. And no matter how good-natured, an out-of-control Beagle in a hospital or nursing home does more harm than good.

If you decide that AAT is for you, you'll need to devote a certain amount of time to it each week or month. People come to expect and look forward to your regular visit, and they often form close attachments to your dog. (The dog enjoys the visits too!) It isn't fair to anyone to make a half-hearted or sporadic commitment. Remember that your visits can make just as much a difference in people's lives as medicine and good food.

## Beagle Rescue

Not every Beagle is as lucky as yours. Some have been abused or neglected, beaten or left to starve. Some have been simply abandoned to shelters, humane societies, roadsides, or garbage dumps. You can help a luckless Beagle by getting involved with a reputable rescue organization. Rescues retrieve dogs from danger, and set about re-homing them. This often involves extensive veterinary or behavioral therapy, lots of time, and a considerable amount of money.

Fortunately, there's room in rescue for everyone who cares about Beagles. Here's how you can make a difference:

- Become a foster parent. This is the most important step between the shelter and the adoptive home. Fosters take in dogs for a period of from one day to one year, nurse them back to health, evaluate their temperaments, and provide perhaps the first human love a dog has ever known. Most rescue groups will reimburse foster parents for medical and training expenses; some will also pay for food.
- Donate money. Rescue is an extremely expensive proposition. The Rescue I work with spends over $25,000 a year on vet bills alone. There are also kenneling fees (when fosters are absent), training costs, phone and postage bills, insurance payments, and dozens of other things. Every dollar you can contribute is a great help.

- Get involved in transport. Sometimes a dog needs to be moved—maybe twenty miles, maybe two hundred miles from a shelter to a foster home. If you can offer the use of your car and your time just one day a month, you'll be doing a service.
- Use whatever talents you have for the benefit of rescue services. If you are crafty, perhaps you can make items to sell at Beaglefests or online auctions. If you have organizational skills, offer to put together a Canine Good Citizenship Test or Fun Dog Show for the benefit of rescue. If you're a teacher or writer, put your talents to use in teaching people about good pet care. With a well-educated populace, the need for rescue organizations will diminish. Nothing would make rescue volunteers happier than to go out of business because they are no longer needed.
- If you have corporate contacts, you might able to arrange for an organization to make matching payments when their employees donate to rescue.

The rewards of rescue work are tremendous. Nothing compares with the feeling you get when you watch your rescued Beagle gradually transform from a frightened, dirty, sick animal into a healthy, happy pet. When your foster dog trots cheerfully off with his "forever family" there'll be a small broken place in your heart amid your happiness—but it can be healed quickly. Take in a new foster dog; get involved all over again.

# Chapter 13

# Backsliding Beagles: Normal "Misbehavior"

In reality, of course, there's no such thing as a bad, or even a backsliding, Beagle. There are only untrained or mis-trained Beagles—or more accurately—untrained, or mis-trained owners. Most "problems" that crop up in the owner/dog relationship aren't even problems in the sense that the dog is exhibiting unnatural behavior. It's just the opposite, in fact. Most of the problems people have with their dogs are due to the dog's being, in effect, altogether *too* natural. Barking, chewing, and chasing small animals are perfectly natural for a dog. They just aren't always appropriate in a civilized society.

The inappropriate behaviors in this chapter are usually correctable through owner training, and without the use of special skills, mechanical devices, or medications.

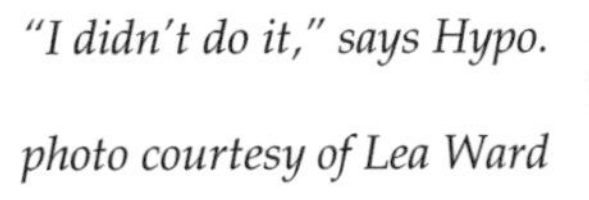

*"I didn't do it," says Hypo.*

*photo courtesy of Lea Ward*

## Bad Habits?

It's important to understand the origins of your dog's "bad" behavior. Although most unwanted behavior has its roots in the genes, it may not pop up unless your dog is feeling bored or lonely. I am not talking about puppy behavior here, of course. A little puppy will tear and dig because he doesn't know yet that such behavior is not acceptable, at least not in the house.

All dogs have a reason for what they do. You may not comprehend the reason, at least not immediately, but rest assured that there is one. In fact, dogs share some common crime-motivators with us humans, such as anger and jealousy. Sometimes there's no subtle emotional component at all. Dogs eat garbage because they like it, not because they're trying to tell you something. But you're the human, and it's your job to figure out the motivation for the offending conduct, and then change it.

## Barking Beagles

Beagles make all kinds of noises; they were bred to do so; it's how they communicated with the rest of the pack (and the huntsmen). In fact, *Dog Fancy* magazine listed them among the top six "barking breeds," along with Yorkies, Shelties, Newfoundlands, German Shepherds, and Dachshunds. The Beagle repertoire includes howling, barking, baying, whining, yelping, yapping, singing, bawling, growling, ahrooing, woofing, yowling, and yipping. Beagles are good at all of them; in fact, one small Beagle can sound like a whole lot of bigger dogs! It's a beautiful sound, really, a whole bunch of Beagles (or even one) howling together, slightly off-key.

All of a dog's vocalizations are just a form of communication. But most owners see barking and other loud vocalizations as a problem—not as a communication tool.

### A Real Howler

The world's most versatile howler is a Beagle named Regal. In fact, Regal won himself a recording session in a 1997 howling contest at the South Street Seaport in New York City. His best known tune is "That's Amore."

*Bonkers*
*photo courtesy of Christine Gaites*

Moreover, the neighbors may not be crazy about the noise. Even people who admire a few minutes of howling can go crazy with a series of barks. That's because most dogs bark in a sharp, piercing monotone. Oh, first it will be the polite, "Ya better shut up yer damned dog or I'm gonna call da cops" routine. It goes pretty much down hill from there. Of course, you don't want things to reach that stage. So, how does one turn a barking Beagle into the small silent type? You probably can't. Not completely. In the first place, barking is a natural and instinctive behavior. Even the so-called "barkless" Basenji makes enough weird (and loud) noises to scare off a ghost.

## Barking for Attention

Although many conditions set off barking, the vast majority of barking episodes are caused by your Beagle's desire to get your attention. He may be saying any of the following things:

- "Hey, there's a weird looking dude in a uniform and a big pouch coming up the steps. He may be dangerous! Look out!"
- "I'm getting very tired of standing around in this backyard by myself with nothing to do. I want you to come out here and play with me right now!"
- "I'm really have fun running around out here and barking at the dog across the street. I wish I could go over there!"

- "I'm cold. Let me in right now!"
- "I hurt somewhere! Help me, please!"
- "I'm the boss around here and I want everyone to know it!"
- "I'm an older dog and I just don't know exactly why I'm barking, but I feel that I must! (In fact, since I don't hear so well any more, I am not sure I really am barking.)"
- "Everybody else in the neighborhood is barking! Something's up!"
- "There's all kinds of activity next door, and I want to make sure that they stay on their own side of the fence! This is my property!"

Dogs have pretty good memories. Your dog has learned to bark because somewhere along the line you have rewarded his barking. Any attention, even negative attention, is a reward for a barking dog.

The first step in reducing the noise your Beagle makes is to understand why he wants your attention. He's probably asking you for something, or telling you something he thinks you need to know. If your dog wants something, and his request is appropriate, grant it. Consider the "I am cold or bored" scenario. If your Beagle gets cold or bored in the back yard, and you've forgotten about him, just how is he supposed to let you know? Would you rather he came to the door and scratched? If that's what you would prefer, then you must reward him when he scratches and not when he barks.

## Territorial Barking

Here's another scenario. Your dog is in his fenced backyard. He barks at a passerby. The passerby actually goes away! The Beagle thinks he is responsible for chasing away the stranger. He feels quite swollen up with pride. The barking worked; the behavior is reinforced. Don't expect your dog to never bark at strangers. He is trying to protect the household and should not be penalized for doing so. Many a burglar has been warned off a house by a barking dog—not because the animal poses any danger but because he will alert the residents and neighbors. It's a mistake to try to eliminate this perfectly natural behavior, but you can control it.

Fenced-in dogs are more likely to bark than free-ranging animals. (Stray dogs hardly ever bark, having no property to defend.) While fences are a necessary protection for your Beagle, they do tend to make dogs territorial—and noisy. It's true, however, that Beagles are less territorial than most breeds, and that barking Beagles usually have another impetus.

As a rule, the more space your Beagle has to run in, the less likely he will be to bark. The worst barkers are dogs kept on a chain all day long. The combination of boredom, loneliness and territoriality make a noisy cacophony that everyone can do without. Dogs left outside at night also tend to bark; it's probably spooky out there.

### Another Good Reason to Spay or Neuter Your Dog

Spaying or neutering your pet will reduce barking in about 50 percent of the cases. It's certainly worth a try.

## Reducing the Decibels

If your dog is barking because he is bored or lonely (as may happen when the dog is left alone for hours at a time), change his environment. Play with him more, take him on walks, exercise him, get him a companion. But don't reward the barking by doing any of these things in response to the barking. If the only time you pay attention to your dog is when he's barking, you are rewarding his behavior. Even yelling out the window, "Shut up!" is better than nothing as far as a dog is concerned. In fact, he may think you're joining in!

You may have to get your grumpy neighbors to help you with a barking dog. Go to them, hat in hand, so to speak, and apologize for your Beagle's barking. (Bring a pie, if you want.) Tell them you are attempting a cure, but you need their co-operation. It's possible that their yelling at your dog may have been enough reward to keep him barking, so ask them if they would simply ignore his barking while you work at reconditioning. Apologize some more, and ask if they would just phone you if the dog is annoying them.

If your dog barks outside when you are away from home, you're better off keeping him inside. He's safer in the house anyway. If he barks while he's inside the house, shut the blinds to reduce the stimulation.

Too much activity or stimulation can also lead to barking. It's exciting to have a bicycle tour go by. For some dogs, even the little old lady with her gardening trowel may be too thrilling for words—so it's bark-time again. Such dogs can be treated either by desensitizing them to the stimulus or removing them from it. In most cases, dogs get used to a certain level of activity, and after a while, ignore it. Our Liz barked wildly for several hours at the road crew outside the house; by the second day she ignored them. If the dog continues to bark from over-stimulation, it's best to bring him in away from the noise.

Regular bark-producing events, like the arrival of the letter carrier can be a challenge. Whether your Beagle adores the letter carrier or hates him—he's anticipating the Big Event. As the magic hour approaches, he may become more and more excited. This is especially true if he's alone in the house, when it's the highlight of the day.

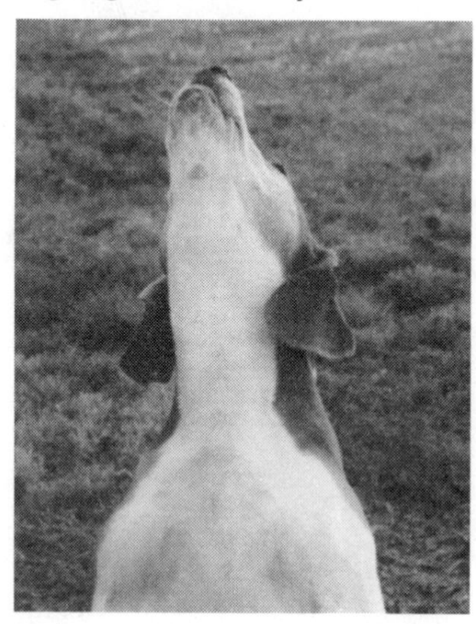

*Louie*
*photo courtesy of Wally Jarrett*

Some dogs bark from sheer pleasure, perhaps somewhat akin to hearing oneself sing in the shower. It all depends on the individual dog. If he seems to be having a great time outside barking for joy, bring him inside the instant he barks. He will soon understand that joy-barking brings an unintended result. You might also try giving the joy-barker a cheese or peanut butter filled Kong toy. Dogs can't bark and chew at the same time, and by the time he finishes the Kong, the thrill of the backyard may have worn off.

Prevention is the best tool. If you know your dog barks in certain situations over which you have control, prevent those situations from occurring. For example, if you know the dog always barks like crazy when the kids next door come home from school, simply don't allow him outside at that time of day. Never use physical punishment to stop barking. In the first place, it won't work. The alternative to giving a reward is no reward. Punishment never teaches a dog anything except to try to avoid the punishment. Using a punishment to suppress a natural behavior will encourage a dog to resort to other, perhaps more destructive actions to get his point across. It can make dogs neurotic, or even aggressive.

### Confused Communication

Elderly dogs suffering from canine cognitive disorder often bark for apparently no reason at all. Your old dog might also be suffering a hearing loss, and not even be aware that he's barking.

## The "No Bark" Command

If your Beagle barks at a visitor, immediately say in mild tone, "Good boy, No Bark." Then touch him, and ask him to "Settle." This acknowledges that his warning has registered and that you see the danger and will deal with it appropriately. After all, it's a good thing for a dog to announce the arrival of guests. It is part of their inheritance, after all. He will soon see that a friend has arrived, and there's no need to give continued warnings.

Teach the "No Bark" command by saying "No Bark" and rewarding your dog with a treat the instant he stops. If he continues to bark, turn your back and walk off. If possible, let him know that strangers are nearly always full of goodwill. If your letter carrier agrees, ask her to speak reassuringly to Oliver, or even hand him a dog biscuit. If you have a very agreeable mail carrier and a letter slot directly into you home, tape a dog biscuit to the outside of the door every day and ask the letter carrier to drop it in. That will be a pleasant event for your Beagle. It may not stop him from barking, but at least he'll feel better about the carrier. If nothing else works, close the blinds and baby gate your Beagle out of the living room.

On the other hand, many people have had success in quieting their dogs by teaching them to "speak." Paradoxical as it may sound, the point is to teach the dog to bark appropriately. The reward is given on the command, "Shush." Soon the dog learns to associate the reward with the word "Shush" and the correct response, silence. You must be very consistent in teaching this behavior, and always use the same commands.

### Contagious Barking!

Dogs copy one another's behavior. Introducing a problem barker into a previously quiet group of dogs can create a whole pack of barkers.

## Anti-bark Devices and "De-barking"

Although electronic anti-bark collar manufacturers use words like "stimulation," "pulse," "vibration," or even "tickle" rather than "electrical shock" to sell their wares, don't be fooled. These devices give your barking dog a jolt of juice. And even trainers who think these collars are effective caution that they shouldn't be used for long periods. They are also completely ineffective when used on a dog with separation anxiety or a neurotic condition. The most effective use for these collars is to curb "joy barkers." Here they seem to work, but it seems unnecessarily cruel—what if someone gave you a shock every time you laughed!

Another kind of anti-bark collar contains citronella oil, which dogs hate. The collar sprays citronella mist in the dog's face when he begins to bark. Although this device is somewhat more humane than an electrical shock collar, it's a poor second best to real training. Besides, Beagles are pretty smart dogs. They know perfectly well when they are wearing any kind of anti-bark collar and when they are not. They will adjust their behavior accordingly.

Some owners keep switching collars around on their dogs, even having them wear two at once—sometimes one of them is an anti-bark collar, and sometimes it isn't. They report good success with "confusing" the dog out of barking, and some research supports the idea that this method works quite well—better than either the punishment or the reward method of conditioning. This is probably true; it's harder to steel yourself against an electric shock when you're not sure whether one is coming. Still, I don't believe that keeping a dog confused is the best treatment for problem barkers, and I suspect their barking only sublimates into other forms of unacceptable behavior.

Other products, like the Super Barker Breaker, use vibrations or a high-pitched sound meant to annoy the dog out of barking. Most Beagles pay no attention to this, and some actually regard the noise as a stimulus to begin barking on their own.

Some experts recommend surgically "de-barking" a dog when all else fails. This is an operation to remove the vocal cords. De-barking does not completely silence the dog; it only "tones" down the barking, leaving with a hoarse, whispery, muted sound. Debarking and electronic collars should be reserved for truly intractable cases.

### Medication

Some kinds of barking, especially those caused by separation anxiety, depression, canine cognitive dysfunction, and obsessive-compulsive disorder, respond well to drugs. (Medication does not work for "normal" barking, however.) Some drugs that have been used successfully include amitrptyline (Elavil) for general anxiety barking, and clomipramine (Clomicalm) for separation anxiety. You should explore the reason for your dog's barking and appropriate medication with your veterinarian. Most dogs don't need drugs at all, and those who do have very individual requirements.

## Begging and Banditry

"But he looks so hungry!" Yes, doesn't he? All dogs specialize in begging, but some breeds can look a lot more pathetic than others. As a matter of fact, Beagles are masters of it. Begging is a natural behavior for canids; weaned wolf cubs beg food from their parents after a hunt. Moreover, in the natural state, wild dogs and wolves eat only once every two or three days. Any meal they can scrounge has to carry them for many miles. The instinct to gobble up as much as possible before it's too late is too powerful for dogs to overcome, even if they wanted to.

Begging probably got dogs to be where they are today—right beneath the dinner table. Although it is possible to teach a dog to come to the table for a tidbit only when called, it's extremely difficult. It's much easier to go by the general rule—never feed the dog at the table. Even if you think it's cute, your dinner guests may not. In addition, begging always escalates. First the dog just looks forlorn. Then he starts to whine. Then he barks sharply. Finally, he just jumps up and grabs whatever takes his fancy. Another reason for this has nothing to do with food, really, but for what food stands for: power. In the animal world the dog with the greatest access to food is the "alpha" dog. If you allow your Beagle to grab food, you are giving him authority you don't want him to have.

Finally, begging Beagles also put on weight quickly. Beagles, along with Bassets, Dachshunds, and Labrador Retrievers, appear to have slower metabolisms than other breeds. So that harmless-looking nibble you hand your dog under the table can turn quickly into extra pounds.

### Stopping Begging

If you don't want your Beagle begging, keep him away from the kitchen. Never offer him food from your plate. If you want him to have a dinner leftover, transfer it from your plate to his own dish when he's not looking. Be consistent about this. You don't want him to get the idea that there's any connection between your dinner and his. If your dog never receives food for humans, he won't know that it's a lot better tasting than dog food. I'll admit, it's hard to keep him from learning this secret, but if you can, he'll be a lot less inclined to beg.

Closely related to begging is counter-cruising—stealing food from the counter. You can try a variety of tricks to keep your dog from doing this, but the safest, surest maneuver is not to leave food unattended on the counter. Although Beagles are usually too short to reach the counter top, a really determined dog is capable of amazing feats.

## Chewing

Chewing and mouthing behavior is normal among dogs, especially puppies. The only way a dog can get familiar with an object is to smell it, and then take it in his mouth to explore it further. Old shoes, new shoes, children's popsicles, children's fingers, they're all part of the wonderful, chewable world! What your dog is most likely to chew on is actually somewhat predictable:

- The most commonly chewed items in the home are new ones. Until the new object—the carpet, the chair, the jacket—absorbs some of the scents of the household, and thus becomes familiar, your Beagle will want to check it out. And although humans examine new objects with their hands and eyes, dogs use their noses and mouths. So until that new drapery starts smelling like everything else in the house, keep your unsupervised dog away from it.
- The second most commonly chewed objects in the house are those that smell strongly like the owner—particularly shoes and used underwear. Both are also popular because they're found lying around on the floor within easy reach. (Some dogs prefer certain material to others. One of mine goes for rubber flip-flops, while another prefers fine leather.)
- The third most commonly chewed items are expensive or irreplaceable ones, such as jewelry, collectible stamps, and furniture.
- The fourth most commonly chewed items are things that are dangerous to your dog. They may contain batteries, or have sharp edges. They may get stuck in the throat or the intestines. Nylon stockings, remote controls, and poisonous plants fit into this category.

Destructive behavior is usually just a normal puppy stage. Puppies chew most during their teething phase, a process that goes through two stages: the first between four and six months, and a second one at around eighteen months, when the back molars come in.

Sometimes, of course, excessive chewing continues past puppyhood. This is especially true of pound or shelter dogs. Perhaps your dog is bored or lonely. Perhaps he isn't given enough chew toys of his own, or enough variety.

Dogs enjoy toys of different shapes and materials. They not only provide amusement for a boring afternoon, but many of them are good for teeth and gums as well. However, it is possible to give a dog too many toys. Usually three or four are plenty; you can keep alternating them so they don't go "stale." A dog with too many chew toys can't keep track of them, and sometimes this makes him nervous or possessive.

*Bonkers chewing on a toy*
*photo courtesy of Christine Gaites*

## Correcting Puppy Chewing

Some people recommend shaking a coin-filled soda (or beer) can at the puppy, but I haven't found this technique particularly impressive to Beagles. A squirt of water works better, although I'd save this ammunition for really serious offenses, such as fighting. It is much better to distract the puppy with a better toy, chew bone, or game. Don't expect to completely eradicate this natural behavior. The best you can hope for is to re-direct it.

Put away things you value, watch your dog carefully, and don't buy anything new for a while. (If you keep forgetting to put away your own valuable items, think how hard it is for a puppy to remember not to chew them!) Some experts recommend using scented or medicated shoe inserts that will hide your scent and make your shoes less tempting for the dog. It's just as easy to stick your shoes in the closet where they belong. If the object isn't movable, such as your new drapes, get a baby gate and keep your Beagle out of that room until he recovers from his obsession with the object. You may have to resort to certain commercial sprays like "No!" designed to keep Beagles at bay. These usually work pretty well, but somehow the dog often manages to find exactly whatever it is you forgot to spray.

Unless you do so for a very brief period, don't lock your dog up in a crate to prevent him from chewing. If your dog is chewing out of boredom or loneliness, this won't solve the problem. Dogs don't get less bored and lonely in crates than they do elsewhere. If at all possible, keep your dog by your side. (Tether him to you if you need to.) This will not only keep him away from tempting

*Bonkers* *photo courtesy of Christine Gaites*

goodies, but also give him some time with the one he loves best—you. This alone will make him more manageable.

You can stop the chewing only when you actually catch your Beagle in the act. Never punish a dog after the fact. He won't have the least idea what the fuss is about, and anything you do other than ignore it is counter-productive.

## When Chewing Turns to Nipping

Puppy nipping often begins as licking, then progresses to chewing, and finally ends up as nipping. You must teach your dog that teeth don't belong on human skin. If your puppy begins to nip, say "Ow!" in a high-pitched, squeaky voice. The puppy should immediately stop nipping, realizing that he's hurt you. If this doesn't work, growl at him, and if absolutely necessary, give him a sharp tap on the nose. Do not jerk your arm away from him. That's too much like a game. The trick is to get him to move first. If he persists, stare in another direction, and walk away. He'll soon learn that nipping means the end of the game.

To help prevent puppy nipping:

- Keep plenty of safe, healthy toys around.
- To ease the discomfort of teething, provide ice or broth cubes.
- Don't play tug of war with your Beagle.
- Pet your Beagle on the chest and back, rather than the head area.
- Exercise your dog a lot. Tired dogs make happy owners.

## Garbage Looting

Garbage is irresistible to Beagles. The smellier it is, the better they like it. Once a Beagle has learned to raid the trashcan, he won't stop. The rewards are potentially too great. Even a tight cover won't keep a really enterprising dog out.

This problem is more than messy and annoying; it can be dangerous to your dog. Not only can he get hold of cooked, dry, splintery chicken bones, but he can also fall prey to the molds and nasty bacteria that have developed in your trash while you weren't looking. Potato skins, apple seeds, and moldy cheese are as bad for your dog as they are for you.

Although you can try booby-trapping the garbage can with balloons, mousetraps, or other scary items, the best plan is prevention. Use childproof locks on cabinets that contain trash cans or keep the trash can behind a closed door.

A few dogs combine trash stealing with food aggression. For some reason, stolen treats are sweeter than those lawfully obtained. I have seen gentle, compliant dogs turn into snarling monsters when they obtain something that doesn't belong to them. It's much better if the situation doesn't occur in the first place. (If your dog does get into something that's actually dangerous, try offering him something really nice as a "trade".)

## Digging

The natural hunting instinct of Beagles leads them to rabbit holes, and the best way to get a rabbit out of his hole is to dig him out. So Beagles dig. There is nothing mysterious about this.

Dogs also have the urge to dig to bury (and so preserve) their food supply. In the wild, wolves who couldn't consume their dinners all at once needed a secure hiding place from other predators and vultures. The earth not only covers food, it also preserves it, since it's generally a few degrees cooler than the surrounding air.

And dogs dig for fun. Just as human children play in a sandbox, digging is a natural and interesting activity for dogs. Digging can also be very productive, for a dog, that is. For one thing, it helps him find interesting things buried in the ground or under snow. Our Liz was an expert mole-hunter. She'd sniff along the ground, and then all of a sudden—*bam!* She'd start digging like a madwoman and then, crunch! No more moles.

Sometimes dogs dig to gain themselves a cool spot. There's nothing nicer on a hot summer day, apparently, than to hollow out a lovely soft bed of cool earth and go to sleep in it. If your dog digs a number of shallow holes, usually in the shade, that's the reason.

Dogs kept outside a great deal are also prone to digging. They are lonely, anxious, and bored, and digging a hole is a good way to pass the time.

Digging near a fence line is an indication that the dog may be trying to escape, while digging near the house may mean he's lonely and desires your company.

### Dogs Who Will Dig

Unspayed females are more likely to engage in digging behavior than are their spayed sisters; it's a form of nesting behavior. Puppies are also more prone to digging than are older animals.

Unfortunately digging around the backyard, whether normal or not, can be destructive, unsightly, and annoying. It's also very hard to stop.

## Dealing with Digging

- Keep your dog inside. The more time he spends inside, the less opportunity he'll have to dig outside. The comfort he'll get from being near you will reduce the anxiety that may lead to digging.
- Reduce his number of toys, especially edible ones. Dogs tend to bury leftovers—not things for immediate consumption. If a dog has too many toys or bones, he will bury some of them to protect them. Dogs also tend to bury the toys that they like the least. If one toy keeps getting buried—your dog is trying to tell you something. Throw it away.

- Exercise him vigorously every day. Tired dogs are good dogs.
- Make him his very own earth-box. Bring along some of his favorite toys or treats, and play with your dog in the box. Praise and treat him for digging in the appropriate place. You might even show him the way by digging a bit in the sanctioned spot yourself.
- Put up a nice Beagle-proof fence to protect your flowers and vegetables. It will give your garden an air of sophistication and be completely secure from your digger as well.

It is useless and counter-productive to punish your dog for performing this natural activity. The best way to stop the objectionable behavior is to offer a palatable alternative. On the other hand, you can let the Beagle find out for himself that digging is no fun. I have heard of people burying a hose in the favorite digging area, hiding in the house, and turning on the hose when the Beagle digs in that spot. In this case, the dog is not associating the soaking with you, but as a consequence of the digging activity. He may stop.

## Bouncing Beagles

In the wild dogs greet each other by giving face-to-face greetings. So, when you arrive home, Sammy is desperately trying to make contact the only way he knows how—by jumping up on you.

*Bonkers goes bonkers…* *photo courtesy of Christine Gaites*

## Jumping on People

The way to dissuade your Beagle from jumping up is not to reward it. When you arrive home, just ignore your dog. I know this sounds hard, but it must be done. The jumping problem has probably been exacerbated because of the attention it has previously obtained for your Beagle. Don't say anything; don't even give eye contact. Turn your back and walk out of the room. Or stare at the ceiling.

When your Beagle is in a calmer state, greet him quietly, and if you like, lean down and put your face near his. Undoubtedly, he'll give you a big Beagle kiss. That gives him the comforting contact he is looking for. Some people recommend asking your dog to "Sit" when he starts jumping. I suppose this is better than nothing, but a dog who must be told to "Sit" so he won't jump is not really broken of any bad habits.

To really cure jumping up, you should not allow your dog to jump on anyone, including children who don't mind it. Your playful jumping Beagle could easily knock over a toddler or a frail elderly person. You *can* teach a dog to jump on command, but you need to work consistently at this. It's usually easier not to let him jump at all.

Beaglers beware! Never knee your dog in the chest or kick him to stop him from jumping. And don't step on his back feet—you could easily break his toes! Dogs learn fast, and pain is a great teacher; but kicking or kneeing a dog teaches him the wrong lesson. If you hurt your dog in any way, he will very quickly associate contact with you with pain. He will become fearful and resentful. Your arrival home will no longer be greeted with joy, but with avoidance.

## Jumping on Furniture

Jumping on furniture is another habit that many dogs have acquired. Some owners don't mind it; they even encourage it. It drives other owners crazy. There are a lot devices designed to train your dogs off furniture; most of them pay homage to Thomas Edison by delivering some variety of electric shock to the poor creature who ventures on the sofa. Some merely emit a horrible noise. One mechanical device, the famous "Snappy Trainer" is really a kind of fancy mousetrap that flaps a scary paddle at the offending dog. Sometimes these work; sometimes they don't. If you are truly averse to having your dog leap up on the furniture while you're gone, stack something on top of the couch that he can't get on, such as a stool laid lengthwise. Or lock the dog out of that room.

# Chapter 14

# Bashful Beagles and Biting Beagles: Serious Behavior Problems

Millions of dogs are abandoned or dumped into shelters every year because of serious behavior problems. The real problem here lies with the owners—people who refused to acknowledge and deal with a behavior issue until it became so troublesome that they felt they could no longer keep the dog.

If you have adopted a shelter or rescue dog, be prepared to inherit a few behavior problems. Some of these problems may have been with the animal since puppyhood, while others were acquired while the dog was a stray or in a shelter.

## Bashful Beagles

Although canine bashfulness is not a serious problem to people the way that aggression or destructive behavior can be, it causes great pain to the dog himself, and significantly affects the quality of his life. Because of this, and because it is so common in Beagles, I consider it among the major problems faced by Beagle owners. Shy dogs, moreover, tend to develop other shyness-related problems. These include barking, housetraining errors, and in serious cases, fear-biting. And if a shy dog gets away from his owner, he can be very hard to catch, since he'll be unlikely to come to strangers.

Some shyness is a natural component of your dog's genetic makeup. For wild dogs, it makes sense to approach new objects and strange situations carefully. But excessive shyness is counter-productive for both wild and domesticated *canids*.

## Causes of Bashfulness

First of all, it's necessary to distinguish shyness from submissiveness. A submissive dog is on the bottom rung of the canine hierarchy. He allows other dogs to precede him out the door, and doesn't push his way into being petted. He may eat last. There's nothing wrong with being submissive; it's an instinctive survival strategy of a weaker animal among stronger, more dominant ones. Since dogs operate on a hierarchical social pattern, one dog has to be at the bottom, at least sometimes.

Excessive shyness is a different matter. A shy dog is a fearful animal—overly afraid of strange people, new situations, or peculiar objects. A shy dog will cringe or squat, even urinate at the approach of stranger—sometimes even with people he knows. A submissive dog can be a happy dog; a shy dog is usually too scared to enjoy life.

Dogs develop excessive shyness for a number of reasons, including:

- Genetic predisposition
- Physical or verbal abuse
- Insufficient contact with humans while still in the litter
- Inadequate socialization with other dogs between weaning and twelve weeks

Unfortunately, genetically predisposed shyness is found with some frequency in Beagles. This makes emboldening your shy Beagle a challenge, but it can be done. The key is early and frequent socialization. Older dogs can be socialized also, but it takes time and patience, particularly if the dog has had a bad experience to overcome.

The earlier you address any dog behavior problem, the better. Dogs have simpler brains and less reasoning ability than humans, and once a behavior becomes thoroughly ingrained, it's difficult to uproot. Be very patient. Impatience will only intensify your Beagle's fear.

## Treating Shyness

To alleviate shyness in dogs, you first have to identify the object(s) of the fear. Is it people in general—or only a certain class of people: a certain age, sex, race, or uniform? Is the dog afraid of crowds? Is it dogs in general—or only bigger (or even in some cases, smaller) dogs, dogs of a different breed, or dogs encountered in a strange place? Is your Beagle fearful of traveling anywhere? Or is the fear reaction triggered by particular places? Perhaps only certain situations scare him, or just specific objects, such as bicycles or vacuum cleaners. (I once had a dog who was terrified of the bird feeder. Nothing else bothered him.) Once you pinpoint the source of the fear, you can begin the desensitizing and counter-conditioning process. Most dogs are afraid of some things, and you needn't panic yourself unless your Beagle is consistently afraid of so many things that it adversely affects the quality of his life—and yours.

The basic principle in counter-conditioning shyness is to make your Beagle understand that he has nothing to fear. Perhaps your Beagle has been hit by a bicycle, abused by a child, or yelled at by a mail carrier. In that case he has good reason for his attitude. Or perhaps he is picking up your own distrust or fear. People with racial or ethnic biases can pass along their attitudes to their dogs. The animal senses that you are uncomfortable or fearful, and since you are his god, his outward actions will mirror your inner thoughts. If an approaching large dog makes you nervous, your Beagle's antennae will pick it up. He'll be nervous too. As with most things in dog training, you have to work on yourself first.

Once you have decided that you yourself are fearless of letter carriers, bicycles, veterinarians, or little old ladies with canes, it's time to begin the desensitization process for your dog. Let's say that your dog fears mail carriers. Enlist the help of a friend with whom your dog is comfortable. Mimic the actions, and, so far as possible, the outfit of the feared intruder, especially the bag. Instead of letters in a pouch, however, your friend will carry dog biscuits! You yourself will be excited and thrilled to observe the "letter carrier" coming up the walk. You will transmit your pleasurable anticipation to your dog.

For each positive movement your dog makes toward the "mail carrier" you will reward him with encouragement or a tiny treat. Encourage your friend to reach out slowly toward your dog, with her palm available for sniffing. (Although it's safer to approach a strange dog with a closed fist, the open palm has a slight positive electric charge that seems more acceptable to dogs.)

Give your Beagle plenty of time to sniff. If he actually makes friendly contact, your friend will reward him with a biscuit from the pouch. Try the exercise again using another friend with whom your dog is not so familiar. Then again with someone who is a stranger to your dog. Encourage strangers to greet your shy Beagle with slow, gentle movements. If they kneel down, your Beagle will be more likely to respond with enthusiasm. Ask your friends to avoid direct eye contact, which can be intimidating to dogs until they get used to it.

The same process is applied to each class of objects or animals or people of whom your dog is fearful. When you observe another dog coming down the street (on a leash, I hope), you become thrilled. With the approval of the dog's owner, you pass out dog biscuits all around. If your dog shows fear, don't try to comfort him. Too much re-assurance will confirm your Beagle's fears that there is something really awful out there, and that he's right to worry. Be upbeat and positive. Speak in a cheerful, happy tone. "Oh, boy, Bowser, look! A nice Setter!" Or whatever. Men in

## Managing Overly Submissive Dogs

Submissive dogs will roll over on their backs at the drop of a hat. If you want to encourage your Beagle to be less submissive, never interact with him when he is rolled over—that reinforces his submissiveness. Likewise, if you have a submissive urinater on your hands—the Beagle pees when you walk in the door—simply ignore it and him. If you scold him, he'll become even more submissive and frightened, and if you praise him you'll encourage the behavior. When he becomes more comfortable, he'll stop.

Some dogs with this problem respond well to obedience training, but this doesn't work in every case. If the instructor doesn't emphasize gentleness, it may increase the dog's anxiety level. So although obedience training is a great tool that helps you bond with your dog, be sure the instructor uses positive reinforcement rather than punishment.

particular need to keep their voices soft and at a higher pitch than usual, just as they would if talking to a baby.

Don't try socializing your dog in a dog park or any place where a lot of dogs are running loose. They can be overwhelming, and some may be truly threatening. If that happens, your Beagle's fears will be confirmed and you'll have a doubly hard time uprooting the problem.

If your dog fears new situations or people, get him out and about as much as possible. He should be exposed to a new place, person, or event at least three times a week. Take him for a ride to the filling station, the bank, the park, and the pet supply store. Walk him downtown.

## Leash-o-phobia

Some dogs, especially rescue or shelter dogs, are afraid of leashes or collars. They may have been choked with a collar or hit with the leash. Or maybe no one ever put a leash on the dog unless he was going to the veterinarian. If you have a dog who has been subject to such abuse (obviously not from *you*, but from the previous bad owners), try using a harness or Gentle Leader rather than a collar. If the leash frightens him, leave it around the house so that it's constantly in view, especially at mealtime. Then, put it on him whenever you give him a treat. Soon he'll associate the leash with something really good. Going for a walk may not be sufficient stimulus to overcome his fear, but over time, food should do the trick.

Some trainers recommend using the leash as a toy to get your dog to overcome his fear of it. They suggest tying some food to the end of it and dragging the leash around. I don't recommend this. Although it may encourage your dog to eventually lose his fear of the leash, it will suggest to him that the leash can be eaten. Then you'll have another problem to deal with—leash chewing.

## Beyond Fear: Phobic Beagles

Beyond bashfulness is phobia. Although many dogs suffer from phobias of one sort or another, the most common is thunder-phobia, or fear of storms. In some ways, thunder-phobia is normal. After all, where there's thunder, there's lightning, and lightning is dangerous. Besides, a dog's keen ears can hear sounds on higher and lower frequencies than our own, so he can hear all the sounds of a thunderstorm—including the ones we miss.

Most dogs tend to "go to ground" during storms, and you'll find them in low, damp places—like behind the toilet. Thunder-phobia seems to be a condition that develops with age, suggesting that some kind of learning experience is involved. Puppies and young dogs don't seem as fearful of thunder as older dogs. It's possible that dogs learn to fear thunderstorms from their nervous owners.

Mild cases of thunder-phobia can be treated relatively simply:

- ▼ Spray some anti-static on your dog.
- ▼ Go the herbal route: valerian, skullcap, St. John's wort, kava kava, chamomile, and vervain have all been used effectively.
- ▼ Try melatonin. This over-the-counter hormone, produced by the pineal gland, is extremely effective in controlling thunder-phobia, and in fact, works better than most other remedies. Although human beings use it for insomnia, in dogs, melatonin will not act as a sedative; it will simply work to reduce your Beagle's fear of thunder, fireworks, or whatever the offending noise happens to be. You can buy melatonin in health food stores. The usual dose is 1.5 mg for Beagle-sized dogs. You can crush the capsules and add it to your Beagle's food.
- ▼ Acupressure works well for some dogs.
- ▼ Counter-conditioning. Don't cuddle or coddle a fearful dog. That will only confirm in his mind something is Very Wrong. Behave as if a thunderstorm were fun, and use it as a time of active indoor play.
- ▼ Try desensitization training. Master's Voice Canine Training has produced a series of CDs designed to help your dog recover from noise phobias. The series includes Thunder, Fireworks, and Gunfire. Each lesson includes slow-rhythm music interspersed with the offending noise. These products work better with dogs who fear gunshots or fireworks, however, than for thunder-phobic dogs. One reason is that thunderstorms have components in addition to loud noise. Besides, audio speakers are not designed to

capture noises in the low range of thunderstorms, and so don't adequately re-produce the effect.

- The Tellington Touch Therapy approach has been used successfully with many dogs. Hold the dog's ear between your thumb and forefinger and stroke it gently from the base to the tip.
- Use a Gentle Leader or a Halti-Collar on your dog. These collars actually act to help calm your dog's fearfulness. Some veterinarians even think they have an acupressure-like effect.
- Try a tranquilizer like a low dose of valium, available from your veterinarian on prescription.

## Home Alone—and Home Destruction

You go out the door, take a little trip to the movies or work, and when you come home, it's like a battle zone. Your Beagle has eaten the living room. Why did this happen? Dogs destroy their homes either because: they enjoy it; they're bored; or they have separation anxiety.

### Let's Trash the Place!

Young, inquisitive puppies don't distinguish between their assigned toys and your furniture. If it's chewable, it might be edible, and should be tried out. The only way to keep a young dog from chewing while you are gone is to restrict his activity to a room where he has nothing but his own safe toys to chew.

While crating a dog obviously protects the furniture and keeps him out of danger, it's cruel to crate a young puppy for more than a few hours (except at night, when he's sleeping anyway). Instead, gate your puppy in the kitchen or bathroom, after puppy-proofing the room.

### Boredom

Any dog, but especially a young one, will eventually grow bored with life alone. Dogs are meant to be companion animals, and that is when they are happiest—as companions. The original dogs followed nomadic human beings on their travels. We made

*Tuny wonders how this happened* *photo courtesy of Polly and Wilson Palacios*

them dependent upon us for their food and comfort; we our responsible for creating their need of us.

You can try leaving on the television or radio, or providing interactive toys like Kongs and Buster Cubes filled with interesting stuff, but these distractions aren't guaranteed to solve the problem. It's much better to provide a companion for your lonely dog. The companion might be a daily dog walker, another dog, or even a compatible cat. You might also wish to consider doggy day care, where your dog can play with other friendly dogs in a home setting.

## Separation Anxiety

Separation anxiety is not a "fad term" for loneliness. It is a serious condition of people or pets recognized by the American Psychiatric Association. In dogs it manifests itself in various symptoms, including salivating, panting, pacing, whining, barking, and behaviors like chewing furniture and destroying rather large portions of the house. Most dogs suffering from separation anxiety fall into two categories: dogs who have been abandoned before, and dogs who enjoy a particularly close or indulgent relationship with their owners. You can avoid the latter situation by not constantly petting and coddling your dog.

From a dog's point of view, it all makes perfect sense. Put yourself in his place.

What would you do if left alone for several days? What if you couldn't read, watch television, get to your computer, or talk on the phone? What would you do if you didn't know when anyone was going to come get you? What if you suspected no one would ever, ever, ever come? This is the world of a dog with separation anxiety. It doesn't matter if you're only gone ten minutes, either. Your dog is alone, he can't think of what to do next, and he doesn't believe you're coming back. Not ever. Separation anxiety sets in the moment the door shuts, and it doesn't get better on its own

Dogs are pack animals. They were never meant to spent long hours alone, and it's unnatural to ask them to do so. Many sufferers of separation anxiety are young puppies, but it can also suddenly manifest itself in older dogs who have shown no previous symptoms of it.

Separation anxiety needs to be approached systematically. And it needs to be approached calmly—don't make a big production of your arrivals or departures. Begin by preparing to leave (getting your keys, putting on your jacket), but don't actually leave. Just hang around. Then put the stuff back. Then try exiting the house for very short periods, just a few seconds at a time. Gradually (over a period of many days) lengthen your absences.

Of course, you have to actually leave the house sometimes. In those cases, resort to problem management like restricting the dog to a safe area like his crate or a dog-proof room. Place an old dirty tee shirt of yours in his bed, the smellier the better. Your smell will comfort him while you are gone. When you return, remain calm, and actually ignore your dog's pleas for attention. When he is quieter, praise him quietly and give him some cuddles and walks.

It's a mistake to lavish too much attention on a separation anxiety prone animal when you are home with him. The contrast between being home with you and receiving lots of attention and being away from you and suddenly receiving none at all is pretty big. I once had a rescue dog who was used to being completely ignored. When she came to live with us, she was surprised and delighted to be smothered with attention. Unfortunately, in about two weeks this insecure animal had become so dependent on the attention she was getting that a mild case of separation anxiety (in the form of house soiling), set in. Luckily, we quickly realized our error, and after a few days of drastically reduced attention, she returned to her calm and housetrained ways.

Give your dog plenty of exercise; a tired dog is a less anxious dog. In some cases, a hyperactive dog may be getting too many carbohydrates in his food. Cut down on them—remember that a dog has no need for carbohydrates in his diet at all. Replace the carbs with protein. (It used to be believed that lowering the protein in a dog's diet would reduce aggression. It doesn't.)

Another way to mitigate separation anxiety is to bore your Beagle a bit. When you leave, he may think you're off somewhere exciting like the dog park or the great outdoors. Dispel this notion. Take the dog out and put him in the car. Then go back in the house. Let him hang out in the car for thirty minutes or so, then bring him in. (Don't do this on a hot or bitter day, of course.) After a few sessions of this, he might decide nothing interesting is going on, and he'd have more fun in the house.

Play a tape of your calming voice to talk to the dog while you are gone. Or call him up and leave a message on the answering machine! You might be surprised to find how much this helps. Music is also soothing to an anxious dog—if it's the right kind. Studies have shown that classical concertos, jazz, and (I'm sorry to say) elevator music, calm jangled canine nerves. Rock and heavy metal, on the other hand, make dogs uptight. I suspect an overdose of country music or blues makes dogs morose, but I can't say for sure. (Most Beagles appreciate "I had a dawg an' his name wuz BLUUE.") No one knows why music is so calming, but I bet that dogs just like it. In human beings, listening to music slows breathing, reduces heart rate, and relaxes muscles, so I suppose it has the same effect on dogs.

If you need to be gone longer than a few hours, ask a neighbor or friend to drop by for a pet visit and walk. If you have no neighbors or friends, consider a pet sitter. It is not natural for dogs to spend long hours alone day in and day out.

In cases of severe separation anxiety that does not lend itself to behavioral therapy alone, a medication called Clomicalm, available by prescription, is a lifesaver. Clomicalm is designed to be used in conjunction with behavioral therapy, *not* as a replacement for it.

It is a receptive-specific tricyclic antidepressant that works by altering the structure of the neural receptors in the brain. It will not change your dog's personality. It enables him to focus and respond better to behavioral training. It is administered in a pill form (2 to 3 mg/kg) every twelve hours.

I have used this medication with several dogs in our rescue organization, and I have found it extremely effective. But it doesn't work overnight (expect to see results in six to twelve weeks.) Be patient, and protect your home while your dog is undergoing drug therapy or behavioral modification. Most dogs can be weaned off the drug after about six months, although some will always need it. Correctly weaning your dog off the medication should take as long as it took for the drug to become effective in the first place.

## Beagles Go Ballistic and Worse: Obsessive-Compulsive Disorder

Obsessive-compulsive disorder (OCD) is a repetitive, purposeless, even destructive behavior over which neither the dog nor owner has any control. It can cause distress or even physical injury to the animal engaging in it.

No one is sure what triggers the condition, although various theories have been advanced, including chemical imbalance, physical or mental stress, or natural behavior which has been foiled by an artificial barrier like a fence—thus producing "fence-running" behavior. The most common obsessive-compulsive canine behavior is licking. Repeated licking may result in a "lick granuloma"—a hard, swollen red sore that takes a very long time to heal. Other common OCD' s include tail chasing or spinning, catching imaginary flies, vacant long-term staring into space, and "checking,"—continually returning to the same spot as if to see that whatever he is looking for it still there—or not there.

Sometimes, if caught early, you can distract the dog from the harmful behavior. For example, paw licking can be discouraged by providing alternative toys or playtime, or even by spraying a bitter "aversion spray" on the problem foot. (Don't use anything containing alcohol if the foot is sore.) Once the behavior becomes established, however, only medication appears to be effective.

The drug of choice for obsessive-compulsive behavior is fluoxetine (Prozac). Prozac is a selective serotonin reuptake inhibitor (SSRI). It is also used to treat anxiety and fear. The drug is administered by weight (1 mg/kg orally) once a day for six to eight weeks.

## Bossy Beagles

Although Beagles are seldom aggressive, some can become dominant and bossy. This is perfectly natural behavior among dogs bred to think for themselves, and owners need to "re-educate" their bossy Beagles into the realities of a civilized family life.

### The Origins of Dominant Behavior

Simply put, it is the owners that allow a dominant dog to take over the household. I have known Beagles who would not surrender their place on the sofa to humans, who snatched food fearlessly from human hands, and who nipped children to get them out of the way. None of this is acceptable behavior, although it's certainly natural enough. A well-behaved Beagle should:

- Move when asked.
- Give up his toys.
- Allow any human to approach his food bowl and pet him while he eats.
- Keep all feet on the floor and jaws out of the way when humans are eating.
- Not nip unless provoked beyond bearing.
- Allow himself to be picked up and carried to the tub.
- Allow his nails to be clipped and his ears to be cleaned without undue complaint.

The basic rule is that all humans should be dominant over all dogs, and if your dog doesn't understand this rule it's because you never taught it to him.

You must establish early that you are boss over your Beagle. This doesn't mean you have to be harsh, but you do have to be firm. Because they are pack dogs, Beagles are always on the lookout for a good leader, who should be you. But you must prove yourself worthy by your consistent training methods, your even temper, and your take-no-nonsense attitude. As leader, it's your job to decide when and where the dog eats, plays, and sleeps.

## Dominance and Furniture

One particular arena in the battle for dominance occurs over furniture. To a dominant Beagle, furniture is not merely a comfy place to sit. It's a fortress, a high place that allows him more status than does the lowly floor. Dogs, especially smaller dogs like Beagles, equate being high up with being in charge. So, if your Beagle tends towards bossiness, don't allow him couch privileges until he is ready to relinquish them to any human being (including a child) without an argument.

If your Beagle growls, snarls, or snaps at a person who tries to remove him from his roost, you must take stern measures. Encourage his leave-taking with a firm "Off!" If he doesn't obey, a light spray of water will accomplish the desired result. Don't make a big deal of it, but be firm. Repeat this routine until you get the desired effect. This is one of the very few situations in which I believe that negative reinforcement has a place in dog training, because here you are responding to a hostile message from your dog. It is absolutely essential that you get the upper hand.

Whenever you are dealing with an overly assertive dog, stand up tall and speak in a firm, no-nonsense voice. You may use food to lure your dog off the couch as an alternative to spraying him. But you can't use food as a lure if the dog has growled or snapped. To a growler, the food lure will seem like a reward to him for his behavior. Don't allow a dominant dog on the couch or bed again.

Non-dominant dogs, of course, may be allowed on whatever furniture you designate as appropriate. Although some trainers recommend that consistency is the key: "If you don't want your dog on the furniture sometimes, never let him on it," it's perfectly possible to train your Beagle to jump on the couch "by invitation." Just teach him the "Up!" command, and he'll be happy to oblige.

### Another Reason to Neuter

Neutering your male dog may lessen his tendency towards dominance and aggression. The Humane Society of the United States reports that unneutered dogs were responsible for six out of ten dog bites.

## Possession Aggression

Possession aggression usually begins in puppyhood. Dogs showing this behavior pattern will stand over their toy or food bowl, and stare hard at anyone who approaches. In cases of food aggression, they will stop eating. The staring may be accompanied by growling, snapping, or biting. Obviously this is something you'll need to nip in the bud, before Buddy nips you.

First, you must realize that such behavior is actually quite natural. Dogs wish to hang on to favored items, and in the wild, they know that if they give up their bone to another animal they won't eat that day. However, even in the wild, dogs *will* surrender a meal to the dominant member of the pack. That's you. And that's the way it should be in your home: you and all other human beings are the "top dog." Dogs aren't born seeing it that way, though; it's something they need to be taught. But you don't teach them by snatching their food or toys away. That only confirms their suspicion that you are not their friend. Dogs first need to realize that they are in no danger of having their food or toys permanently removed.

So when approaching a dog who seems to be guarding a treat, dog bowl, or toy, try trading with him. If he's eating kibble, he'll be happy to come over for a piece of cheese. In established cases of food aggression, it's wise to start by taking away the dog's food bowl completely and feeding him by hand until he becomes used to the basic idea that all food comes from you. If your dog seems suspicious of your approach, drop a tender morsel of food in the bowl every time he eats.

In less serious cases, it helps to keep the food bowl in a big, empty space rather than in a corner that's easier to protect. Don't give the dog his "special place" to eat in, either. Move the bowl around and remove it immediately after the dog has eaten. Stay in the room while your Beagle eats, reinforcing the fact that you have control over his food.

Teach your Beagle to sit and wait before you place his food bowl before him. If possible, teach him to wait until given permission before he actually eats. Reward him for obeying by feeding him something better than what is in the bowl. (Let him know you have it first, or he'll wolf down the entire meal before you dig the piece of cheese out of your pocket.)

Note that in addition to guarding toys and food, some dogs take to "guarding" their owners and will growl or snap at the approach of other dogs or people. While most flattered owners assume the dog is protecting them, think again. What he's actually doing is "guarding" you—treating you like a favorite piece of rawhide. The dog is telling everyone—including you—that he owns you. This kind of bad behavior in Beagles is very, very rare.

## Biting Beagles

Every year American insurance companies pay out a total of one billion dollars in settlements and lawsuits over biting dogs. (The average claim is about $12,000, according to State Farm Insurance.) Luckily, Beagles are *extremely* unlikely to be aggressive dogs. As rule, they are gentle and playful, and any "biting" they do is more likely to be from accidental play-nipping than true aggression. However, never assume that your dog won't bite. Any dog, given the right (or wrong!) circumstances will bite.

If your Beagle has ever bitten anyone, especially for "no reason," take him to your veterinarian for a thorough physical workup, especially if the behavior is new or sudden. It's possible he has a physical ailment. For example, he may have developed cataracts or another condition that limits his vision. This could lead to misidentification of a person or a general insecurity that could produce biting. Chronic pain, like back or spinal problems, can also lead to aggressive behavior.

### Fear-Induced Biting

Timid Beagles may bite out of fear. Medications can be used to help treat this condition. In the meantime, never provoke a situation where the dog may bite. Don't chase him, and don't attempt to pull him out of a hiding place. You're just asking for trouble.

If he is healthy, make an immediate appointment with a qualified animal behaviorist, not just any old dog trainer. Take careful notes of the circumstances under which the dog bit. Some biting dogs are "alpha dominant"—the dog is under the impression that he is the owner of the house. Many cases of biting are limited to the biting of children or other members of the family that the dog considers weak and low-status. Most dog bites, in fact, involve family members or other people well known to the dog.

Most dogs bite because they have been allowed to believe that they are the boss and that biting carries no negative consequences. The average biting dog is an unneutered male, poorly socialized, in his early adolescence. His first victim is probably a young child.

Most dogs who bite have preceded the attack with a whole bunch of warning signs—which were usually covered up or ignored. The dog was probably allowed to mouth and chew on human fingers when he was puppy. He may have grabbed at a child's clothes or ankles as the child ran away, or have snatched food out of someone's hand. He may have growled and refused to relinquish his place on the sofa to a person. He may have snapped when someone leaned over him. It should come as no surprise whatever when he finally bites someone.

It is commonly believed that aggressive dogs have been abused at some point in their lives, but this is not true. Most aggressive dogs have been treated with kid gloves and the families of biting dogs are usually quiet, gentle people. They are truly shocked when their beloved pet shows some trace of wolf-like behavior. They are afraid and heartbroken.

Never make excuses for an aggressive dog. Telling yourself or others "He didn't really mean it," or "You must have done something to him" is simply putting your head in the sand. Biting is a very serious problem that can cause you to lose a lawsuit or your dog if you don't get it under control. Seek professional help immediately.

## Treating Canine Aggression

If your dog is aggressive, take the following steps:

- Get your dog vet-checked for any possible physical problems.
- Enroll your dog in *special* obedience classes for aggressive dogs. Regular obedience class may make a dog more anxious.

- For at least two weeks, keep your interactions with your dog down to a bare minimum; make him beg for your attention.
- Keep the dog off the bed and the furniture.
- Make the dog sit or lie down before feeding him; always give him a command he must obey before a meal.
- Give your dog twice the exercise he's getting now—outside the yard. Working dogs are less stressed and much happier, thus less apt to bite.
- If necessary, keep a soft muzzle on the dog while working with him. Keep a spray bottle of water and lemon juice handy as well.
- Keep small children completely away from the dog at all times unless the dog is muzzled.
- Consult your vet about possible antidepressant medication (Elavil has worked well for some dogs.)
- Avoid any competitive games such as tug of war and the like. If you do play them, make sure you always win. Always. (If you have a shy Beagle, let the shy dog win.)
- Don't give the dog any chew toys—or any possessions at all.
- Use a head halter rather than a conventional or choke collar.
- In cases of extreme aggression, consider having the canine teeth removed. Amazingly, once the dog discovers his biting is useless, he stops trying. This is a complicated and expensive procedure, however, and should be used only as an alternative to euthanasia.

Behavior therapy, sometimes combined with medications (tranquilizers and antidepressants) is usually effective in curing dog aggression—as long as everyone in the family cooperates to help the dog. The American Society for the Prevention of Cruelty to Animals has recently opened a behavioral therapy center in New York City. The center is equipped to deal with common behavioral problems like aggression, house soiling, barking, and anxiety in dogs. Costs will vary, but animals adopted from the ASPCA Placement Program will be treated for free. For further information, contact the ASPCA, 424 E. 92nd Street, New York, NY 10128; or call (212) 876-7700, ext. 4357.

# Chapter 15
# Beagle Well Being

Everybody wants a healthy dog. And it's surprisingly easy to keep your Beagle in tip-top form. Prevention is the best, easiest, and cheapest way toward that goal. Prevention is fourfold:

- Watch your dog's diet. Feed him healthy portions of good quality foods.
- Exercise your dog. Most dogs lie around the house far too much—like their owners. Get out there and play hard and vigorously with your dog for at least thirty minutes every day. It will make both of you feel better.
- Keep your dog well groomed (including his ears, teeth, and feet).
- Find a good veterinarian, and form a partnership with him for your dog's good health.

## Exercise

Beagles are premier hunting dogs, and they require much more exercise than their small size indicates. A big, well-fenced yard is a definite plus in Beagle ownership. But it's not enough. You must be willing to exercise with your Beagle, especially if he has no canine companions. Beagles crave company as much as they need to run. Young dogs can get sufficient exercise running around the backyard, but to keep your Beagle, happy, healthy, trim, and out of trouble, a sustained exercise program is best. And the best-sustained exercise programs include dogs and their owners working together.

Learn to play cooperatively, not competitively, with your Beagle. Competition merely encourages your Beagle to try for a leadership role in opposition to you, and that's bad pet policy. Tug of war, excessive roughhousing, and other "fighting" games should be avoided. Fetch, catch, and hide and seek are better choices. (Beagles aren't natural retrievers, but you can sometimes get them to bring back a ball for you.)

## Veterinary Care

An important step toward helping your Beagle to a life of good health is developing a healthy relationship with your veterinarian. You need to find a vet with whom you are comfortable, and of whom you can ask questions. Never be afraid to question your veterinarian about a vaccination, medication, test, or treatment plan. If you don't understand something, ask him to explain it again.

### Diagnostic Tests

Your veterinarian has access to many kinds of tests to help him diagnose and treat your dog. These include blood tests, urinalyses, chemistry panels, fecal tests, skin scrapings, and screenings for particular suspected organisms. Much of the time, however, your vet will take just one blood sample and order a complete screening on it. This saves time and money. The screening test panel includes a complete blood count (CBC), to measure the number of red and white blood cells and a chemistry panel. The chemistry panel is designed to detect levels of different enzymes, waste products, cholesterol, and the like.

The urinalysis can give information about the levels of sugar, proteins and blood in the urine, as well as urine sediment, the urine specific gravity (how concentrated or diluted it is). Admittedly, it's not always easy to collect a urine sample, but the information it provides is very helpful.

## Your First Visit

If you possibly can do so, select a veterinarian before you get a dog. You'll have time to evaluate the vet and his office in an unhurried frame of mind. Assess the place carefully. Do the staff members seem relaxed, friendly, and compassionate? What services do they provide? Are any of the staff specialists in orthopedics, holistic treatments, behavior, or cardiology? What hours is the clinic open? Is someone there evenings? Weekends? Who answers the calls when the office is closed? Does the clinic offer boarding or grooming services? Telephone conferrals? Home visits? Does the clinic accept pet insurance? Is it a member of a spay/neuter program? How many Beagles does the practice care for? How close is the clinic to your home? Adding up the answers to all these questions may make it easier to decide on the right vet for you.

## Your Dog's First Visit

Make the first visit to the veterinarian a fun and interesting one for your dog. If necessary, top it off with a trip to the park. If all goes well, the first trip will be for a checkup only, so your dog won't have any painful associations with the visit. If you are calm and happy yourself, your mood is bound to rub off on your Beagle. If you regard the vet and his staff as friends, so will he. It's really important to use this initial visit as an opportunity to establish a cordial relationship between your veterinarian and your dog.

## Saving Money on Veterinary Bills

Although price should not be your first consideration, (especially since dogs always end up costing more than you think they will), there are ways to save without getting substandard care.

The best way, of course, is to do your part by feeding your dog a good diet, and providing him regular exercise, and good maintenance care in the ears, nails, and dental department. A penny of prevention is indeed worth a dollar of cure.

Some vets offer discounts to senior citizens, or to people with multi-pet households. Some accept spay/neuter certificates, available through Spay USA (800-248-7729) and The Friends of Animals (800-321-7387). Others give coupons, or provide special deals during "dental month" or "spay and neuter week." It certainly doesn't hurt to inquire. In general, spaying/neutering will cost between $70 and $200, depending largely on where you live. (Our excellent veterinarians also give a helping hand to rescue groups.)

When purchasing medication, you should know that some kinds are available in generic form. These are almost always cheaper and usually of the same quality as the "name brand." Ask your veterinarian about each generic versions of specific drugs.

One thing I would not do is order medications and immunizations through the mail and administer them to the dog yourself, even if you know how to give shots. You may save some money, but in the long run you'll doing your dog a disservice. Here's why: When you take the dog to vet, you are doing more than getting him immunized and going home; it's a chance to speak with your vet about your concerns. It's important for the veterinarian to see the dog when he's healthy as well as when he's sick. A good veterinarian will always give your dog a checkup at the same time. From a more selfish standpoint, I always feel that going to my regular vet for routine care gives me the right to call him up at home at midnight (which I have done) during an emergency.

## Pet Insurance

Dogs are living a lot longer than they used to, and many a Beagle sees his late teens and beyond. With these increasing life spans, and the high-tech medicine available to sustain them, come increased medical costs. The medical advances that have allowed veterinarians to perform kidney transplants, heart-valve replacements, and orthopedic surgery don't come cheap.

Pet insurance is the best option for many people. Most plans cover accidents, poisonings, illness, surgery, X-rays, anesthesia, diagnostics, chemotherapy, and radiation. Some provide for preventive care. A variety of plans are available, so evaluate them thoroughly to see what's covered, and what the monthly and annual premiums are. You'll also need to verify that your veterinarian accepts pet health insurance and that the insurer covers the vet of your choosing. Most plans have both an annual benefit maximum and a maximum per incident.

Many pet insurance policies do not cover pre-existing conditions. Sound familiar? Check the fine print. It's also important to verify that the insurance company is licensed. Contact your state's insurance department if you are not sure.

## The Home Health Exam

Even if you have found a veterinarian you adore, as I have, you are your dog's first line of medical care. Your careful, close, continuous observation of your dog's looks and habits are an invaluable tool in diagnosing, treating, and even foreseeing any problems your dog may have. Only you know whether your dog's coat, temperament, eating or elimination habits have undergone any changes recently. For example, some dogs have normally redder eyes or runnier noses or dryer noses than others. You know what is normal for your dog. Furthermore, a good owner is aware of emotional as well as physical changes in her dog. Since the two are often related, a depressed, lethargic, or irritable dog may be telling you he has a physical problem.

These types of observations are very informative to your veterinarian. It's even a good idea to keep a notebook or checklist of your dog's major systems. Taking notes not only keeps your memory fresh; it also helps you observe more carefully.

*Louie looking healthy* *photo courtesy of Wally Jarrott*

## General Appearance

How does your dog look overall? Is he too fat, or too thin? How is his coat? Is it thick and shiny? Is it free of fleas and ticks? Is there hair loss? Does he have any bumps or cyst-like growths? Ruffle the fur backward to check for dandruff and flea dirt.

Normal dogs have elastic skin. If you pull gently at the skin behind the shoulder blades, it should slide quickly back into place without sagging. If it does not, your Beagle may be dehydrated. Because the amount of elasticity may vary from dog to dog, it's a good idea to check out your own dog when you know he's healthy, so you can note any changes. Move your hands over the dog's body and note any tender areas.

It's important to manually examine your dog's lymph nodes. Although dogs have many lymph nodes throughout their bodies, three common sites for trouble are beneath the ears, where the jaw meets the skull; the prescapular area where the neck meets the shoulder; and, in the back legs, behind the knee joints.

## Movement and Feet

Observe your dog at a walk and jog. Note if he moves fluidly, or if you notice signs of incipient arthritis. Does he favor one leg? Is he hesitant to reach out?

Examine your dog's paws. Look for cracks or tears in the pads. Cracks on all four feet could indicate allergies, a zinc deficiency, or problems with the immune system. If your Beagle has just one crack on one foot, it's probably an injury. Make sure that he has no thorns or other foreign matter lodged in his feet. The nails should be short enough so that they don't touch the floor. Check to see that they are of the proper length, and not split or cracked. If your dog tends to develop cracked nails, consider adding more fatty acids, or a package of gelatin to his diet once a day. Dogs whose nails tend to crack should have them trimmed as close as possible.

If the nails exude a black, gummy or pus-like substance, your dog probably has a nail infection. These are nasty, and very difficult to treat. Call your vet. In some cases, the nails may actually have to be removed. Poor nail condition could also indicate other exotic diseases with names like pemphigus, and canine lupus. Any strange-looking nails warrant the attention of your veterinarian.

## Head

Examine the head region. Are the eyes bright and clear? Check for any lumps or bumps on the eyelids. It is important to notice the color of the tissue around the eyes (the conjunctiva). It should be a nice healthy pink. Red can indicate infection or allergies, yellow might mean liver disease, and white suggests anemia. Any cloudiness in the eyes themselves should be checked by a veterinarian, although a greenish glaze in the eyes of older dogs is normal. Dogs accumulate "gunk" in the corners of their eyes because their tears naturally wash away minute debris that has accumulated in there. If the discharge has a greenish color, however, it may signal an infection, especially if the discharge is from both eyes. If you see this type of discharge, take your Beagle to the vet.

Dog noses are usually wet, but don't panic if your Beagle has a dry nose. Some dogs are just like that. Any thick or crusty discharge from the nose, however, can be a sign that something is seriously wrong. Take your dog to the vet.

The ears should be pink, clean, odorless, and free of dark brown or red residue. (Don't be afraid to sniff the ears. Any "off" smell or yeasty odor could be an indicator of trouble.) Dogs with hanging ears like Beagles may be prone to otitis, or ear infection, so you need to keep a careful watch. If your dog has a mild yeast or bacterial infection, you may be able to get rid of it with a solution of vinegar and water (50 percent of each). Never use an alcohol product. Use a bulb syringe or cotton swabs to clean the ears, but don't clean too deeply.

Since the ear lining is part of your dog's skin, any problems your dog has with his skin can also appear in his ears. Once a dog gets an ear infection, he may be a candidate for repeat bouts of the same. If your dog shakes or tilts his head, or scratches at his ears, it could mean trouble. Loss of hair around the ears may mean he has been scratching there.

Ear mites can leave black, gritty material that looks like coffee grounds in your dog's ears. You can buy a commercial product to get rid of them.

Another sign of possible ear problems is if your normally compliant dog fusses or snaps when you attempt to touch or clean his ears. In any case, never neglect the ears. Untended ears can lead to chronic pain, and even hearing loss in your pet.

If there is any chance your dog has punctured an eardrum, do not use any vinegar, or any other product on the ears. Take your dog to the vet's office immediately.

The teeth and gums should be pink and healthy looking. Pale or bluish gums could indicate anemia, while red gums could be a sign of an infection. Every dog's normal gum color is slightly different, and it's good to know what your Beagle's gums look like under normal conditions. If you press gently on the gum until it's white, the pink color should return immediately. The gums should also be moist and contain plenty of saliva. A dry mouth could indicate dehydration.

Irritation or pimples around the muzzle could indicate an allergic reaction to food or to your dog's food or water bowls. It is not uncommon for dogs to be allergic to plastic dishes.

Foul odors coming from the mouth may indicate an abscess, indigestion, kidney problems, or periodontal disease. About 85 percent of dogs over the age of three have some kind of gum disease, a problem that is more than cosmetic. The accumulating tartar can not only destroy your dog's teeth but harbor bacteria that can find its way through the gum line straight to your dog's heart.

## Genitalia

Check the visible reproductive organs. Intact males should have both testicles descended. In both males and females, any excess discharge, or a discharge that is not clear, could signal an infection. The mammary glands should be regular. Any hard, irregular lumps, or lumps that appear attached to a bone may be dangerous. Never poke at a lump or try to squish it; you might make a potential problem worse. Always ask your veterinarian to examine any suspicious lumps.

## Anal Sacs

Your Beagle's two anal sacs (sometimes mistakenly called "anal glands") are located under his tail at the four and eight o'clock positions. Each is lined with glandular cells that produce a strong, foul odor. When your dog poops, the sacs are compressed. They then release through the anus some of this bad-smelling material. The whole purpose behind this procedure is apparently to allow your dog to announce his presence to the world. The sacs serve no other function.

Anal sacs can be annoying to owners for one of two reasons:

- They can empty spontaneously. When this happens, an excited or fearful dog might release the smelly contents of the sacs on your furniture or clothing.
- They can also not empty at all. Anal sacs can get impacted, a condition often associated with gastrointestinal problems or obesity. Once anal sacs become impacted, they are also at risk for infection. Your veterinarian can "express" the glands.

Examine the anal sac area. Any sore-looking, red, or blistery spots could indicate disease. A dog who "scoots" as he walks along may have blocked anal glands. (He could have worms, too, or some other irritation, but the anal glands are the more likely culprits.)

Don't get in the habit of expressing the anal glands yourself as a part of routine grooming. It is not only unnecessary, but could lead to further problems down the road. Most of the dogs I see with anal sac problems are dogs who have had them regularly expressed. Dogs on poor diets, or who receive too little exercise, are also more likely to have anal sac problems. Eventually, many of these animals have had to have their anal sacs surgically removed.

## Taking Your Dog's Temperature

Although you won't be taking your dog's temperature every day, it's a good skill to learn in case you suspect something is wrong with your dog. So the first time you try it, it's best to work with a healthy animal. Purchase a rectal thermometer specifically designed for dogs. (Unfortunately, you can't use one of the stick-it-in-the-ear probes for dogs. The L-shape of a dog's ear canal makes an ear probe inaccurate. You'll have to do it the old-fashioned way.)

- Put your Beagle on a table, the smaller the better. This makes the temperature reading easier for you, and your dog is more likely to hold still. It's best to have a friend help you.

- Clean the thermometer with alcohol and shake it down until it reads about 96° F or 35° C. (Keep a moist towelette nearby to clean it afterward.)
- Lubricate the thermometer with mineral oil or petroleum jelly.
- Lift your Beagle's tail gently and place the end of the thermometer into the rectum. Slide it slightly upward about until it's halfway inserted, and let it remain for about two minutes.
- Remove the instrument, wipe it, and read it. Normal canine temperature should read between 100.5 and 102.5° F or between 38.1 and 39.2° C. A variation of more than a degree may warrant a call to your vet, especially if tied to other symptoms.

## Vaccines and Vaccinations

Vaccines are lifesavers, and a definite "must" for puppies. They have also recently become one of the most controversial elements of veterinary medicine. How much, how often, and what diseases should be covered are an ongoing discussion. Different veterinarians have different protocols for spacing of these injections. Have a talk with your veterinarian about his own vaccination protocol. In any case, expect a full round of vaccines to cost between $85 and $140.

Since everyone agrees that young puppies need to be vaccinated against certain diseases, I'll start with the critical ones:

### Distemper

Distemper, a highly contagious viral disease, is a major, worldwide killer of unvaccinated puppies and even of older dogs. It is an airborne virus, but it can also be spread by contaminated objects. About 80 percent of puppies who contract the disease will die, as will about 50 percent of older dogs. And even a dog who survives a bout of distemper may have a permanently damaged nervous system. He might lose some of his vision, hearing, or even his sense of smell. Puppies who contract distemper usually lose significant tooth enamel, resulting in a brown band around the tooth. Once a dog contracts distemper, it is very difficult to treat, and, as I noted above, often fatal.

## Pinniped Peril

Dogs catch distemper by coming into contact with sick dogs, or possibly raccoons. Some researchers have hypothesized that distemper can also be carried by seals and sea lions, but unless your dog is regularly in contact with large marine mammals, I wouldn't worry about them as a source. The dog next door is the more likely culprit. Still, just to be on the safe side, keep your Beagle away from seals. You never know. Besides, seals and Beagles don't have all that much in common.

Distemper comes in two stages. In the first stage the dog will exhibit fever, loss of appetite, a discharge from his eyes and nose that gets progressively thicker, a cough, diarrhea, vomiting, and pustules on the abdomen. It may seem that he just has a bad cold. Many dogs experience a temporary recovery from this stage. The second stage affects the brain and nervous system, and manifests itself by convulsions. There is no excuse whatever for failing to vaccinate against this dread disease.

Luckily, distemper is pretty rare these days, precisely because of effective vaccines against it. The virus has *not* disappeared, however, and the best way to make certain it doesn't get hold of Rover is to vaccinate him against it.

### Hepatitis

Hepatitis is a serious disease caused by an adenovirus. It is spread by contact with an infected dog, or his urine or feces. The white blood cell count drops and some dogs experience clotting problems. It is most serious in puppies and affects the kidney and liver. Signs include high fever, red mucus membranes, depression, and loss of appetite. Little blood spots may appear on the gums, and the eye may take on a bluish tinge. Even animals who recover may have chronic illnesses, and continue to shed the virus for months. Fortunately, the vaccines for this disease have rendered it pretty rare.

## Titering

Most vets recommend that puppies be vaccinated at eight, twelve, and sixteen weeks. Your dog will probably receive a booster shot at one year of age, and then every three years thereafter. This new, less frequent vaccination schedule seems to be safer and just as effective as the traditional annual round of vaccines. Some veterinarians recommend getting your dog "titered," rather than automatically given a booster shot.

Titering measures the amount of antibody in the blood, and some vets use this measure to determine whether or not your dog actually needs another shot. A lot depends on how prevalent a particular disease is in your area, how many other dogs your pet encounters, and you and your vet's personal preferences. Titering is expensive, and each disease antibody requires a separate test, but it may be appropriate for dogs who have had prior reactions to vaccines. Most of these reactions are minor, similar to what a sensitive dog might experience if stung by a bee, but sometimes shock or even death could result.

### Leptospirosis

Leptospirosis is caused by spirochetes. It comes in two strains and it affects the liver and kidneys. It thrives in wet conditions and warm temperatures. It is transmitted in the urine of infected animals, which can include mice, rats, possums, and raccoons, and skunks (the usual suspects). The dangerous organisms make their way into the victim's body through a sore or other broken place in the skin. It takes from five to fifteen days to incubate. Signs of the disease are extremely variable, with some animals showing almost no symptoms. Others become listless and lose their appetites. Jaundice may appear. Therapy includes a course of antibiotics.

One variety of leptospirosis can be transmitted to people and animals that contract it and then recover can be carriers. Always wash your hands carefully after coming in contact with a dog's urine—but then you would anyway, I'm sure.

## Parvovirus

Parvovirus, first noticed in the 1980s, attacks the intestinal tract, bone marrow, and immune system, which leaves the dog open to secondary infection. Signs of the disease include vomiting, diarrhea, and bleeding. Most dogs who contract this disease die, even with excellent veterinary care. This is a cold-hardy virus, surviving in infected feces in temperatures as low as 20 degrees. The incubation period is from two to seven days.

## Coronavirus

Coronavirus causes symptoms similar to those of parvo, but they are less severe. Most dogs recover with proper fluid therapy. Symptoms include diarrhea and vomiting. It can incubate in twenty-four to thirty-six hours.

## Bordetella (Kennel Cough)

Many organisms can cause kennel cough, which is like a bad cold in older dogs, but serious in puppies. It can spread very rapidly through a kennel. The official name for the most common kind is tracheobronchitis.

## Lyme Disease

Carried by deer ticks, Lyme disease is endemic in many parts of the country, especially in the northeast. The incubation period is from two to five months. It causes intermittent lameness, as well as heart and kidney disease. If untreated, your dog can have permanent arthritis from contracting Lyme disease.

## Rabies

Every mammal can be affected by rabies, including human beings. Rabies is caused by a virus that is shed in the saliva. It is usually transferred by animal bites, and attacks the central nervous system. Once the symptoms appear, rabies is 100 percent fatal. It seems to be on the rise in certain areas, too, particularly in suburbia. It is the law in every state to vaccinate your dog against rabies. Puppies usually get a rabies vaccination at four months of age, and have it repeated either once a year or every three years, depending on the type of vaccine.

### Storing Medications

Be sure you keep all medications—especially the chewable kind—well out of the reach of a your inquisitive Beagle. Beagles are extremely open-minded about what is edible. One of my eight dogs once ate an entire bottle of chewable Rimadyl tablets. Since I was unable to identify the culprit—I spent the entire day making all eight dogs throw up. Then I got to poke through their vomit and clean it up afterwards. It wasn't one of my better days.

Read the label careful about proper storage. Some medications need to be refrigerated, and all have optimal temperature ranges. Many need to be stored away from sunlight or moisture. Homeopathic medications also need to be kept away from electromagnetic fields, and strong odors, even natural herbal ones.

## Spaying and Neutering

Nearly all owners of companion Beagles should have their pets spayed and neutered. Here's why:

- Although any Beagle is apt to run off at any moment, spayed and neutered dogs are less eager to do so. Intact males try to get out of their yard to visit neighboring females, and even securely fenced females who have not been spayed draw throngs of admirers from around the neighborhood.
- Spayed and neutered dogs are healthier. Unaltered dogs are prone to mammary cancers, testicular cancers, prostatitis, prostate cancer, and pyometra, a life-threatening infection of the uterus.
- Unneutered animals are messy around the house; males tend to mark territory with their urine, and females in heat leave spots of blood on the furniture and carpets.
- Unneutered animals tend to be more aggressive.

The traditional age to spay pets has been six months for females and nine months for males, but many experts and shelter groups are now recommending earlier altering, to help stave off the plague of unwanted puppies around the country. Modern

*Tuny* *photo courtesy of Polly and Wilson Palacios*

surgical equipment makes early neutering easy. A new procedure uses laser beams, and takes only about five minutes. A tiny incision is made over the scrotum, the testicles removed, and the veins tied up. The skin is closed with a few drops of glue.

Moreover, unneutered males may become aggressive toward other males and if you wait too long to neuter your dog, you may not be able to alter this pattern. The same is true with marking behavior.

"But what if I want to breed my dog?" Unless you are an expert in Beagle bloodlines and genetics, don't even think about breeding your companion Beagle. It's a job better left to people who have a real knowledge of what they are doing. Your job is to love and care for your dog. That's enough for most people.

# Chapter 16
# Beagle Bugs

Although bloodsucking seems like a miserable way to make a living, it's positively amazing what a successful career choice it is for so many of our fellow beings. Fleas, ticks, lice and mites specialize in this horrible habit, much to the detriment of your Beagle—and you.

## Please, No Fleas

Fleas are cosmopolitan creatures that can live on almost any warm-blooded animal they happen upon. Some prefer cats, some dogs, and some rabbits, but these enterprising entrepreneurs aren't terribly picky. Although really high altitudes and extremely dry areas set them back, they can live in diverse climates. Still, with more than 2400 species world wide, it's a rare place that can't boast at least a few fleas. It doesn't help that an adult flea can live for up a year without eating anything, and jump 150 times its own length, about eight inches. When a flea bites, it sucks up an amount of blood equal to its own body weight. And for every flea that you see on your dog, there are about 100 more in various life stages lurking very near by. Like in the rug. No wonder American dog owners spend more than $1 billion every year to control them!

The flea that likes dogs the best is the cat flea. I'm sorry about that, but there it is. About 99 percent of the fleas on dogs are cat fleas. The cat flea, more politely known as *Ctenocephalides felis*, will put up with cats too, but it really prefers a good dog. *C. felis*, like all other fleas, has a four-stage life cycle: egg, larva, pupa, and adult. It spends most of its adult life feasting on your dog's blood and laying smooth little eggs that contain yet more fleas. In fact, an industrious flea can produce forty to fifty eggs every single day for her entire adult life of about 100 days. Although factors like humidity, temperature, and available hosts play a role in flea egg development, it generally takes between eight and twelve days for them to go through an entire cycle to become great big fleas.

While fleas can carry numerous diseases, their most common effect on the family dog is a flea dermatitis itch. This itch is more than a mild annoyance; it can progress to allergies and infections and make your dog truly miserable. Just because you don't see any fleas on your dog, it doesn't mean you should relax your guard. It only takes one fleabite to set up an allergic dermatitis. An extreme number of fleas can actually kill a puppy by literally exsanguinating him—sucking out too much of his blood. Fleas are also a vector for tapeworm, which I'll discuss in more detail later in this chapter. They can carry bubonic plague, too, as they proved so well in 1348, but as a rule that's something the average person doesn't have to worry about. Much. (They also carry typhus.)

To check for fleas on your dog, look for those telltale black specks, especially around the dog's back end. These particles are flea excrement, composed largely of your dog's blood. If you wet the things, they'll turn red to prove it.

## Terrible Ticks

Ticks are worse than fleas, if possible. Although a tick or two doesn't seem to cause any discomfort to the affected dog the way a flea infestation does, all 850 species of ticks are extremely dangerous. They carry an almost interminable list of filthy diseases, including Lyme disease, Rocky Mountain spotted fever, Ehrlichiosis, Babesiosis, Tularemia, and tick paralysis. The most famous tick-borne disease as far as humans are concerned is the arthritic-like Lyme disease, but there are others, such as Ehrlichiosis, that are more dangerous. Ehrlichiosis has been reported in every state, although it's most common in the southeast and southwest. A recently discovered tick-borne disease is called *Hepatozoon americanum.* It causes fever and attacks bones, muscles, and white blood cells.

The principal carrier of Lyme disease, the northern deer tick, is a "hardshell" tick of tiny size when it hatches. It takes about two years for it to molt into its nymphal state, when it does the most damage, although it's a nasty piece of work at any age. As far as "tick season" goes, the beasts can become active any time the temperature rises above 40° F, but what I call "high tick season" is from April to September. You can find them under leaf debris, on walls, and on grass and leaf tips, where they lie in wait for dogs, deer, or white-footed mice to show up. If you have a lot of deer and white-footed mice where you live, you have deer ticks.

Lyme disease was first noted in humans in 1975, when it appeared among children in Old Lyme, Connecticut. Since then it has been found in every state on the continent. Lyme disease is caused ultimately by the bacterium *Borrelia burgdorferi,* named for its discoverer Willy Burgdorfer. That's the nice thing about bacteria. If you find a new one, you can name it after yourself. The disease can be treated with antibiotics if it is caught early. Lyme is a tricky disease, though, and is often over-diagnosed, because its symptoms—fatigue, lameness, fever, and loss of appetite, are also signs of many other conditions. Also be aware that dogs who have been vaccinated against it may test false positive. Untreated dogs can develop a permanent arthritis in the joint.

Other kinds of ticks include the brown dog tick (*Rhipicephalus sangineus*), which carries Rocky Mountain spotted fever, Tularemia, and tick paralysis, *Babesisa canis, Erhlichia canis,* and *Hepatozoon canis.* It carries a few other diseases, too, but I didn't want to frighten you. These particular ticks are often found around kennels in cracks between the wood. Spray kennel areas to get rid of them.

## Removing Ticks

*Never* touch a tick with your bare hands. The Lyme disease spirochete (and some others) can penetrate through infinitesimal openings in the skin. Use tweezers, gloves, or at least a piece of paper towel or tissue. If you find a tick when you're in the woods and have no tweezers on your handy Swiss army knife, use a leaf—anything to keep your hand away from direct contact with that thing. (Not your Beagle, of course, the tick). Grasp the tick as closely to the head as possible, and pull it out with a straight motion. Some people claim that using a corkscrew motion gives better results, but I haven't found that to be the case. Don't worry about leaving the tick's head in the skin. You won't.

Throw the tick in the toilet and flush. It won't get out. Scrub your hands thoroughly with hot soapy water.

Never try to burn or smother a tick with petroleum jelly. Burning ticks is dangerous, and smothering them takes too long. By the time they die, they could have transmitted something deadly.

## Preventing Fleas and Ticks

Fortunately, today there is no reason at all for your dog to have fleas or ticks. These pests can be controlled with safe modern insecticides, some of which are available over the counter. Some work by topical or spray application; others are administered orally in tablet form. Some are shampoos or dips. Some need to be given monthly, others are good for up to three months. Some products kill both fleas and ticks, others only fleas.

Amitraz collars kill embedded ticks and mites, and do it much better than any other product tested. They cause paralysis of the tick's mouthparts. Currently amitraz is available in two products, both from Virbac: Preventic and Tick Arrest. If your Beagle is often out in tick-infested areas, an amitraz collar is a must.

Some products kill adult fleas; other products like lufenuron, methoprene, and pyripoxyfen (nylar), are insect growth regulators (IGR), which do not allow fleas to reproduce. Pyrethins (which come from the chrysanthemum plant) and imidacloprid kill fleas on contact; while permethrin and fiprinil do the same to both fleas and ticks. Some work for repelling mosquitoes also, which is very important in places where heartworm is prevalent. Effective as these products are, however, *never* combine them without direct instructions from your veterinarian. It *does not* follow that because one product is good, two must be better.

Popular insecticides for your dog include:

- Frontline TopSpot (fiprinil, Rx): This topical medication is applied to the back of the neck every thirty to ninety days. (The back of the neck is chosen since the dog can't lick it off from there.) The medication moves through the oil glands of the skin, and becomes completely effective within twenty-four hours. It blocks the action of the neurotransmitter gamma amino butyric acid (GABA) in fleas and ticks.
- Advantage (imidacloprid, Rx): A topical medication applied to the back once a month. Advantage kills fleas but not ticks.
- Biospot (permethrin and pyripryfen; over the counter): This is a topical insect growth regulator (IGR). It is applied once a month to the base of the neck and tail. It works by inhibiting the insect growth hormones, and does not enter the bloodstream of the dog. It kills adult fleas, eggs, and larvae, ticks, and mosquitoes. It also repels them.
- Defend EXpot (permethrin, over the counter): This is a topical medication applied monthly between the shoulder blades and to the base of the tail. It repels fleas, ticks, and mosquitoes. This product is safe for puppies four weeks and older, as well as pregnant, or nursing bitches. Re-apply if the dog swims or is bathed.
- Program (lufenuron, Rx): This product is available in liquid or pill form and is given once a month. It circulates in the dog's bloodstream, and stops flea eggs from hatching because it makes lady fleas sterile. This kind of control is called an Insect Development Inhibitor. Program can be used in conjunction with Frontline.
- Sentinel (lufenuron and milbemycin oxime, Rx only): This is a chewable tablet administered once a month. This product combines two others: Program (fleas) and Interceptor (worms). It works as an IGR for fleas, and kills heartworm, hook worm, roundworm, and whipworm. It is safe for use on puppies, and for pregnant, and nursing dogs; however it does not kill ticks or adult fleas.

- Revolution (selamectin, Rx only): This topical medication is applied between the shoulder blades once a month. Selamectin prevents heartworm, kills ear mites, adults fleas, acts as an IGR, treats sarcoptic mange and kills American dog ticks. However, it is expensive, and does not kill roundworms, hookworms, or other kinds of ticks, such as the deer tick. Another serious disadvantage of Revolution is that, like all topical medications, it's easy to misapply. And if you do, you could have a bigger problem than fleas or ticks—your dog could get heartworm. I prefer an oral medication for heartworm. An effective year round flea control product will cost about $35.

Beaglers beware! Read all labels carefully before treating your dog and follow the directions. Some of these products are not safe around cats, birds or tropical fish. Most medication labels provide a toll-free number to call if you have questions, or you can check with your veterinarian.

You can also find many products on the shelves that rely on "natural" insect repellents like garlic, brewer's yeast, citronella, vinegar, vitamin B1, or cedar. Many natural flea remedies come in a chewable, wafer-like form. Some contain soothing emollients or herbal fragrances. A few natural citrus products, such as linalool and di-limonene are effective against fleas, but have some serious side effects for dogs unless used with extreme care. One new product, Ark Natural's lemon-scented Neem Bug Free repellent can be used every seven to ten days, as long as your Beagle doesn't get wet, in which case you must reapply it. An eight-ounce bottle costs $10.25. These products have varying degrees of effectiveness, but at least most won't hurt your Beagle. Still, my advice is that unless you have compelling reasons to do otherwise, use one of the traditional medications listed above.

One "high tech" device that doesn't work is the so-called ultrasonic collar. These products emit a high-frequency noise in the area of 25,000 to 65,000 hertz, well above the range of human hearing. They're supposed to drive fleas mad. But the fleas aren't bothered by the noise one little bit. Dogs, however, can hear noises up to about 50,000 hertz, so the collars may be very effective on their psyches.

Improving your dog's diet may also help control fleas. Give your dog top quality meats and fresh vegetables, or add them to your dog's good commercial food. Although this won't get rid of fleas, it will help your dog fight them.

Whatever flea control product you choose, remember that in case of a flea infestation, you must treat your dog's bedding, collar, toys, and the household carpets as well. A good vacuuming of the carpets, and thorough washing of the pet's bedding can reduce the flea population. Fleas could also be living in your car. Vacuum that too. Keeping your grass cut short and your bushes trimmed will also help keep away those nasty bugs.

Some people opt for a more "total" approach to flea-fighting and treat their yards with organophosphate sprays that kill not only fleas, ticks, and ants, but every other insect. They can also be dangerous to cats. I would stay away from these products unless you have a very serious infestation. Use these products with extreme caution.

### Managing Lice

Although lice aren't common in dogs, they *can* get them, especially if the kids catch them at school and bring them home. Most lice actually prefer people, but will live on the family dog if nothing better happens along. There is a dog-loving louse, however: *Trichodectes canis*. This critter causes irritation and severe itching as well as hair loss. If untreated, your dog may get a secondary infection. Luckily, lice are usually controlled with flea medication.

## Mites

Altogether there are over 30,000 kinds of mites, but only a dozen or so infect dogs. This is a good thing; otherwise this book would have to be a lot longer.

The most common sort of mites are ear mites, nearly microscopic little beasties that cats and dogs pass along easily to one another. They live upon shed particles of skin. Infected dogs dig frantically at their ears. They also shake their heads. In severe cases, ear mites, can actually pierce the eardrum!

Several medications, such as rotenone, amitraz, and methyl phthalate, pyrethrins, and piperonyl butoxide are available to treat this problem. The first step is to clean the ear gently, then apply the mite-killer.

## Demodectic Mange

Demodex mites are nearly always present on dogs, but some individuals and some breeds (including Beagles), seem prone to developing the "red mange" associated with it. (Actually, people have demodex mites too, in the follicles of their eyebrows. They have been living there quietly for millennia, if it's any comfort to you. You cannot "catch" demodex from your dog.)

Apparently, there is a connection between demodectic mange and a susceptible immune system. There is also a hereditary component to the disease and puppies are most generally affected. When the disease is present, the mites crowd out the hair follicles, causing them to fall out. In addition, the follicles often become infected and the skin red and inflamed. A skin scraping can be made to confirm the diagnosis. Mange in puppies usually resolves itself, but it can be also treated with insecticides. Adult onset demodex is very serious and requires almost continual attention. Sadly, the outcome is far from assured, however.

## Sarcoptic Mange (*Sarcoptes scabei*)

If you think you detect the word "scabies" in the scientific name for this creature, you are correct. Its other name is "itch mite," and with good reason. The lady mite burrows into the skin and lays her eyes there. When the eggs hatch into larva, the larva dig around even more. The results are lesions on many parts of the body and secondary infections are common. Both humans and dogs can get sarcoptic mange. The mites burrow in the skin and cause itchiness, redness, and hair loss in both people and dogs. (This mite can affect almost any kind of animal, by the way, and seem to have a particular liking for livestock.)

This mange is treated with special shampoos, dips, pills, or injections.

### Walking Dandruff (*Cheyletiella yasguri*)

The charming name of this mite is indicative of its not so charming habit of producing crud and hair loss on your dog. It doesn't cause the severe itchiness of the other mites, nor is it as dangerous. Your veterinarian can treat it easily with amitraz.

## Worms

Studies show that one out of every three dogs will be afflicted as one time or another with an internal parasite. The major kinds include roundworms, hookworms, tapeworms, heartworms, whipworms, and giardia.

Worms are troubling parasites of both puppies and adult dogs. There are dozens of varieties and different species infect different parts of the dog's body. Some kinds attack the esophagus and stomach; others go for the small intestine. Still others, like whipworm, target the cecum and colon. In fact, almost every organ of the dog's body can be prey to one kind of worm or another: the liver, nasal cavity, trachea, lungs, heart, kidney, nervous system, arteries, and veins. Some of these worms, including hookworms and roundworms, can be passed on to humans. In fact, hookworms are a real public health concern.

To prevent your dog from getting worms, use a regular de-wormer on him, and keep his quarters and your yard clean and picked up. Some worms are transmitted though food. Freezing meat to minus 40° F for two days, or heating it to 140° F kills them. Of course, unless you live in a laboratory, finding a place to freeze anything to minus 40° F is a bit of a challenge.

### Heartworm

Heartworm is the most deadly of all the worms that can attack your dog. These spaghetti-shaped creatures damage the heart by restricting its blood flow; they also damage other internal organs. Carried by more than twenty-two species of mosquitoes, heartworm is prevalent wherever mosquitoes are common, usually in warm, wet areas of the country. Your veterinarian can look for heartworm by taking a blood sample from your dog.

Several products are available to control heartworm; I use Interceptor. However, whatever choice you make, your dog should be on heartworm preventative all year long. This costs about $75. If your Beagle contracts heartworm, he can be treated, but the procedure is long, expensive, dangerous, and by no means guaranteed. Untreated dogs will die.

## Roundworm (*Toxocara canis*)

Roundworm is the most common worm of all. Nearly every single puppy ever born is born with roundworms, which are acquired from the mother. Roundworms penetrate the small intestine and can be carried through the bloodstream to the liver and lungs, and even up the trachea, where they are swallowed. At that time the worms begin their life cycle all over again, producing eggs that are excreted with the feces. Older dogs are less likely to be infected, but they can pick roundworms up from contaminated soil.

Here's another good reason to keep your yard cleaned up: Children playing in areas where dogs have defecated can get roundworm if they place their dirty fingers in their mouths. Children with roundworms present a variety of symptoms that may be misdiagnosed as flu.

## Hookworm (*Ancylostoma canium*)

Hookworms are nasty critters that attach to the intestinal wall with their little teeth. Hookworms cause intestinal bleeding; just a few dozen of them can kill a puppy. The larvae are deposited in feces from which they can be easily picked up again, either through the skin or by mouth. They like shady, sandy areas best, and barefoot children are particularly at risk. Remember, hookworms don't have to be swallowed; the larvae can actually penetrate the skin and cause lesions. Children infected by hookworms can develop chronic intestinal bleeding, and consequent pain and anemia. Because they absorb nutrients, they can also cause malnutrition. Not a nice thing at all.

### Diagnosing Worms

To find out whether your dog has worms, you may have to collect a stool sample to take to your veterinarian. Use a baggie and roll it inside out after collecting the sample. That way you'll keep air out of the bag and your hands clean. You don't need to bring in a whole lot, but the softer and fresher it is, the better, since live worms are easier to detect than dead ones.

### Whipworm

Whipworms are one of the most difficult of all worms to destroy. Their eggs seem impervious to time and cold weather, and a lady whipworm can lay 2000 eggs a day. Those aren't good statistics. Severe infestations can give a dog a terrible case of colitis, something that happened to the dog next door, who nearly died.

### Tapeworm (*Dipylidium canium*)

If you see something that looks like grains of rice emerging from your dog's backside, look out. It's tapeworm. Tapeworms are carried by fleas and are contracted by dogs when one or more fleas are swallowed. If your dog has fleas, there's a good chance that he has tapeworms too. The worms are easy to eliminate with medication, but they won't be gone long if you don't also get rid of the fleas.

## Fungus

Despite its name, ringworm is a fungus, and a highly contagious one at that. Dogs can pick up ringworm from an infected dog, or even from the ground. It is more common in puppies than in adult dogs. Classical signs include scabs or an irregularly shaped area of skin infection. There may be rapid hair loss at the site. People, especially kids, can get ringworm from dogs, so get it treated immediately.

# Giardia

This tiny organism, oddly harbored by beavers of all things, is present in many water sources—including bubbling "pure" mountain springs. Many species exist. Since the stuff is everywhere, it's practically impossible to prevent except by vaccination, which can be administered at seven or eight weeks of age. Giardia infects the intestinal tract. Signs of giardial infection include dehydration, cramps, and loose, mucoid feces. More rarely, the infection can cause diarrhea and vomiting, and in young or debilitated animals, can even be fatal.

Giardia has a direct life cycle, and infects the host when its cysts are ingested. The cysts can outlive the host by several months, especially in cold wet areas. If humans step on infected feces, they can track the organism into their homes, where the family dog could be infected. Most mammals, including human beings, can get giardia. Dogs most at risk are the obvious ones: strays, outdoor pets, and dogs in multi-pet households. Many dogs carry giardia and show no, or only mild, symptoms. Unfortunately, the cysts are shed only intermittently, and giardia may not be seen on routine smears or flotation tests. Several samples over several days are often required.

## Treatment for Giardia

Treatment commonly involves administering metronidazole, which also kills off other diarrhea-causing organisms. Infected animals should be separated from healthy ones. The best way to prevent giardia is to keep your dog from drinking contaminated water, it also helps to keep your yard clean of dog feces.

# Chapter 17

# Beagle Blights: Common Health Problems

Although they are generally brimming with well-being, Beagles can have health problems just like everyone else. As a conscientious dog owner, you should be aware of the major health problems Beagles encounter, their signs and symptoms, and possible methods of treatment.

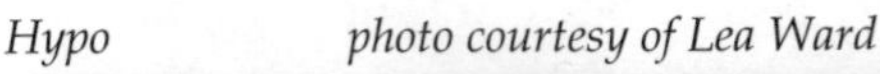

*Hypo* *photo courtesy of Lea Ward*

## Symptoms

Many illnesses manifest themselves by the same set of symptoms, such as diarrhea, constipation, or vomiting. These symptoms are not a disease, but indications of a problem, often nothing more serious than poor judgment about a meal. Since dogs are basically scavengers, they are designed to expel toxins the easiest way possible. However, if symptoms persist, call your veterinarian. As a general rule, call your vet if diarrhea persists for more than twenty-four hours, or if the dog vomits more than four times in an hour, especially if the vomiting is accompanied by blood or abdominal pain. Dogs with diarrhea need access to fresh water at all times, as they may become dehydrated. Don't feed a dog who has been vomiting recently; give his system time to rest.

## Skin Problems and Allergies

Healthy skin is the result of good nutrition, a healthy environment, and freedom from parasites. A shortcoming in any one of these areas can lead to skin trouble.

S-C-R-A-T-C-H!!! There's Riley, digging away at his skin—again. What's wrong? How can you stop it? And keep it from happening in the future? The canine itch is one of the most common and troublesome ailments in dogdom. The biggest challenge is trying to discover why your Beagle is scratching, because it could be almost anything. Itching in dogs can be caused by any of the following conditions, and more: allergies (food or environmental), parasites (flea and scabies), fly bites, chemical irritations from pesticides sprayed on garden plants or field crops, acute infections, adverse reaction to medications, psychological problems and neurological disorders.

### A Beagle Bummer

Beagles are prone to a variety of skin problems, including demodectic mange, which is considered in Chapter 16, "Beagle Bugs."

The most common cause for dog itch is allergy. Although dogs aren't born with allergies, many dogs acquire them during their lifetime and Beagles more so than many other breeds. Although allergic tendencies are inherited, most allergies don't show up until the dog is between six months and three years of age.

Dogs get several kinds of allergies: inhalant allergies, contact allergies, and food allergies. Dogs tend to respond to all types by developing skin problems, rather than by sneezing.

## Inhalant Allergies

Between 10 and 15 percent of all dogs suffer from one or another kind of inhalant allergy and if one or both parents suffer from inhalant allergies, the chances are increased that the puppies will also. The most common culprit is the common household dust mite. Other allergens include trees, particularly elm, maple, and walnut; weeds like lamb's quarters, Russian thistle, ragweed, cocklebur, and English plantain; and various species of grasses. Some dogs are even allergic to human dander! Better get out the Head and Shoulders—for you.

## Contact Allergies

Dust, smoke, and certain plants are usually the culprits in contact allergies. Unlike inhalant allergies, contact allergies are usually not inherited.

However, some dogs can contract atopic dermatitis. This is a chronic skin problem that can often be traced to increased production of reaginic (IgE) antibodies, which is an inherited condition. It may also stem from some inhalant allergies, including allergies to pollen and mold. Affected dogs can develop lesions, and spend a lot of time chewing their paws. The best treatments are to remove the allergen from the dog's environment or submit the dog to a series of hyposensitization shots. Another approach is the use of antihistamines or alternate-day glucocorticoid therapy.

Some Beagles are also prone to systemic lupus erythematosus, an immune complex disorder in which the dog may develop mouth ulcers and reddish, scaling skin on the face. This disease can actually be psychosomatic in dogs—as it can in human beings! Treatment includes corticosteroids, antibiotics, and keeping the animal out of the sun.

Another autoimmune skin disease affecting Beagles is pemphigus, which starts on the head and works its way down. Here again the treatment of choice is corticosteroids.

Many dogs are allergic to flea saliva; it appears that some families of dogs are more susceptible than others. Even one chance bite can produce a reaction. It's not the flea itself that dogs are allergic to, but an anti-coagulant present in the flea's saliva. Dogs show a reaction with a few minutes of being bitten; a second reaction occurs twenty-four hours later. Crusty scabs will appear toward the rear of the dog. Keep your Beagle flea-free by using the many effective preventative products now on the market. (See Chapter 16 for more details.)

## Food Allergies

Although food allergies are less common than the other two types (seen in 5 to 10 percent of dogs), many dogs develop allergies to corn, soy, wheat, and certain proteins, including pork, beef, chicken, and eggs. Allergic responses to food will be seen within four to twenty-four hours of eating, at least in the early stages. Later on, the dog will show symptoms constantly. As in other types of allergies, skin problems are the common signs, but some dogs also vomit, and have diarrhea or gas. If your dog has a year round itch that doesn't seem affected by weather, I would suspect a food allergy. To find out, he must be placed on a strict elimination diet, which forbids even treats. (Rawhide and dog biscuits often contains dyes to which your pet may be allergic.)

The new diet must also contain a protein to which the dog has not previously been exposed, such as venison, fish, or rabbit. Further, the dog must stay on that diet for at least four weeks (but six weeks are even better). Gradually, suspect foods are added back one at a time. However, the precise substance to which your dog is allergic can be hard to pin down.

If you suspect your dog has a food allergy, several manufacturers produce hypoallergenic diets. DVM Pharmaceuticals, for example, has developed a hypoallergenic test diet composed of hydrolized liver, casein (milk protein) oats, and pinto beans. Luckily, food allergies do not seem to be inherited. A good way to help prevent your Beagle from becoming food allergic is to provide him a varied diet from puppyhood. Don't be afraid to switch foods; it's good for him and challenges his immune system in a positive way.

## Dealing with Dermal Allergic Reactions

To help protect your dog, take these important steps:

- Prevention: Get your dog on flea medication immediately. Clean all bedding. Even one bite can start a flea dermatitis in your dog. Probably the most common canine allergy is to fleas, but with the wonderful flea control medicines now on the market, fleas never have to be a problem with your dog again.
- Bathe your dog. Use a shampoo appropriate to your dog's needs. Some shampoos are moisturizers; others assist in keeping the skin dry. Some contain soothing aloe, oatmeal, or other natural products. Some are more strongly medicated than others. Some can be bought by prescription only. Choose the shampoo that is right for your Beagle and use it. If you use the right shampoo, you cannot over-bathe your Beagle, no matter what your great-aunt Hattie says.
- Some dog itching is due to poor skin conditioning. If necessary, use a supplement containing omega-3 fatty acids. Most dog foods, particularly grocery store brands, are lacking in these vital aids to your dog's coat.
- Try an antihistamine, either topical or oral. Benadryl works well for many dogs, but make sure you get plain Benadryl—not Benadryl for colds or even for allergies, which can contain ingredients dangerous to dogs. The usual dose is one to three milligrams for every pound of dog. Many creams or ointments are also available to help reduce itching. None of these products cure the actual allergies, but they do alleviate the symptoms. But when dogs don't itch, they don't scratch, and it's the scratching that can produce inflammation and hence infection.
- Cortisone treatment may be used as a last resort for short-term use only. I would avoid this unless your dog is suffering acutely and no other treatment is beneficial. Cortisone injections can be quite dangerous.

- ▼ Quit smoking. Smoke allergies are common, and if your Beagle suffers any other kind of allergy, the smoke will only make it worse. Quit now.

Your veterinarian can test your dog for inhalant allergies by using blood tests such as the Enzyme-Linked Immunosorbent Assay (ELISA), the Radioimmunoassay for Antibody Test (RAST), or the Indirect Fluorescent Antibody Test (IFA). However, blood testing is still fairly inexact. Better results can be obtained with more invasive and time-consuming skin tests. Treatment may involve allergy shots, antihistamines, and fatty acid or vitamin E supplements in the diet. The latter is especially good for chronic conditions.

Allergies can cause more than itching, however. In response to the allergen, the sebaceous glands of the skin may become over-productive, altering the normal condition of the skin. This leaves the skin open to infection (pyoderma). Pyoderma causes not only *more* itching, but also pain and inflammation, ear infections, or even abscesses beneath the skin. Antibiotics are usually used to treat cases where pyoderma, but many of the more commonly prescribed antibiotics won't work, and your vet may need to take a culture. The course of treatment may be long—over a month.

Skin problems can also be a sign of other, more serious problems. If a dog has persistent skin problems, it may because something else is out of joint. (It's "safer" for a dog to express these problems in skin ailments than in liver or kidney dysfunction.) In cases like these, just treating the skin is not enough. It's time to look for the real culprit.

## Sebaceous Gland Tumors

Several types of benign, sebaceous gland skin tumors exist. Unless they are infected, no treatment is required. They are very common, especially in older animals.

A gland tumor is not the same as a so-called "sebaceous cyst," which results from malformation of the hair follicle. These cysts should be removed.

## Amyloidosis

Amyloidosis is actually a whole group of disorders, including lupus erythematosus, neutropenia, and spleen tumors. Many dogs with this condition also have cancer or an inflammatory disease, which may precipitate it. It's caused by the accumulation of an abnormal protein in the kidney. Older dogs are most commonly affected. They exhibit signs of increased thirst and urination, lethargy, and vomiting. Unfortunately, the outlook for affected dogs is poor.

## Blood Disorders

Beagles suffer from several blood clotting disorders, caused by a deficiency of a "clotting factor." The most common of these is von Willebrand's Disease (vWD), also called Factor VIII-related antigen. This is the most frequently inherited disease of dogs, affecting all breeds and mixes. Although the cause is different, it is similar to hemophilia, in that the dog's blood fails to clot. Not all dogs are equally affected. Dogs who suffer severe bleeding episodes may need transfusions.

## Immune-Mediated Hemolytic Anemia (IHA)

IHA destroys the red blood cells. The spleen is also affected. Although this problem usually appears as a primary or idiopathic disease, it can also result from vaccinations and other underlying conditions, including bacterial or viral infections. Signs of the disease include weakness and fever. The disease is treated with corticosteroids such as prednisone or dexamethasone to decrease production of the destructive antibody. Blood transfusions may also be needed.

## IgA (immunoglobulin A) Deficiency

A lack of immunoglobulin A can predispose the dog to a large number of infections, including infections of the digestive, respiratory, and reproductive systems. It may also cause ear infections, which are so common in Beagles.

### Intervertebral Disc Disease (Herniated Disc)

In a herniated disc, the inner layer of the donut-shaped disc that lies between the vertebrae protrudes through the outer layer, and puts pressure on the spinal cord. It is caused by a degeneration of the disc. This can occur in dogs as young as one year. Dogs with this condition suffer intense pain. The disc can slip anywhere along the spine, and the placement of the slipped disc produces different symptoms. A herniated disc in the lower back is often quite serious, as it may lead to paralysis.

In mild cases, the disease can be managed with anti-inflammatory drugs, primarily corticosteroids and muscle relaxants. Crate rest is required. More serious cases demand surgery and it's important to act right away. The best results are obtained when surgery is undertaken within eight hours of the event.

## Bones and Joints

One of the most common conditions to affect your Beagle's bones and joints is arthritis, a word that can refer to over one hundred specific conditions! All of them, however, cause pain and inflammation of the joints, just as they do in humans. As with people, arthritic joints suffer deterioration of the cartilage, and well as loss of the synovial fluid and eventually the development of bony "spurs" or chips. In fact, there's not much difference between human arthritis and dog arthritis, except that dog arthritis progresses much faster. For example, a dog who receives an injury could develop arthritis in as little as two or three weeks after the event; the same thing wouldn't occur in humans for many months, or even years. Traumatic injury, or repeated stress on a joint can lead to this condition.

Arthritis can occur in any part of a dog's body—however, the most common sites are the hips and legs, where the cartilage is subject to the most wear and tear. Although there is no cure for arthritis, or for many similar bone disorders, you can make your aching dog's life a lot easier.

### Pain Relief from Joint Problems

Talk with your veterinarian about the best pain relief for an arthritic dog. The most effective anti-inflammatory drug, Rimadyl (carpofen), has rare but serious side effects in some dogs. This hugely prescribed medication can, in a very few instances, damage the liver. Some veterinarians recommend that it not be used long term. Another drug in its class, Etogesic, is probably safer, although I don't think it has the same high level of success as Rimadyl. Unfortunately, human pain relief drugs like aspirin, ibuprofin, and Tylenol are not safe for dogs over time.

Some dogs respond to intra-muscular injections of Adequan, which is used to replace the synovial fluid. This treatment is expensive, however, and not suited for all cases. Alternative medical practice offers dietary changes (more fresh foods, no preservatives), nutraceuticals such as glucosamine and condroitin sulfate (to replace synovial fluids and rebuild cartilage), flaxseed and primrose oil, and acupuncture.

### Preventing Arthritis

You can help avert arthritis by feeding your dog a healthy diet rich in omega-3 fatty acids. Many quality commercial foods also contain glucosamine, chondroitin sulfate, and the correct balance of meats and vegetables. And plenty of exercise is important. Be sure that your dog gets a fair amount of exercise throughout his life.

## Epilepsy

It is estimated that as many as 4 percent of all dogs suffer from epilepsy, and it is the fourth leading killer of dogs, yet the cause and cure of the disease remain elusive. We do know, however, that genetics play a major role.

Epilepsy is a brain disorder characterized by sudden seizures, which result from an uncontrolled electric discharge of neurons in the brain. Some experts characterize it as an "electrical storm" in the brain. Seizures can be precipitated by any number of factors: inflammation, infection, congenital malformations, tumors, cysts, and trauma. Other causes might include toxins, liver or kidney disease, hypoglycemia, electrolyte imbalances and hypoxia. More often, the cause is unknown; such cases are called "idiopathic epilepsy." The seizures associated with epilepsy may be accompanied by loss of consciousness, memory loss, odd muscle movements, hallucinations, excessive salivation, and loss of bowel or bladder control. In some cases, the dog exhibits rage or terror. Seizures first appear in dogs aged one through three. Many dogs suffer only partial seizures, affecting only one part of the body. The goal of therapy is to reduce the frequency and severity of the seizures, many of which are more frightening to the owner than they are dangerous to the dog, although this can vary considerably.

The most dangerous type of epilepsy is "status epilepticus," in which the dog suffers a continuous series of seizures without any recovery time between events. This is a medical emergency, for the dog could die from hyperthermia, acidosis, circulatory collapse, or hypoxia. In such cases, the usual treatment is the administration of Diazepam intravenously or rectally, followed by Pentobartital or Phenobarbital.

Epilepsy can usually be managed by Phenobarbital, but there is no cure. To help your dog avoid seizures, try to keep his life to a predictable and quiet routine. This will lower his stress level.

## Ear Infections

Ear problems are common in Beagles, as they are in all lop-eared dogs. If your dog produces a lot of wax in his ears (this varies from dog to dog), has hair growing in the canal, swims a lot, or lives in a humid environment, the chances for problems are increased. Ear infections are more than uncomfortable. They can be really agonizing, and can permanently damage your dog's hearing. Infection of the outer ear is called otitis externa. This is the most common condition. When the infection involves the middle ear, it is called otitis media. This is more serious and can develop from otitis externa.

Signs of ear infections include redness, or a foul odor. Your Beagle may tilt his head to the side, shake his head, or scratch repeatedly at his ears. (Some of these actions can result in your dog developing a blood blister in the earflap, making everything worse.)

Infections can be caused by bacteria, fungus like yeast, or by an external irritant. It's important to understand what the cause of the problem is before it can be correctly treated, and you'll

*Louie*

*photo courtesy of Wally Jarrett*

need to take your Beagle to the vet. Your veterinarian may prescribe an ointment that contains antibiotics, antifungals, and cortisone (to fight inflammation). Make sure you follow the veterinarian's advice and give the entire course of treatment. In some cases, photon laser therapy has been used to reduce inflammation, as have holistic treatments. In cases of serious, painful infection, or inflammation, the veterinarian may need to anesthetize your dog for a thorough cleaning. In very serious cases of long-standing, surgery may be the only option.

Be wary of treating infections yourself. Using the wrong kind of treatment will not only be ineffective, but may permanently damage your dog's hearing, particularly if the ear drum has been punctured.

If your dog has persistent ear problems, he may have an allergy or trouble with his immune system. In fact, allergies to substances such as pollen are the most common cause of ear problems. Sometimes, repeated ear infections are the only sign of the allergy. About 75 percent of dogs who have allergies also have ear infections of various sorts.

Keeping your dog's ears clean as part of a regular grooming program will help prevent ear problems. Do this at least once a week, using a good commercial cleanser that is non-irritating to your dog. When you notice your Beagle sleeping, see if you can put his ears up to dry them out. And when bathing your Beagle, be sure to use cotton balls in his ears to keep out the water.

*A clear-eyed gaze from Louie*

*photo courtesy of Wally Jarrett*

## Eye Problems

Beagles suffer from a variety of eye problems, most of them inherited. The Canine Eye Registry Foundation (CERF) promotes eye health and genetic screening of all breeds.

### Cataracts

This common condition typically affects young or middle aged dogs, not the elderly, as in the case with human beings. Cataracts are characterized by an opaque lens or lens capsule. The condition comes on over time; the eye usually becomes cloudy first, and then gradually develops a white "veil." Surgery can remove the cataract.

Frequently owners mistake the greenish haze that is often visible in the eyes of older dogs for cataracts, but that condition is a normal result of aging, and doesn't seriously affect vision.

Not all cataracts lead to blindness. They are largely inherited, and in fact, Beagles are among the breeds that tend to inherit canine cataracts. Accordingly, the best way to reduce the likelihood of cataracts is to avoid breeding dogs who carry the gene, which is an incomplete, dominant one in Beagles. However, other factors like diabetes and inflammation may also play a part. Currently, the only treatment for cataracts is surgery, which is very successful.

### Glaucoma

Beagles are one of the breeds that are genetically disposed to primary glaucoma. In this disease the fluid that helps maintain the eye doesn't "flow" the way it should, and it builds up, causing terrible pressure on the retina. The eye itself will look enlarged, red, and cloudy. An acute episode of glaucoma is usually preceded by a milder condition that has gone unnoticed, because the signs are so subtle.

Primary glaucoma can be divided into several types: open-angle, narrow-angle, and closed angle. Diagnosis is made by a gonio-scopic examination of the iridocorneal angle. For Beagles, primary open-angle glaucoma is inherited as an autosomal recessive trait.

These glaucomas are exceedingly difficult to treat, either medically or surgically, and the treatment is very expensive. In serious cases, surgical removal of the eye may be necessary. Sadly, most dogs go blind within a few months after contracting glaucoma. When purchasing your Beagle, find out if any of his relatives has suffered glaucoma, and beware.

### Progressive Retinal Atrophy (PRA)

Progressive retinal atrophy is an inherited condition in which the retina slowly deteriorates, eventually leading to blindness. In Beagles, this is an autosomal recessive disorder—the dog inherits the defective gene from both parents. The first symptoms are night blindness, but eventually the loss of vision becomes total. The condition develops so slowly, however, and dogs adapt so well to loss of vision, that many owners aren't aware that anything is wrong until the disease is far advanced. No treatment is currently available, but there are two tests available to detect the presence of the gene that causes PRA.

### Retinal Dysplasia

Retinal dysplasia is becoming increasingly more common in dogs. Beagles are most likely to acquire "multifocal retinal dysplasia," which can cause visual impairment but not blindness. Still, this genetically based condition could be eliminated by careful breeding.

## Cancer

As with people, cancer is seen more and more frequently in dogs. In fact, about one out of every five dogs will eventually get the disease. This is about the same rate as for humans. To make matters more complicated, cancer is not one disease—it's a name for over 200 different types of malignancies that can occur. And although Beagles are among the least likely breeds to contract cancer, the disease is still more common than we'd like to see. This is partly because dogs are living longer than they used to. About 45 percent of dogs who reach the age of ten will die from cancer or a related condition. Another reason for the increase in cancer cases is due to increased exposure to noxious substances and toxins. In addition, there is a strong genetic component to the disease. The most common form of cancer is skin cancer.

The Veterinary Cancer Society has provided owners a list of cancer warning signs; these include unexplained lumps, especially a hard lump that appears attached, or lumps that continue to grow quickly; weight and appetite loss; sores that don't heal; bleeding or discharge; foul breath; constant fatigue; difficulty in swallowing, urinating, eliminating, or breathing.

Unspayed females are at a high risk for mammary tumors, usually seen as a firm, painless swelling around a nipple. Mammary tumors in dogs are not so serious as they are for human beings, but early detection is still important. Check out your dog's nipples during every grooming session. The nipples closest to the tail are the ones most likely to develop tumors. Surgery is the accepted treatment for mammary tumors.

Cancerous tumors are divided into three types: simple carcinomas, complex carcinomas, and carcinosarcomas. No kind of tumor is good, but complex carcinomas, which are composed of more than one cell type, are probably the least likely to spread to other organs. Carcinosarcomas originate from embryonic connective tissue and are very dangerous. Simple sarcomas are somewhere between the other types are far as seriousness goes. Early diagnosis is critical, since cancers can spread so quickly—usually to either the lymph nodes or to the lungs. That is why your veterinarian will often recommend an X-ray before surgery. If the tumors have spread to other organs, surgery may not be an effective option.

In addition to surgery, some veterinarians treat cancer patients with radiation and chemotherapy. Radiation is not yet widely available, and is designed only to reduce the swelling and pain from the tumor. If the tumor has spread, radiation is not a useful treatment. Chemotherapy for dogs has fewer side effects than in humans, probably because of the lower doses required for effective treatment.

Fortunately, several experimental treatments are on the horizon, in addition to standard surgery, radiation, and chemotherapy. These include acupuncture (blocks pain and boosts the immune system), cryosurgery (treats with extreme cold); "flip and nuke surgery," (the surgeon removes the affected bone, but leaves the joint attached, radiates it, and then re-attaches it); herb therapy (promotes relaxation and may help heal); hyperthermia radiation therapy (heat plus drugs and radiation); liposome treatment (activates immune cells); photodynamic therapy (uses a laser beam to activate the chemical only within the tumor); and slow-release chemotherapy (medication is contained in a slow-release polymer right under the skin).

## Radiation Therapy

One experimental alternative is an implantable radiation treatment that uses radioactive beads, a procedure known as brachytherapy. Doctors can insert a plastic "after-loading tube," into the tumor area (after most of the tumor has been removed) and radioactive beads are fed into the tube. This is an exciting therapy because practitioners can precisely control the dose. The beads also target the cancerous area pretty exactly. The downside of this treatment is that while medication is going on, your pet is mildly radioactive and must be kept in isolation from other animals and their owners. And only veterinarians licensed to handle radioactive substances can treat such animals. On the other hand, in many ways, the treatment is much kinder than traditional radiation, in which the animal must undergo anesthesia several times. Brachytherapy requires anesthesia only for the insertion and removal of the beads.

## Cancer Therapy Diets

Dogs affected with cancer have special dietary requirements, usually involving high fat foods, including plenty of omega-3 fatty acids. The acids, found in marine fish, have proved to inhibit the spread of cancer cells.

It was formerly believed that antioxidants and selenium were beneficial in preventing or treating cancer, but this has been found to be questionable. Other suggested supplements include grape seed extract, vitamins A and K, arginine, garlic, and glutamine, an amino acid.

## Heart Problems

Beagles are subject to a number of heart problems, particularly malfunctioning valves, and heart malformations. Veterinarians check for heart disease using both radiography (X-rays) and echocardiography. These tests permit them to detect abnormalities in the heart valves or heart enlargement. They also use an electrocardiogram to observe abnormal heart rhythms. Treatment varies with the nature and severity of the disease and can include diuretics to reduce fluid accumulation, vasodilators, diet therapy, moderation in stress and exercise, as well as surgery.

## Thyroid Disease

The thyroid gland, located near the windpipe, is a two-lobed organ that regulates cell metabolism. Beagles can be affected by several thyroid diseases.

In a properly functioning system, a dog's thyroid, hypothalamus, and pituitary gland all work together in a complex way. The hypothalamus, located in the brain, excretes a special hormone, TRH; which travels to the pituitary gland and triggers the release of another hormone, THS. This hormone then travels to the thyroid where it asks the thyroid to release its own special thyroid hormone.

Hypothyroidism is the most common hormonal disorder in dogs. Dogs with this endocrine disorder produce an abnormally low level of the thyroid hormones, usually because of an inflammation that destroys the thyroid-hormone producing cells. Several types of the disease are known, and it can vary considerably in severity. Most often the disease first occurs in dogs between the ages of three and six years.

Symptoms may include lethargy, obesity, cold skin, weak limbs, and non-itchy hair loss, although many dogs exhibit no signs at all until their entire supply of hormones are used up—which may take several years. Blood tests can confirm the diagnosis. Dogs with hypothyroidism can suffer heart damage, and they are more at risk for developing certain other serious conditions.

Testing for hypothyroidism is done through a T4, or thyroid hormone test, that measures thyroid hormone levels in the blood. Because the test can be expensive ($60 to $80), it is not performed unless a malfunction is suspected. Treatment consists of a thyroid hormone supplement, usually taken twice a day. It is very effective—and not too costly ($12 to $20 a month). You should notice behavioral improvements in a matter of days, but skin and coat problems usually take longer to resolve.

## Urinary Tract Problems

The main problems associated with the urinary tract include: incontinence, inability to urinate, urinary stones, blood in the urine, cystitis, or abnormal discharges. Each of these symptoms may indicate more than one condition.

Incontinence is a condition associated with older, spayed females. In plain terms, they "leak," especially at night, often wetting their bedding. It is not serious, but it is very annoying, at least to the owner. Several effective, inexpensive treatments are available. The opposite problem, an inability to urinate, is extremely serious, and may indicate an obstruction in the urinary system such as a urinary stone or a tumor. More rarely, the dog is afflicted with an atonic bladder—one that has lost the ability to constrict.

Very often dogs develop increased thirst and the urination that goes along with it. Vets call this condition polyuria/polydipsia (PU/PD). It can have many causes; everything from normal aging to diabetes and Addison's or Cushing's disease. If you see these symptoms, bring your dog to the veterinarian for a checkup. Most conditions causing PU/PD respond well to treatment.

Seen more often in females than in males, cystitis is an infection or inflammation of the bladder. Usually the cause is a bacterial infection, which enters the urinary duct from the outside. (This is why females are more prone to bladder infections. Their urethra is very short, enabling bacteria from the outside to migrate up into the bladder.) A dog with cystitis will urinate frequently, but only a small amount of urine will come out each time. This is because the dog doesn't really need to urinate; the irritation in the bladder is just making it feel as if she does.

Some dogs develop stones in the urinary tract, nearly always in the bladder. Many times a therapeutic diet will dissolve the stones; but if the stones are causing a blockage, surgery may be necessary. The exact course of treatment may depend on the kind of stone involved. In Beagles, struvite crystals are the most common kind of stone. Females can sometimes "pass" the stones. To treat struvite stones, the urine is made more acidic, often by adding cranberry juice or capsules to the diet.

## Surgery and Anesthesia

Most pet dogs undergo surgery at least once in their lives—for neutering or spaying. Accident or disease may make surgery necessary at other times as well. Fortunately, we live in an age when surgery is not only more effective than ever, it's safer, too, thanks to the new generation of anesthesia now available. The type of anesthesia your veterinarian chooses depends on many factors including the age and health of your pet, the type of surgery, and financial concerns. Don't be afraid to talk to your vet about any of these issues. If you are anxious, ask your vet how often he has performed this type of surgery, and what the results have been. Ask how the dog will be monitored during surgery. The protocols for anesthetizing dogs are well established, and a veterinary surgeon generally has plenty of experience in this respect.

Most vets recommend (and some require) that you obtain a pre-surgical blood screen for your pet. Because some kinds of anesthesia may have adverse effects on the kidneys or liver, your vet needs to know as much as possible about how these organs are functioning before the surgery. Even if you have an option, it's wise to choose a pre-surgical blood screen, especially for older dogs. If you don't, you are increasing the risk to your dog's life.

Be sure to follow all your veterinarian's advice about pre-surgical procedures, which will include fasting your dog. Equally important, of course, if to obey all instructions about post-surgical care, which may include a series of antibiotics or painkillers.

# Chapter 18

# Beagle Boo-Boos: First Aid Emergencies

An emergency is a situation in which you need to get your Beagle to the veterinarian as quickly as possible. Of course, not every ailment needs professional treatment, and even professional treatment can sometimes be scheduled somewhat at your leisure. But these symptoms require immediate action:

- Bleeding from the nose or mouth
- Spurting blood (arterial bleeding)
- Seizures or disorientation
- Problems with breathing or swallowing
- Repeated vomiting
- Diarrhea lasting more than eighteen hours
- Refusal to eat for forty-eight hours
- Muscle tremors
- Broken bones
- Unusual swellings, especially sudden, hard, or fast-growing ones

## Your Veterinary First Aid Kit

You don't need a special box; anything handy will do, but a fishing tackle box works quite well. On the outside of the box, write "Dog First Aid Kit" in bold letters all over the place. Put it in an obvious place, because someone else might need to find it! In fact, you might tape on your bathroom mirror: "Dog First Aid Kit is in the __________."

To the inside of the box lid, tape any special information someone might need about conditions or allergic reactions your dog may have. Tape a special card with the name, address, and phone number of your veterinarian. Also write down the use and dosage for each medication your dog is likely to need in an emergency, so you, or someone else, won't have to try to figure it out then.

The First Aid Kit is also a good place to keep a copy of your dog's medical records, including his rabies certificate.

If you have a chance, take a Red Cross or similar course in first aid. Sometimes special clinics are given in first aid for animals. It is very helpful to learn to perform artificial respiration, mouth-to-mouth resuscitation, and the Heimlich maneuver. You never know when you might need them for animals or people.

## Be Wary of Pain Relievers

Do not give your dog Tylenol, ibuprofin, or aspirin, all of which are dangerous to dogs.

Here it is: the ultimate Canine First Aid Kit. Get everything on the list and you can open a clinic:

- Canine first aid manual
- Gauze and cotton pads (to clean and cover wounds)
- Baking soda (for burns caused by acids)
- Vinegar (for burns caused by alkaloids)
- Bandages or New Skin (the latter is especially useful for cuts on paw pads)
- Antibiotic soap or Nolvasan (skin and wound cleanser)
- Betadine (treating wounds)
- Antibiotic cream
- Hydrocortisone cream (minor inflammation)
- Gentle eye wash
- Petroleum jelly (numerous uses)
- Mineral oil (numerous uses, including constipation)

- Aloe vera (for minor burns)
- Activated charcoal (for poisoning)
- Immodium or Kaopectate (for diarrhea: one milligram for every fifteen pounds, one to two times a day; or one tablespoon for every ten pounds every six hours.)
- Ipecac or 3 percent hydrogen peroxide (in order to induce vomiting)
- Benadryl (one to two milligrams per pound, every eight hours; or two to four twenty-five milligram tablets every eight hours)
- Witch hazel (insect bites, minor injuries)
- Pepto-Bismol (digestive upsets and diarrhea; one teaspoon for every five pounds during a six-hour period)
- Epsom salts (soaking wounds, especially on the feet)
- Milk of magnesia (constipation, administer with equal amounts of mineral oil)
- Saline eye solution and artificial tear gel
- Rubber or latex gloves (to protect your hands and prevent contamination of wounds)
- Styptic powder (stops minor bleeding)
- Thermal blanket (prevents shock by preserving the dog's body heat)
- Syringe (without needle), or turkey baster (to apply oral medication)
- Canine rectal thermometer
- Round-tip scissors
- Eye dropper
- Clinging wrap heat or ice pack
- Tweezers or hemostat
- Magnifying glass
- Soft muzzle (injured dogs tend to bite)

### Moving an Injured Dog

If you must move an injured dog, wrap his head in a towel (allowing him, of course, nose room to breathe). This action will keep him calm and will prevent you from being bitten.

## Administering Medication

Medicating a dog is an integral part of both regular and emergency care. The easiest way to give a Beagle a pill is to stick it in a piece of bread, American cheese, or even a seedless grape. Sometimes you can just coat the pill in butter. But for those times when this is impossible, it's still not hard to pill your Beagle. Simply open the little guy's jaw and place the pill as far back on the tongue as you can. Hold his jaws gently closed, and stroke his throat. Bingo! The pill is gone. You can also try this: while holding the dog's mouth closed, blow gently into his eyes. The natural blink reflex will also cause the dog to swallow the pill.

If you are giving your dog a homeopathic remedy in pill form, be careful not to touch the capsule. Contact with your skin is said to neutralize the remedy. You should also not feed your dog for fifteen minutes or so before administering a homeopathic medication, since tiny food particles in the mouth can interfere with the action of the remedy.

Liquid medications can be given with an oral syringe, or in a pinch, a turkey baster. Tuck the syringe neatly down the "pocket" of the dog's mouth, and hold the jaws closed, with the lips firmly together. Don't ram the thing directly down the Beagle's throat, because you might get the medication into his lungs by mistake. Keep the dog's head tilted upward. After giving the oral medication, stroke your dog's throat gently.

## Diarrhea

Diarrhea is not a disease in itself, but a symptom. Diarrhea can be symptomatic of many conditions, and caused by many things, including bacteria, viruses, parasites, poisons, and organ dysfunction. Even psychological upsets and undue excitement may be a cause. Usually it's not classed as an emergency.

Diarrhea as a result of eating something untoward is a not serious problem for adult dogs. But for puppies, any diarrhea can be serious, because puppies have few "reserves" to draw on, and they can get dehydrated or even develop low blood sugar.

If you have an adult dog, you are usually safe waiting a day for the diarrhea to improve. Do not feed your dog for twenty-four hours; he won't starve. This will give the stomach and bowel plenty of time to settle down. Make sure your dog has plenty of water to drink, however, so he doesn't dehydrate. Do not give him any supplements.

Follow with a bland diet of boiled white rice (50 percent), boiled, diced, skinless chicken (25 percent), and low-fat cottage cheese (25 percent). Also helpful (although harder to come by) is liver from organically fed beef, cottage cheese (or tofu) with brown rice and chopped vegetables in meat broth. Dogs recovering from diarrhea should eat smaller, more frequent meals (three to six times a day). Wean the dog back to his normal diet after a week or so.

Lots of dogs develop temporary diarrhea when they are stressed out, or bothered by something. I had one who always developed a brief episode whenever he went anywhere new and exciting. Luckily, this sort of thing is short-lived, which is good, since most of the time there's not a lot you can do about it. Diarrhea can be treated with Kaopectate, Immodium A/D, or Pepto-Bismol.

## Constipation

Constipation can be caused by the ingestion of foreign substances, insufficient water, or a number of diseases. Mild cases can be cured by giving your dog an equal amount of milk of magnesia and mineral oil. Give one teaspoon of each for every five pounds of weight. But use laxatives infrequently, as they are habit forming. If the treatment doesn't work, call your vet.

If your dog suffers from continual constipation, try adding milk or brewer's yeast to his diet. You may want to switch to a dog food with a high fiber content. Get your Beagle to increase his exercise level also.

## Vomiting

Dogs vomit readily, but vomiting more than once an hour could be a sign of serious trouble.

Bad food, poisons, ulcers, worms, or swallowed foreign objects can all produce vomiting in your dog. Dogs who have a vomiting episode need to rest their tummies, so don't feed your dog for at least twelve hours afterward. Try to limit the amount he drinks also, unless he is in danger of becoming dehydrated, which may be the case if the vomiting is accompanied by diarrhea. Vomiting accompanied by diarrhea or fever is quite serious. Check with your veterinarian for specific advice.

## Choking

Dogs are in the habit of swallowing large objects such as sticks, rocks, and tennis balls that subsequently get caught in the throat. Don't try to remove these objects yourself, unless the dog is choking and you have absolutely no choice. Try easing the object out gently, not tugging or pulling, which could cause further damage. Use heavy gloves if you have them readily available, so you won't get bitten by a panicky dog. If you have no gloves at hand, it's usually safe to wait a few seconds until the dog's air supply has decreased to the point where he's too weak to bite you. You can then usually pull out the offending object safely.

The canine Heimlich maneuver can also be helpful. Kneel behind the dog and lift him off the ground by his hindquarters. Squeeze the abdomen quickly and hard (really put the pressure on); then shake gently. The offending object will probably pop right out. In serious cases, you may end up breaking a dog's rib, but that's preferable to having him choke.

In addition to classic choking signs, dogs who pant heavily, even though they haven't exercised, may also be struggling to breathe. If you have been trained in cardiopulmonary resuscitation (CPR) you may use external pressure on the dog's ribcage to get the blood flowing through his heart. This procedure requires training, since it's easy to break a dog's bones if done improperly. On the other hand, nothing is more important than to get your dog breathing again.

### Artificial Respiration

To perform artificial respiration on your dog, remove the collar and lay the dog on his side with his neck straight. Open his mouth, and pull out his tongue to make sure his airways are open. Check to see if there are any obstructions in his mouth, and if there are, remove them if possible.

Close the dog's mouth, inhale to the count of five, and blow slowly and gently into his nose, again counting to five. Blow five or six breaths a minute into your dog's nose. Massage the chest gently at the same time, to help the blood flow. If a dog stops breathing for five minutes, brain damage may result! When the dog begins to breathe again, elevate the hind end slightly, keep him warm, and call your veterinarian.

If you are dealing with a drowning case, hold the Beagle upside down by the hind legs for about thirty seconds to help drain any water from the lungs.

Beagles have such powerful noses that they can use them to vacuum up debris. All kinds of weird stuff have been found in Beagle noses, including sticks and small stones. An easy way to discover whether or not your Beagle has inhaled something is to place a mirror under his nose, and see if it mists under both nostrils. If it doesn't, you should suspect a nasal obstruction. If you try removing it yourself, you risk shoving the article even further up his nose. Take your dog to the vet to have it removed, unless he is positively not breathing at all.

Sometimes a dog's breathing will be affected by an allergic reaction. See the topic "Allergic Reaction" later in this chapter.

## Hypothermia

Hypothermia, in which the body temperature is below 99° F or 37° C, often manifests itself as frostbite. The ears, tail, and paws are especially vulnerable. The skin will be pale, perhaps even turn dead white, and the respiration and heart rate will be slow. To treat it, warm your dog's skin very gently and slowly by applying warm (not hot), damp towels. If possible, give the dog a warm bath for fifteen minutes or so. In any case, dry the dog thoroughly with a hair dryer if possible. Keep him warm in blankets, on a heating pad, or in front of the heater. Most dogs recover well, but keep an eye on any parts possibly damaged by frostbite. If they turn dark, gangrene may be setting in and you need to call your veterinarian immediately.

### Bundle Your Beagle Up

Beagles sensitive to cold weather should wear sweaters outside. Your dog will be more comfortable and he'll look quite sporting at the same time.

## Burns and Hyperthermia

A conventional burn should be rinsed with cold water for at least ten minutes. This not only makes the burned area feel better, but will help reduce swelling and blisters. If the burn is not serious, simply dry it carefully and apply an antibiotic cream to the completely cooled skin. Applying a cream to hot skin will only seal in the heat.

If the burn was caused by a chemical, identify the offending chemical, and apply an ointment of the opposite nature. For example, if the chemical was acidic, use an alkaline substance like baking soda or soap. (Acid chemicals, like sulfuric acid or hydrochloric acid end in the word "acid." That's handy.) Alkaline chemicals include ammonia, lye, and drain cleaners. Use diluted vinegar to treat burns from these chemicals.

Hyperthermia is often termed "heatstroke." It occurs when your dog's body temperature rises to about 104° F or 40° C. Most sufferers are dogs left in cars on warmish days. To check for yourself how miserable this experience can be, shut yourself up in closed car on a 70-degree day for ten minutes. It's twice as bad for your dog, who cannot sweat to cool himself.

Signs of hyperthermia include heavy panting, or even foaming at the mouth. The condition may be accompanied by dehydration. You can check for dehydration by pulling at the loose skin at the shoulder blades. If it doesn't immediately spring back into place, your Beagle is probably dehydrated.

Put your dog in a cool bath to lower his temperature, or put cold, wet towels on him. Take him to the veterinarian, since further treatment, including intravenous fluids, may be necessary.

## Bleeding

Bleeding often looks worse than it actually is, especially when it occurs in the ear or foot. Both are well supplied with blood vessels, and in both cases, gravity keeps the blood flowing. Naturally, this makes such wounds slow to heal. Cuts near the joints and in the groin area are also slow in healing. However, cuts that are less than an inch long (and not very deep) will heal on their own with minimal attention from you or your veterinarian.

Using a non-adherent wound dressing (such as polyurethane sponges) will speed healing.

Any serious bleeding requires two critical actions from you:

- Use pressure. Place a clean cloth directly to the wound and apply pressure. If blood starts to seep through, do *not* remove the cloth. Simply apply a second cloth on top of the first, and continue the pressure. If you take off the first cloth, you might pull off a necessary clot that is forming to stanch the bleeding. Usually a little compression, possibly coupled with bandaging, will stop the bleeding. Keep the pressure on for about five minutes. If you cannot control the bleeding, you'll obviously need to see the veterinarian

- Clean the wound. The biggest danger from most wounds is infection. Wash the wound gently but thoroughly for several *minutes*. A few seconds isn't enough. You can use soap and water, but even better is a special product like Nolvasan, a skin and wound cleanser. Then pat it dry with a clean cloth. Do not use gauze or cotton balls, because the tiny fibers can irritate the wound. Follow with a non-alcoholic antiseptic like Betadine.

Don't bandage a wound too tightly. If you notice swelling in the area within the first minute or so, re-bandage it.

## Arterial Bleeding

Much more serious than regular cuts, of course, are cuts that slice across arteries. Arterial blood is usually very bright red, and comes in spurts, rather than the steady flow of darker blood characteristic of venous cuts. In case of arterial bleeding, you must stop the blood flow at once. Use anything you have at hand. If you can't find a clean towel, use your dirty underwear or your bare hand. Nothing is more important than stopping the bleeding. Apply strong pressure to the blood flow. If the bleeding continues, apply pressure to the pressure point closest to the wound, between the wound and the heart. Pressure points are located in the "armpits," the groin, and just below the base of the tail. Press firmly until the bleeding slows. You will have to relax the pressure for a few seconds every few minutes, so you don't cause tissue and nerve death.

If your dog suffers from von Willebrands or another blood disease that inhibits clotting, bleeding can go on for long time. Bleeding from the nose may indicate your Beagle has gotten into a household poison. Wounds caused by bites are very serious, and almost always need veterinary attention.

## Blood in the Urine

Bloody urine usually indicates a urinary tract infection (UTI), especially in male dogs. (Urinary tract infections in females are more often characterized by painful, frequent urination.) In most cases this is easily treated. In addition, drinking plenty of water will help your Beagle flush out any harmful bacteria that might be causing the problem. It also dilutes the urine that may be irritating the tract further. It may help to dose a Beagle in early stages of UTI with vitamin C in the form of cranberry concentrate. You can get it in capsule form, and one or two capsules a day should do the trick. This acidifies the urine and makes it difficult for bacteria to thrive.

Blood in the urine may have other causes, including internal injuries, poisoning, clotting disorder, chronic infection, tumors, polyps, or stones. If your male dog's urine contains both blood and a yellowish pus, he might have a prostate infection. Whatever the source, it must be identified by your vet, who may use urinalysis, ultrasound, or X-rays to diagnose the problem.

Straining to urinate could indicate a kidney problem, UTI, bladder stones, or in males, prostate disease.

### Uterine Disease

Unspayed females can develop a life-threatening infection called pyometra, a disease of the uterus. Dogs with pyometra discharge a foul-smelling substance from their vaginas. Your dog must get to the veterinarian immediately, or she could die. This is just another reason why you should spay your female Beagle.

### Blood in the Stool

Blood in the stool is more common in dogs than in people. It is most often caused by a parasite infection, particularly whipworms or hookworms. (Hookworms tend to make the stools look tarry; whipworms make it redder.)

Other causes for bloody stool include bacterial or viral infections, and ingestion of sharp objects that scrape the intestinal lining. Puppies are in greater danger from any kind of bleeding than are adult dogs.

## Broken Bones and Accidents

Broken bones are usually characterized by sharp pain, swelling, and a distortion in the shape or size of the injured area. Usually the dog will not be able to support his weight.

Sometimes a bone will not be broken, but dislocated, or out of position. The symptoms are similar to those of a broken bone, and you should take the dog to the veterinarian. Do not try to move it back into place yourself.

If the bone breaks through the skin, it's called a compound fracture, and is thus a both wound and a break. Simple fractures that are not properly handled can easily become compound fractures. Some varieties of broken bones, such as greenstick fractures, are not readily apparent, even by visual or tactile examination. These are really partial fractures and can be detected by X-ray.

## Brewster the Beagle

About six months ago, I got a call from our excellent veterinary clinic. A Beagle had been struck on the interstate and left to die. A kind passing motorist brought him to our clinic, where he was found to have broken a shoulder on one side and a broken elbow on the other. No one ever called to claim him. We named him Brewster. Brewster was in a body cast for six weeks—and a very guarded prognosis. The vets were afraid he would be paralyzed in one leg. But that kind of thinking is too pessimistic when it comes to Beagles. While in the cast, Brewster learned to climb stairs. After six weeks, the cast was removed—and we all held our breath. Brewster simply stepped out of his body cast and trotted off, for all the world as if he had just awakened from a nap. He's now living with the vet who rehabilitated him.

### Responding to a Broken Bone

Obviously, your dog needs to be taken to the veterinarian if he has a broken bone. He may require an emergency splint for transport. Because he will be hurt and frightened, he may bite, so muzzle the dog first.

If you have no muzzle handy, you can make one from a nylon stocking, a scarf, a piece of gauze, or even a rope. Wrap the material a few times around the snout about halfway between the nose and eyes. Double-knot the cloth under the chin and then tie the ends back under the ears and behind the head.

To make a splint, use a piece of wood, or try a magazine and a lot of tape. Straighten the leg as much as possible without exerting force. Surround the leg with the magazine and tape everything up together firmly, but not so tightly that you cut off circulation.

If your Beagle has been struck by a car, take him to the vet for a checkup, even if you don't see anything wrong. He could be suffering internal injuries, or an injury to his spine. The latter may be indicated by a wobbly gait, or paralysis. Make a stretcher out of any solid piece of wood—even a door, and keep the animal as still as possible, and his spine as straight as possible, while you transport him.

## Allergic Reaction

Hives, or soft swellings around the nose, ears, and eyes, are caused by a severe allergic reaction, often to insect stings. Strong reactions can also cause your dog to stop breathing. Give your dog Benadryl and get him to the veterinarian as soon as possible. He may need a shot of cortisone or adrenaline. (One of my hounds is so allergic to insect stings that I keep a supply of cortisone injections in my refrigerator all summer long!)

## Poisoning

If a dog swallows poison, he may have telltale chemical breath. The ASPCA National Animal Poison Control (800-548-2423 or 900-680-0000) will dispense telephone help for poisoned animals. The cost is $45 per call, with no extra charge for follow-up calls. So get out your credit card. Don't try to medicate your pet until you talk to a professional. Have at hand all the evidence you can muster about the material your Beagle has eaten.

If indicated, get your dog to the veterinarian. Bring with you in a Ziploc bag a sample of the vomitus, to help your vet make an accurate determination for treatment.

In general, try to *induce vomiting* in your dog if he has consumed any of the following: Actetone, alcohol, antifreeze, diazinon, drugs, insecticides, lead, or rat poison. To induce vomiting, give your dog a tablespoon of hydrogen peroxide. Do this every ten minutes until the dog vomits, and get him to your vet. If you have no hydrogen peroxide, use a teaspoon of salt or a tablespoon of dry mustard. Ipecac also works, but it takes about thirty minutes. Use the hydrogen peroxide if possible.

*Do not* induce vomiting if the dog has eaten: Bleach, cleaners, cleaning fluid, fertilizers, furniture polish, gasoline, kerosene, paint thinner, or pine oil. Get the dog to the vet, along with a sample of the vomit if you can obtain one.

### Antifreeze

Unlike your car, Beagles do not benefit from antifreeze. Conventional antifreeze is mostly ethylene glycol, two ounces of which can kill your dog. To make things worse, ethylene glycol apparently tastes good, and cats and dogs (and children) are attracted to it. Safety conscious Beagle owners should switch to a safer kind of antifreeze, such as Sierra, that is based on propylene glycol, a less toxic choice. No antifreeze is actually safe, of course, and you should mop up all spills and keep your Beagle away from areas where antifreeze may be spilled.

## Seizures or Convulsions

Signs of a seizure include twitching, shaking, drooling, staring, and stiffening of the body. Many causes are possible, including recent vaccinations, poison, and epilepsy. Not much first aid is possible or necessary, but you may want to wrap the dog loosely in a blanket. Don't muzzle a dog with seizures. When the seizure is over (usually in a minute or two), make an appointment with your veterinarian.

# Chapter 19
# Senior Beagles

Your baby Beagle has become a senior citizen. His muzzle is tinged with gray, and the eyes are slightly hazy. The spring in his step is a little less springy, and his heart, while true as ever, beats a little more hesitantly. How did this happen? Because you took good care of him, and Beagles are tough cookies.

Beagles live a very long time, for dogs. In fact, they are one of the longest-lived of all breeds. While this is very good news indeed, it's also a reminder that your Beagle will be a senior dog for a lot longer than he'll be a puppy. Dogs' life spans have been extended, thanks to good veterinary care, better nutrition, and responsible owners. About 18 percent of dogs seen by veterinarians are ten years and older, and it's estimated that there are about twenty million senior dogs in the United States today.

Senior dogs have their own special needs, and of course, it's up to you to fulfill them. Pamper your pet; he certainly deserves it after his many years of faithful companionship.

Aging is a very gradual process; it doesn't happen all at once, and there are great variations among individuals—even two dogs from the same litter may age at different rates. It is also a normal process of life; it is not a disease and it doesn't have to be an uncomfortable or unhappy time for your dog.

Be sure your dog gets regular veterinary checks—twice a year is best. The vet will routinely do a thorough physical exam, and may do blood tests, a urinalysis, or even X-rays or an electrocardiogram, depending on your dog's medical history. In between professional dog-doctor visits, be vigilant in noticing any changes in his behavior or physical condition that may indicate a problem. Most problems that plague older dogs will be apparent to the observant eye! Early diagnosis allows most geriatric diseases to be treated successfully.

### Luxury Beds

Your senior dog deserves a comfortable bed away from drafts and close to you. Hard wood and tile floors are tough on old bones. Orthopedic beds, raised beds, heated beds, and even special cooling beds are now available to make your dog's golden years more enjoyable. For example, the Soothsoft Company (www.soothsoft.com) manufactures the Cool Spot, a thermoregulating bed. This cushioned bed needs no refrigeration, stays dry, and uses no electricity.

## Keeping Your Dog Fit

If anything, fitness is even more important for your senior dog than it is for a young adult. Losing a few days exercise won't hurt a young adult, but a senior who misses his exercise regimen is likely to suffer from arthritis and similar ailments. Exercise also keeps your dog's metabolism working well, and helps maintain bone density and muscle strength. Cold weather, hot weather, and stress are also more problematic for the older animal; he has fewer resources to cope with them. (This is because the endocrine function has dropped by as much as 30 percent, and it's the thyroid and adrenal glands of that system that help regulate temperature.)

Exercise is not only good for your Beagle's health and yours, but gives him a sense of belonging and companionship. All too often, I see a family get a new puppy as their senior dog grows older. All their attention goes to the new dog, and old Rover gets "forgotten." Make some special "alone time" with your older dog. It will do you both a world of good.

In fact, your older Beagle may try so hard to "keep up" that you should not mistake his enthusiasm for his abilities. Don't let him get overtired, which could seriously hurt his joints and ligaments.

Keep your older dog in trim condition. A fat dog is an unhealthy dog at any age, but fat seniors suffer even more. Obesity is the single most common health problem in older dogs. I know, I know. Your Beagle loves to eat. Well, he can. Feed him less, but feed him more often. Get rid of dog biscuits, and use nutritious low calorie carrots for a treat instead. Take him for more walks. This is really very simple. Just keep an eye on your dog's weight, and feed him accordingly—you don't need any fancy charts.

## Diet

Monitor your dog's eating habits carefully. Increases in thirst (and consequent urination) can indicate kidney problems, Cushing's disease, or diabetes.

Senior dogs tend to gain weight because they get insufficient exercise, perhaps because of arthritis or other age-related problems. But it's not age per se that makes your dog require fewer calories. Most senior dogs have about a 20 percent drop in caloric needs, but this is a very individual thing, and it depends more on lifestyle than anything else. Senior dogs need the same amount of nutrition as any other dog does for his exercise level.

Senior dogs do have a few special nutritional needs, however. They require about 50 percent more protein than does a young adult dog. Only dogs with kidney problems should be on a reduced protein diet. Check your dog food and make sure that the protein content is high for your healthy older dog—25 to 30 percent high quality protein is not too much for a senior dog. High quality protein comes from good meat, not plants or by-products.

### Arthritic Diet

If your senior dog suffers from arthritis, it's important that he is getting the correct ratio of omega 3 and 6 acids in his diet. The ideal ratio is one part omega 3 to five parts omega 6. Giving your arthritic dog a glucosamine-chondroitin sulfate supplement such as Cosequin will reduce his need for non-steroidal anti-inflammatory drugs.

### Supplements

Many senior dogs benefit from a judicious use of supplements. Vitamins C and E are safe, non-toxic anti-oxidants. Vitamin A is an anti-oxidant also, but since it is fat-soluble, it can be stored in your dog's body, and overdoses are possible. Additional levels of B-complex vitamins benefit older dogs. This is because B vitamins help dogs handle stress, infections, and allergies, all of which are increased problems as they age. Older dogs may also require selenium and zinc. Some people recommended adding digestive enzymes, the omega 3 and 6 fatty acids that I mentioned before, and the coenzyme $Q_{10}$.

Older dogs are also subject to senile friability of the nails. This just means that your old Beagles' nails become easily cracked and broken. Keep the nails as short as possible and add a packet or so of Knox gelatin to his diet once a day.

## Dental Hygiene

Dental hygiene is particularly important for senior dogs, most of whom suffer from periodontal disease. The tartar that can build up over time is more than unsightly and smelly. It is dangerous—and not just to teeth. Tartar contains filthy bacteria that can migrate under the gum line and into the blood stream. From there they can cause damage to the heart, liver, and kidneys. In addition, painful dental conditions can lead to loss of appetite. The dog may go off his food, become emaciated, and fall prey to nutritional or other diseases.

Scrub those teeth with a good canine toothpaste whenever your think of it. Once a day is not too often, but be sure to do it at *least* one a week. While you're at it, look for red or swelling gums, broken teeth, and bad breath, all danger signs.

## Slowing Down With Age

As dogs (and people) grow older, their physical and mental state undergoes some inevitable deterioration. One way of coping with these problems is simply being aware they exist. Your awareness will help you compensate for the trouble they can cause.

## Hands-On Dog Care

Groom your older dog thoroughly and frequently. The brushing action is good not only for getting rid of dead hair, but keeps his skin in tiptop condition as well. And everyone, including your elderly Beagle, likes a nice massage. Like grooming, it makes your dog feel good.

## Hearing Problems

Older dogs are likely to lose some hearing as they age. They may not hear you come in the door, or respond to you when you call them. People and dogs suffer hearing loss in the high-frequency range first, so some noises, like the loud low booms of thunderstorms, may sound even scarier to dogs than they did before, and they may become fearful of them.

Deafness is common in older dogs. It can manifest itself in incessant barking (is the dog trying to hear himself?) and obliviousness to the owner's voice. Of course, your Beagle may never have paid any attention to your commands, but if he doesn't respond to the sound of the refrigerator door being opened, something is probably wrong.

Another ear condition, old dog vestibular disease, stems from an inner ear problem. Dogs with this disease typically shake their heads; they may circle around or even fall. (I once heard of a dog who did this; it was later discovered that a plug of ear wax had managed to settle on his eardrum; when the wax was removed, the dog recovered.) The disease can be treated with anti-motion sickness medications and perhaps antibiotics. Afflicted dogs usually recover well.

## Coughing

Some older dogs seem to cough a lot, especially during the night. One reason is that old lungs produce more mucus, and more mucus equals more coughing. Although it seems harmless, bronchitis can result. Even more ominously, coughing can be an early symptom of heart problems.

## Arthritis and Joint Pain

The most common disease of older animals (including humans) is arthritis. Nearly all old dogs have at least a touch of it. As dogs age, they get creaky. You may notice your Beagle having difficulty getting up in the morning. He may be reluctant to climb stairs.

Most older dogs, like older people, get the form of arthritis called geriatric osteoarthritis, caused by a lifetime of wear and tear on the joints. (This condition, which used to be called rheumatism, famously gets worse in cold and wet weather—even for Beagles.)

Some excellent anti-arthritis medications are now on the market. Carpofen and etodelac have been used effectively with many dogs. Buffered or coated aspirin, and glycosamine products are also useful in controlling pain, but always consult your veterinarian before giving your dog a pain killer. Acupuncture is another option that many say has worked wonders for their pet's arthritis.

## House Soiling Issues

Your older, arthritic dog may start having accidents in the house because it's simply too hard for him to get to the door in time. (His bladder control probably isn't what is used to be, either.) Try taking your dog out more frequently. If your dog is still pulling at the leash after all these years, switch to a harness or a head halter; it's kinder for both of you. Not only will this help his bladder problems, but the exercise will also make him feel better.

Many older, spayed females lack estrogen, a hormone that helps keep muscles in good working order. The telltale symptom is "leaking" at night while the dog is asleep. Luckily, a hormonal prescription medication is available to help this problem.

Older dogs are also likely to suffer from loss of kidney function. This is because the tiny tubes inside the kidney (neprons), which are responsible for filtering body wastes like urea and creatinine, are gradually lost during the aging process. However, the remaining nephrons grow larger, and take up some of the slack, providing older dogs with about 75 percent of their former kidney function. Most dogs do quite well on that. Dogs with kidney problems should be on a reduced protein diet.

## Heart Trouble

Old canines are apt to suffer from degeneration in the heart valves, allowing the blood to leak backward into the heart and producing a heart murmur. Signs might include coughing, heavy breathing, and an inability to tolerate exercise.

## Lungs

Seniors can develop scar tissue in their lungs that makes them less elastic. If such a dog then comes down with pneumonia or a similar disease, the lungs have an extra hard time doing their job.

## Vision Problems

Like people, senior dogs often encounter vision problems, and your dog will probably lose some visual acuity as he grows older. Since dogs can see moving objects more clearly than stationary ones, I always move my arms around when I try to attract the attention of my senior dogs.

Older dogs' eyes may have a greenish haze to them; this is fairly normal and doesn't seriously affect their vision. But cloudiness, redness, obvious pain, or evidence of vision problems should be attended to immediately by a professional. It may be nothing but a pollen-related conjunctivitis. Your dog may suffer from cataracts or glaucoma (which I discuss in more detail in Chapter 17, "Beagle Blights"). Many older dogs suffer from "dry eye," (keratoconjunctivitis sicca). Dogs with this condition are unable to produce sufficient tears, and may need a daily regimen of artificial tears to keep them in shape.

Of course, some older dogs go blind. This seems to be more of a problem for the owners than for the dogs. Blindness is not the tragedy for dogs that it is for people, and most dogs learn to compensate for the loss of vision rather well. They rely upon their noses for most of their information, and the nose is one organ that usually keeps working. You can also help your dog navigate around the house by using a number of relatively simple techniques.

- Keep the furniture where it is now. Groping about sightless is hard enough without your making it more difficult for your Beagle by changing room arrangements on a whim.
- Use a navigational guide like vinyl or carpet runner rugs to indicate important pathways. Your Beagle will soon learn to feel his way about.
- Spray furniture with a non-harmful, good smelling substance like lemon oil; that's another marker for your dog.

- Hang a sweet-scented non-edible object like a small potpourri bag from door handles. That way your dog will know which door to sit in front of when he wants to go out.

## Cancer

The risk of cancer increases as your dog ages. Check your dog's body for unusual lumps and if you find one, especially a hard lump that seems attached to the bone, get moving. Any lump that is large, fast growing, or in a lymph node, should also be attended to at once. Make an appointment to see your veterinarian right away. For a more detailed discussion of cancer, see Chapter 17, "Beagle Blights."

## Cognitive Dysfunction Syndrome

Cognitive dysfunction syndrome is a common form of "canine senility." If your dog seems to be having house soiling accidents, accompanied by withdrawal, change in personality, or disorientation, he may well be a victim of this progressive condition. Even sadder is the fact that senior dogs, like humans in the early stages of Alzheimer's, seem to know that something is wrong. They understand they can't think as quickly or respond as well as in days of old. This in turn makes them sad or despondent, depressing them even more.

Don't give up training or interaction with your afflicted dog. Don't allow him to languish in the corner. Work patiently with your dog, understanding that his attention span is probably not what it used to be. Provide carrot pieces or other nutritious low-cal treats to encourage your dog to interact. Don't be surprised if he has apparently forgotten a skill or two. It happens to the best of us. Pretend your old friend is a nine-week-old puppy, and use the same level of tolerance. He deserves it after all these years.

Cognitive dysfunction syndrome can now be treated with selegiline (which used to be called L-deprenyl), a drug that is also used to treat Parkinson's disease in human beings. The brand name is Anipryl or Eledpryl, and results have been very good. These drugs cannot be used with all dogs, however, particularly ones suffering from epilepsy.

### Anesthesia

Senior dogs who need surgery are at a higher risk from anesthesia than younger ones. This is why most veterinarians want to do a pre-surgical blood screen on older animals, to check for any problems that might interfere with a successful procedure.

## Saying Good-bye

Although Beagles live a lot longer than most dogs, most Beagle-owners still have the sorrowful task of saying good-bye to their beloved pets. I was luckier than most. My dear Liz died in my arms at age seventeen after suffering a brief illness. More often, however, we have to make a painful decision. Pets need to be euthanized for only two reasons: incurable, painful illness, or uncontrollable aggression (after all alternatives have been explored).

For sick dogs, it's easy to let one day slide into the next, with the dog gradually getting worse. You need to ask yourself about the quality of life your pet is experiencing. Sometimes we wait too long not for the pet's sake, but for our own. We just can't let go. This is the time to have a heart-to-heart with your veterinarian. By this time, I hope you have built up a solid and trusting relationship with him. Listen to what he is telling you—not to what you want to hear.

Your Beagle will also let you know when the time has come to say good-bye. In his final illness, failure to eat or drink, general lethargy, and non-responsiveness to petting are all indications the hour is near. Some veterinarians will come to your home, a policy that is most considerate to your pet. Other times, you will need to take your pet to the doctor. Whether or not you wish to stay during the procedure is up to you. If you can be calm and comforting, your Beagle will appreciate your being there in his final hour. You will find that the procedure is very quick and painless to your pet. However, if you are too distraught to deal with it without breaking down, it might be best to let the veterinarian and his sympathetic staff members take care of the procedure. Your Beagle will forgive you. If you are extremely distraught, your presence then might make him feel worse. Remember that whatever your choice, you are releasing your dog from suffering. Many people, like me, believe that Beagles enjoy an afterlife with their humans. Heaven without our dogs doesn't sound like any fun whatsoever.

Of course, you will grieve after your pet is gone. This is natural—don't listen to anyone who says "It's only a dog" or any other such thoughtless remark. Give yourself both time and permission to grieve. Doing so confirms your membership in the circle of those who can extend their love and caring to others—even if the others are of a different species.

Just as with human beings, you can have your pet cremated or buried in a pet cemetery. Some people prefer to bring the ashes home and scatter them over a favorite meadow. No matter what you decide, you will know that your Beagle's joyous spirit will live on in your heart forever.

Talk honestly with your children about the dog and his death, in language they can understand. If appropriate, use your own religious belief to explain death and comfort the child. Some children withdraw and clam up after the death of a pet. Don't make the mistake of thinking the child doesn't care or has forgotten. In many cases, this is a child's first experience with death, and it is extremely traumatic.

## The Next Step

People seem to have to diametrically opposed ways of dealing with pet loss. Some need a period of months or years to grieve before they can bring themselves to get another dog. Others want to get a new dog immediately. There is no right or wrong feeling. Just go with what you know is right for you. If you feel a huge hole in your heart that only a Beagle can fill, but feel guilty about "betraying" your old dog, please don't. Go to your local Beagle rescue and save a dog from death. Do it in honor of the dog who has passed away. And make a contribution to your local shelter in his name.

# Appendix A
# Resources: Books, Websites, Associations, and Institutions

## Activities

Delta Society Pet Partners Program
289 Perimeter Road East
Renton, WA 98055-1329
(800) 869-6898
www.deltasociety.org

North American Dog Agility Council
HCR 2 Box 277
St. Maries, ID 83861
www.nadac.com

U.S. Dog Agility Association
PO Box 850955
Richardson, TX 75085-0955
(972) 231-9700
www.usdaa.com

*The Whole Dog Journal*
Editor in Chief; Nancy Kerns
Subscription Services: P.O. Box 420234
Palm Coast, FL 32142
800-829-9165
wholedogj@palmcoastd.com
For Canada: Box 7820 STN Main
London, ON NY5 5WI

*Your Dog: A Magazine for Caring Dog Owners*
Tufts University of Veterinary Medicine
Subscriptions:
PO Box 420234
Palm Coast, FL 32142
(800) 829-5116

## Therapy Dogs

Delta Society Pet Partners Program
289 Perimeter Road E.
Renton, WA 98055
(206) 226-7357 / (800) 869-6898
Email: deltasociety@cis.compuserve.com

Therapy Dogs, Inc.
P.O. Box 5868
(877) 843-7364

Therapy Dogs International
6 Hilltop Road
Mendham, NJ 07845

88 Bartley Road
Flanderd, NJ 07836
(973) 252-9800
email: tdi@gti.net

Pets and People: Companions in Therapy and Service
P.O. Box 4266
Meridian, MS 39307
(601) 483-8970

Bailey, Joan. *How to Help Gun Dogs Train Themselves—Taking Advantage of Early Conditioned Learning*. Sun City, AZ: Doral Publishing, Inc., 1993.

Daniels, Julie. *Enjoying Dog Agility—From Backyard to Competition.* Sun City, AZ: Doral Publishing, Inc., 2001.

# General

The Friskies Company has a great pet care Website, www.friskypet.com. Especially good is the section that answers your questions about your dog's behavior.

American Kennel Club
5580 Centerview Drive
Raleigh, NC 27606
(919) 233-3725
www.akc.org

United Kennel Club
100 E. Kilgore Rd.
Kalamazoo, MI 49002
(616) 343-9020
www.ukcdogs.com

# Health

## Acupuncture and Acutherapy

Canine Acupressure Therapists, Amy Snow and Nancy Zidonis:
www.animalacupressure.com
(888) 841-7211
Email: acupressure4all@earthlink.net.

Snow, Amy and Nancy Zidonis. *The Well-Connected Dog: A Guide to Canine Acupressure.* Larkspur, CO: Tallgrass Publishers, 1999.

## Arthritis

Beale. Brian D.V.M. *The Arthritis Cure for Pets: How to Halt, Reverse, and Even Cure Your Pet's Osteoarthritis.* New York: Little, Brown, and Company, 2000.

## Epilepsy

Canine Epilepsy Network Worldwide Web Site
www.cvm.missouri.edu/cen

## First Aid

Copeland, Sue and John A. Hamil, DVM, *Hands-On Dog Care: The Complete Book of Canine First Aid.* Sun City, AZ: Doral Publishing, Inc., 2000.

## Holistic

www.naturalpetvet.com is a website devoted to holistic medicine and natural treatments. The site provides information about essential oils and herbals extracts that can be used to treat your pet holistically. (1-877-PESDOC).

Flower Essence Society
P.O. Box 459
Nevada City, CA 95959
Telephone: 800-736-9222
Voice mail: 530-265-9163
Fax: 530-265-0584
Email: Mail@flowersociety.org
Web Site: www.flowersociety.org

American Holistic Veterinary Medical Association
2218 Old Emmorton Road
Bel Air, MD 21015
Tel: 410-569-0795
Fax: 410-569-2346
Email: ahva@compuserve.com
Website: www.altvetmed.com/ahvmadir.html

Hamilton, Don. *Homeopathic Care for Cats and Dogs: Small Doses for Small Animals*. Berkeley, CA: North Atlantic Books, 1999.

Pitcairn, Richard and Susan Pitcairn. *Dr. Pitcairn's Complete Guide to Natural Health for Dogs and Cats*, by Richard and Susan Pitcairn. Emmaus, PA: Rodale Press, 1995.

Jones, Linda Tellington-Jones and Sybil Taylor, *The Tellington Ttouch: A Revolutionary Natural Method to Train and Care for Your Favorite Animal*. New York: Penguin Books, 1992

## Massage

Furman, C. Sue. *Canine Massage: A Balancing Act*. Wolfchase Press, 2000.

Hannay, Pamela. *Shiatsu for Dogs*. J.A. Allen & Co. Ltd., 1998.

## Nutrition

Cusick, William D. *Canine Nutrition: Choosing the Best Food for Your Breed*. Sun City, AZ: Doral Publishing, Inc., 1997.

Duno, Steve. *Plump Pups and Fat Cats: A Seven-Point Weight Loss Program for Your Overweight Pet*. New York: St. Martin's Press, 1999.

Gianfrancesco, Cheryl. *Doggie Desserts: Homemade Treats for Happy, Healthy Dogs*. Sun City, AZ: Doral Publishing, Inc., 2001.

Morgan, Diane. *Feeding Your Dog for Life*. Sun City, AZ: Doral Publishing, Inc., 2002.

### Traditional

American Veterinary Medical Association
1931 N. Meacham Road, Suite 100
Schaumberg, IL 60173
(847-925-8070
Website: www.avma.org

International Alliance of Animal Therapy and Healing
Ardsley, NY
(914) 378-5295.
Web site: www.IAATH.com

## Products

Ark Natural Products for Pets
6166 Taylor Road, No. 105
Naples, FL 34109
(800) 926-5100
(941) 592-9388
www.arknaturals.com

## Training

Association of Pet Dog Trainers
P.O. Box 385
Davis, CA 95617
800-PET-DOGS

Bennett, Bill. *Beagle Basics: The Care, Training and Hunting of the Beagle*. Sun City, AZ: Doral Publishing, Inc., 1995.

Bulanda, Susan. *Ready! The Step by Step Training of the Search and Rescue Dog*. Sun City, AZ: Doral Publishing, Inc., 1995.

Dodham, Nicholas. *Dogs Behaving Badly: An A-to Z Guide to Understanding and Curing Behavioral Problems in Dogs*. New York: Bantam Books, 1999.

Haithcox, Anet. *A-1 K-9*. Sun City, AZ: Doral Publishing, Inc., 2002.

Lachan, Larry and Frank Mickadeit. *Dogs on the Couch: Behavior Therapy for Training and Caring for your Dog*. New York: Overlook, 1999.

Owens, Paul with Norma Ecroate. *The Dog Whisperer: A Compassionate, Nonviolent Approach to Dog Training*. Avon, MA: Adams Media Corp., 1999.

Pryor, Karen. *Don't Shoot the Dog: The New Art of Teaching and Training*, Revised edition. New York: Bantam Books, 1999.

## Travel, Kennels, and Sitters

Pet Sitters International will give you tips and provide references for finding a petsitter in your area. Check out www.petsit.com

National Association for Professional Pet Sitters Referral Network
800-296-PETS
www.petsitters.org

United States Department of Agriculture (USDA)
The USDA produces a brochure, "Traveling with your Pet" (#1536) that gives helpful advice and explains airline regulations concerning pet travel.
Phone (800) 545-USDA to obtain a copy.

www. petswelcome.com is an up to date website listing travel spots and hotels that welcomes pets.

AAA Publishing. *Traveling with your Pet: The AAA Petbook.* Heathrow Publishing.

Barish, Eileen. *Vacationing with Your Pet*, 4th ed. Petfriendly Publications, Scottsdale, AZ. 1999.

# Index